*Transformations of the State*

Series Editors: **Achim Hurrelmann**, Carleton University, Canada; **Stephan Leibfried**, University of Bremen, Germany; **Kerstin Martens**, University of Bremen, Germany; **Peter Mayer,** University of Bremen, Germany.

Titles include:

*Outlines of the themes of the series:*

---

**Transformations of the State**
**Series Standing Order ISBN 978-1-4039-8544-6 (hardback)   978-1-4039-8545-3 (paperback)**

You can receive future titles in this series as they are published by placing a standing order. Please contact your bookseller or, in case of difficulty, write to us at the address below with your name and address, the title of the series and  the ISBNs quoted above.

Customer Services Department, Macmillan Distribution Ltd, Houndmills, Basingstoke, Hampshire RG21 6XS, England

---

# Internationalization of Education Policy

## A New Constellation of Statehood in Education?

*Edited by*

Kerstin Martens, Philipp Knodel and Michael Windzio
*University of Bremen, Germany*

palgrave
macmillan

First published 2014 by
PALGRAVE MACMILLAN

Palgrave Macmillan in the UK is an imprint of Macmillan Publishers Limited, registered in England, company number 785998, of Houndmills, Basingstoke, Hampshire RG21 6XS.

Palgrave Macmillan in the US is a division of St Martin's Press LLC, 175 Fifth Avenue, New York, NY 10010.

Palgrave Macmillan is the global academic imprint of the above companies and has companies and representatives throughout the world.

Palgrave® and Macmillan® are registered trademarks in the United States, the United Kingdom, Europe and other countries

ISBN: 978–1–137–40168–7

This book is printed on paper suitable for recycling and made from fully managed and sustained forest sources. Logging, pulping and manufacturing processes are expected to conform to the environmental regulations of the country of origin.

A catalogue record for this book is available from the British Library.

A catalogue record for this book is available from the Library of Congress.

# Contents

# List of Tables and Figures

## Tables

## Figures

# List of Abbreviations

| | |
|---|---|
| AACRAO | American Association of Collegiate Registrars and Admissions Officers |
| AERES | Agence de l'évaluation de la recherche et de l'enseignement supérieur (Evaluation Agency for Research and Higher Education) |
| ANECA | Agencia Nacional de Evaluación de la Calidad y Acreditación (National Agency for Quality Assurance and Accreditation) |
| ANPE | Asociación Nacional del Profesorado Estatal-Sindicato Independiente (National Association of Teachers-Independent Union) |
| ANR | Agence Nationale de la Recherche (National Agency for Research) |
| APQN | Asia Pacific Quality Network |
| ASEAN | Association of Southeast Asian Nations |
| AUNP | ASEAN University Network Programme |
| BA | Bachelor |
| bac | Baccalauréat (French Secondary School-leaving Examination) |
| BBT | Bundesamt für Berufsbildung und Technologie (Federal Office for Professional Education and Technology) |
| BDA | Bundesvereinigung der deutschen Arbeitgeberverbände (Confederation of German Employers' Associations) |
| BFS | Bundesamt für Statistik (Swiss Federal Statistical Office) |
| BIS | Department for Business, Innovation and Skills |
| BMBF | Bundesministerium für Bildung und Forschung (Federal Ministry of Education and Research) |
| BTS | Brevets de technicien supérieur (Technician certificates) |
| CAFTA | China-ASEAN Free Trade Area |
| CANAE | Confederación Estatal de Asociaciones de Estudiantes (Federal Confederation of Students' Associations) |
| CE | Confédération étudiante (Confederation of Students) |
| CEAPA | Confederación Española de Asociaciones de Padres y Madres de Alumnos (Spanish Confederation of Parents' Associations) |

| CEDEFI | Conférence des directeurs des écoles françaises d'ingénieurs (Conference of the Directors of French Engineering Schools) |
| CEE | Consejo Escolar del Estado (State School Council) |
| CEUNE | Consejo de Estudiantes Universitarios del Estado (National Council of University Students) |
| CFDT | Confédération française démocratique du travail (French Democratic Confederation of Labour) |
| CNE | Comité national d'évaluation (National Evaluation Committee) |
| CNER | Comité national d'évaluation de la recherche (National Research Evaluation Committee) |
| CNESER | Conseil National de l'enseignement supérieur et de la Recherché (National Council of Higher Education and Research) |
| CNKI | China National Knowledge Infrastructure |
| CNRS | Centre National de la Recherche Scientifique (National Centre for Scientific Research) |
| CONCAPA | Confederación Católica Nacional de Padres de Familia y Padres de Alumnos (Catholic Confederation of Family Parents and Parents of Pupils) |
| CPU | Conférence des présidents d'université (Conference of University Presidents) |
| CRUE | Conferencia de Rectores Universidades Españolas (Spanish Rectors' Conference) |
| CSI-F | Central Sindical Independiente y de Funcionarios (Central Independent Union and Union of Civil Servants) |
| CVCP | Committee of Vice-Chancellors and Principals of the Universities of the United Kingdom |
| CVP | Christlichdemokratische Volkspartei der Schweiz (Christian Democratic People's Party (Switzerland) |
| dbb | Deutscher Beamtenbund (German Association of Civil Servants) |
| DEPP | Direction de l'evaluation, de la prospective et de la performance (Evaluation department of the French National Ministry of Education) |
| DfES | Department for Education and Skills |
| DGB | Deutscher Gewerkschaftsbund (German Federation of Trade Unions) |

| | |
|---|---|
| DHV | Deutscher Hochschulverband (German Association of University Professors and Lecturers) |
| ECTS | European Credit Transfer System |
| EDK | Swiss Conference of Cantonal Ministers of Education |
| EDU | Eidgenössisch-Demokratische Union (Federal Democratic Union of Switzerland) |
| EHEA | European Higher Education Area |
| ESEA | Elementary and Secondary Education Act |
| EU | European Union |
| FAEST | Federación de Asociaciones de Estudiantes (Federation of Students' Associations) |
| FAGE | Fédération des associations générales étudiantes (Federation of General Student Associations) |
| FCPE | Fédération des Conseils de Parents d'Élèves (Federation of Councils of Parents of Secondary School Pupils) |
| FDP | Freisinnig-Demokratische Partei der Schweiz (Free Democratic Party (Switzerland)) |
| FE-CC.OO | Federación de Enseñanza de Comisiones Obreras (Educational Federation of Workers' Commissions) |
| FEN | Fédération de l'éducation nationale (Federation for National Education) |
| FETE-UGT | Federación de Trabajadores de la Enseñanza-Unión General de Trabajadores (Federation of Educational Employees-General Workers' Union) |
| FHSG | Fachhochschulgesetz (Swiss framework legislation for universities of applied sciences) |
| FSIE | Federación de Sindicatos Independientes de Enseñanza (Federation of Independant Unions in Education) |
| FSU | Fédération Syndicale Unitaire |
| fzs | freier zusammenschluss von studentInnenschaften (National Union of Students in Germany) |
| GATS | General Agreement on Trade in Services |
| GEW | Gewerkschaft Erziehung und Wissenschaft (Trade Union for Education and Science) |
| GDP | Gross domestic product |
| HarmoS | Intercantonal agreement for harmonization of obligatory schooling |
| HEFCE | Higher Education Funding Council |
| HE | Higher education |

| HEI | Higher education institutions |
|---|---|
| HFKG | Hochschulförderungs- und -koordinationsgesetz (Swiss law on coordination and financing of universities) |
| HLPF | High Level Policy Forum |
| HRK | Hochschulrektorenkonferenz (German Rectors' Conference) |
| IEA | International Association for the Evaluation of Educational Achievement |
| IHEP | Institute for Higher Education Policy |
| IMF | International Monetary Fund |
| INEE | Instituto Nacional de Evaluación Educativa (National Institute of Educational Evaluation) |
| IOs | International Organizations |
| jfs | Jungfreisinnige Schweiz (Young Liberals of Switzerland) |
| KFH | Rektorenkonferenz der Fachhochschulen der Schweiz (Swiss rectors' conference of Universities of applied sciences) |
| KMK | Ständige Konferenz der Kultusminister der Länder in der Bundesrepublik Deutschland (Standing Conference of the Ministers of Education and Cultural Affairs) |
| LCH | Lehrerverband Schweiz (Swiss Teachers' Union) |
| LMD | Licence, Master, Doctorate |
| LOCE | Ley Orgánica de Calidad de la Educación (Education Quality Act) |
| LOE | Ley Orgánica de Educación (Federal Education Act) |
| LOMCE | Ley Orgánica para la Mejora de la Calidad Educativa (Education Quality Enhancement Act) |
| LRU | Loi relative aux libertés et responsabilités des universités; also Loi Pécresse (law regarding the liberties and responsibilities of universities) |
| MECD | Ministerio de Educación, Cultura y Deporte (Federal Ministry of Education, Culture and Sports) |
| MEDEF | Mouvement des entreprises de France (Movement of the Enterprises of France) |
| MEN | Ministère de l'éducation nationale (French National Ministry of Education) |
| MESR | Ministère de l'enseignement supérieur (Ministry of Higher Education and Research) |
| MET | Mouvement des étudiants (Movement of Students) |
| MINT | Mathematics, informatics, natural sciences, and technology |
| MSTP | Mission scientifique, technique et pédagogique (Scientific, Technical and Pedagogical Mission) |

| | |
|---|---|
| NAFSA | National Association of Foreign Student Advisers |
| NCLB | No Child Left Behind Act |
| NRW | Nordrhein-Westfalen (North Rhine-Westphalia) |
| NUS | National Union of Students |
| OECD | Organisation for Economic Co-operation and Development |
| PDE | Promotion et défense des étudiants (Promotion and Defense of Students) |
| PIRLS | Progress in International Reading Literacy Study |
| PISA | Programme for International Student Assessment |
| POS | Political opportunity structure |
| PP | Partido Popular (People's Party, Spain) |
| PRES | Pôles de recherche et d'enseignement supérieur (Poles of Research and Higher Education) |
| PSOE | Partido Socialista Obrero Español (Spanish Socialist Workers' Party) |
| RAE | Research Assessment Exercise |
| RIHED | Regional Centre for Higher Education and Development |
| R2T | Race to the Top |
| SAV | Schweizerischer Arbeitgeberverband (Swiss Employers' Confederation) |
| SBFI | Staatssekretariat für Bildung, Forschung und Innovation (State Secretariat for Education and Research) |
| SE | Sindicato de Estudiantes (Students Union) |
| SEAMEO | Southeast Asian Ministers of Education Organization |
| SES | Socioeconomic Status |
| SEU | Subjective Expected Utility Theory |
| SGEN | Syndicat Général de l'Éducation Nationale (General Union of National Education) |
| SMEC | Shanghai Municipal Education Commission |
| SNES | Syndicat National de l'Enseignement Secondaire (National Union of Secondary Education) |
| SNI | Syndicat National des Instituteurs (National Union of Primary School Teachers) |
| SP | Sozialdemokratische Partei der Schweiz (Social Democratic Party (Switzerland)) |
| STES-I | Confederación de Sindicatos de Trabajadoras y Trabajadores de la Enseñanza-Intersindical (Confederation of Workers and Teachers Unions) |
| SUD Education | Solidaires, Unitaires, Démocratiques (Solidary, Unitary, Democratic Education Union) |

| SUK | Swiss University Conference |
| SVP | Schweizerische Volkspartei (Swiss People's Party) |
| TSCS | Time-series-cross-section |
| UDE | Unión Democrática de Estudiantes (Democratic Union of Students) |
| UFG | Universitätsförderungsgesetz (Swiss framework legislation for universities) |
| UIS | UNESCO Institute for Statistics |
| UK | United Kingdom |
| UMAP | University Mobility in Asia and the Pacific |
| UMP | Union pour un mouvement populaire (Union for a Popular Movement) |
| UNEF | Union Nationale des Étudiants de France (National Union of Students of France) |
| UNESCO | United Nations Educational, Scientific and Cultural Organization |
| UNI | Union Nationale Universitaire (Inter-University Union) |
| UNL | Union Nationale Lycéenne (National Union of Secondary Students) |
| UNSA | Union nationale des syndicats autonomes (National Union of Autonomous Unions) |
| U.S. | United States |
| USO | Unión Sindical Obrera-Federación de Enseñanza (Union of Workers-Educational Federation) |
| UUK | Universities UK |
| VSS | Verband schweizerischer Studierendenschaften (National Union of Students in Switzerland) |
| VET | Value-Expectation Theory |

# Notes on Contributors

**Alexander Akbik** is a PhD student at the Central European University, Budapest, and an Associated Research Fellow in the project C4 on "Internationalization of Education Policy" within the TranState Research Center "Transformation of the State" at the University of Bremen. He is currently writing his thesis on the democratization process of hybrid regimes in post-Communist states. Among his research projects are the internationalization of education in China, democratization in the post-Communist world as well as regional security studies.

**Tonia Bieber** is a Senior Research Fellow in the project "Internationalization of Education Policy" within the TranState Research Center at the University of Bremen. She holds a PhD in political sciences from the University of Bremen and the Bremen International Graduate School of Social Sciences (BIGSSS). Her thesis deals with the domestic impact of voluntary international initiatives, prominently the Bologna Process, the PISA Study and the Copenhagen Process on reforms in education and training policies using the example of Switzerland. Her areas of expertise include policy convergence, education politics, European integration and international organizations, in particular the EU and OECD. She has published on recent reforms in public education and training policies, with a special focus on internationalization processes in Europe and the United States.

**Michael Dobbins** is an Assistant Professor of Education Policy at Frankfurt University. He completed his dissertation on higher education policy in Central and Eastern Europe, which focused on the impact of Europeanization and the Bologna Process on existing higher education governance structures. He is also associated with the project "Internationalization of Education Policy" within the TranState Research Center at the University of Bremen. His research interests are higher education policy, secondary education policy, the European Union and American politics, Central and Eastern Europe and the Caucasus region.

**Timm Fulge** is a Research Fellow in the project "Internationalization of Education Policy" within the TranState Research Center at the

University of Bremen. He is also an affiliated PhD Fellow at the Bremen International School of Social Sciences. In his dissertation, he studies the political economy of higher education and the implementation of policy reforms associated with the Bologna Process. Further research interests include quantitative methodology, political communication and international relations.

**Philipp Knodel** is a Research Fellow in the project "Internationalization of Education Policy" within the TranState Research Center at the University of Bremen. He is also Senior Research Associate at the Centre for International Studies at the University of Oxford and affiliated PhD Fellow at the Bremen International School of Social Sciences. He works in the field of comparative politics with a special focus on higher education policy. His research interests are international initiatives in education policy and the political economy of higher education. His areas of expertise include global trends of higher education such as massive open online courses (MOOCs) and international branch campuses. He has published several papers on the Bologna Process in England and is co-editor of *Das PISA-Echo: Internationale Reaktionen auf die Bildungsstudie* (2010).

**Kerstin Martens** is Associate Professor of International Relations at the University of Bremen, Germany. Her research interests include theories of international relations, international organizations, global governance and global public policy, in particular education and social policy. She heads the research project "Internationalization of Education Policy" and is in charge of the research area "International Relations and World Society", both located at the University of Bremen. She is co-editor of *New Arenas of Education Governance* and *Transformation of Education Policy* (2007 and 2010), *Education in Political Science – Discovering a Neglected Field* (2009) and *Mechanisms of OECD Governance – International Incentives for National Policy Making?* (2010). She holds a PhD in Social and Political Sciences from the European University Institute, Florence, Italy.

**Dennis Niemann** is a Research Fellow in the project "Internationalization of Education Policy" within the TranState Research Center at the University of Bremen. His research interests include the internationalization of education policy and the role of international organizations in global governance. In his PhD thesis he is currently analysing the soft governance influence of international organizations on domestic policy-making using the example of the OECD's PISA Study and its impact on German education policy. He has published on recent internationalization processes in education policy, with a special focus on secondary and higher education reforms in Germany.

**Marie Popp** is a Schoolteacher at the Gymnasium Heidberg in Hamburg and an Associated Research Fellow in the project "Internationalization of Education Policy" within the TranState Research Center at the University of Bremen. Her research interests include the role of international organizations in the field of education, especially the impact of the OECD's PISA Study on education reforms. She has a special interest in Southern Europe and Latin America.

**Janna Teltemann** is a Senior Researcher in the project "Internationalization of Education Policy" within the TranState Research Center at the University of Bremen. She holds a PhD in Sociology from the University of Bremen. Her research interests are quantitative methods, migration, integration and education. In her PhD project she analysed the impact of institutions on the educational achievement of immigrants with data from the OECD PISA Study. She has published several papers on determinants of educational inequality, results and methodological implications of the PISA Study as well as on OECD activities in the field of migration.

**Eva Maria Vögtle** is a member of the research staff of the German Center for Higher Education and Science Research (DZHW), Hannover, an institute for higher education research under the auspices of Germany's federal and state governments (*Länder*). After finishing her PhD in Political Sciences at the University of Konstanz, she was a short-term research fellow at the TranState Research Center at the University of Bremen. Her research interests are diffusion and network theory, higher education policies, lifelong learning and the European Union. She has published several papers and contributed to monographs on the impact of the Bologna Process on higher education policy convergence in the field of study structures and quality assurance as well as on patterns of student mobility.

**Michael Windzio** is a Professor of Sociology at the University of Bremen. His research interests include the sociology of education, migration and urban studies, quantitative methods with a focus on longitudinal data, network analysis, social structure, sociology of organizations, and delinquency. He has been a fellow at the Criminological

Research Institute of Lower Saxony where he conducted large school surveys. Recently he published "Integration of Immigrant Children into Interethnic Friendship Networks" in *Sociology*; "Are We Just Friends? Immigrant Integration into High and Low-Cost Social Networks" in *Rationality and Society* (with E. Bicer), "Religion, friendship networks and home visits of immigrant and native children" in *Acta Sociologica* (with M. Wingens) and is editor of *Integration and Inequality in Educational Institutions* (2013 and co-editor of *A life-course perspective of migration and integration* (2011).

**Chenjian Zhang** is an Associate Senior Researcher in the project "Internationalization of Education Policy" within the TranState Research Center at the University of Bremen. His research interests include organizational sociology, education reform and social network studies. His research in education focuses on how internationalization of education impacts education reform in China and how different social groups react to this process.

# Acknowledgements

This book is part of a research project on the internationalization of education policy that started in 2003. The aim of this project is to explore new international dynamics in education politics and their effects on states, corporate actors and individuals. In 2007 we published the first findings examining the international level of education policy (*New Arenas of Education Governance*). The research showed how international organizations have expanded their governance capacities in education policy and have become influential players in this field. A second book analysed the impact of internationalization, in particular the PISA Study and the Bologna Process, on the domestic level by comparing policy changes in a variety of countries (*Transformation of Education Policy*). The present book marks the third and final publication of our "trilogy on education policy". It explores the outcomes of international initiatives and actors' reactions to new constellations of statehood in education.

Our research project is part of the TranState Research Center in Bremen, funded by the German Research Foundation (Deutsche Forschungsgemeinschaft – DFG). Over the years many people contributed their expertise on education policy to the project. Former colleagues include: Carolin Balzer, Tilman Brand, Daniel de Olano, Frederik Elwert, Nadin Fromm, Anja Jakobi, Bettina Kohlrausch, Kathrin Leuze, Alexander-Kenneth Nagel, Alessandra Rusconi, Reinhold Sackmann, Raphaela Schlicht-Schmälzle, Heiko Walkenhorst and Ansgar Weymann. We extend our special thanks to Dieter Wolf and Stephan Leibfried for answers to all the questions that occurred to us while working on this book.

When we were deeply immersed in thoughts about reactions, outcomes and new constellations, we received helpful feedback from an anonymous Palgrave reviewer. Finally, we are grateful that so many interview partners participated in our research. During the different stages of this book we received outstanding research assistance from Nicole Henze, Lukas Röber, Tim Hildebrandt, Sarah Bose, Valentin Jandt, Jenny Fuhrmann, Lisa Kühn, Keith Wirrell, Romy Siegert, Atiqah Fairuz Md Salleh, Jana Pittelkow, Ramsey Wise and Mehmetcan Sinir. Last but not least, we want to thank all the contributors to this book for their patience during our meetings. Quite often they had to listen to our reactions to our kids' new skills before we started discussing actors' reactions to internationalization.

*Bremen, December 2013*

# 1

## Introduction: Outcomes and Actors' Reactions on Internationalization in Education Policy – A Theoretical Approach

*Philipp Knodel, Michael Windzio and Kerstin Martens*

### Introduction

Education systems in Europe have undergone profound changes within the last ten years. In response to demands of the labour markets, increasing costs for public education institutions or demographic challenges, the education sector has successively come under pressure. New contexts, procedures and arenas of governance emerged that, beside the established actors involved, shape education policy. Although traditionally assumed to be a genuinely 'national' policy field, various international initiatives and programmes have triggered fundamental education system reforms in many countries. What we can observe by now in the education landscape is different from the status-quo *ante* internationalization processes and presents a *new constellation of statehood in education policy*.

While most research in this field focuses on international governance and policy changes, the consequences of internationalization on the domestic level have not yet been analysed in sufficient depth. Although various studies have provided a picture of the structural and political changes that have been triggered by the transformations taking place in the field of education policy, yet, the implications have not been analysed expansively. We know little about the outcomes of educational systems and the political actors' reactions to these changes.

In order to fully understand the phenomena of internationalization, this study seeks to answer a set of questions: *Does the internationalization of education policy trigger domestic policies that have the desired effects on*

1

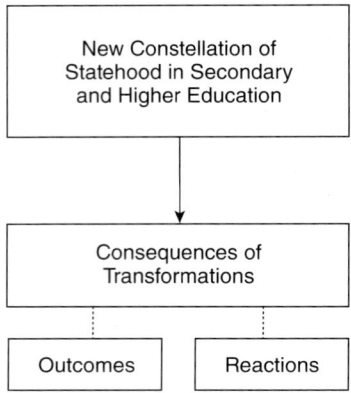

*Figure 1.1*  Studying the dynamics of internationalization.

*the outcomes at the levels of secondary and tertiary education? How do those actors affected by internationalization and resulting domestic reforms respond to new constellations of statehood? How can these reactions be explained, and what are the similarities or differences between countries?* Figure 1.1 presents the approach of this book.

In this introductory chapter, we develop a theoretical framework for capturing the changes in outcomes as well as the diversity of actors' reactions. The first part introduces different perspectives on the transformation of the state in the field of education. Two prominent examples for internationalization in secondary and higher education, namely the Bologna Process and the Programme for International Student Assessment study (PISA), will be discussed in more detail in part II. By critically reviewing current literature on internationalization, part III identifies lacunas in research. Part IV specifies our dependent variable, namely educational outcomes and reactions on internationalization in the field of education policy. In order to analyse the outcomes, we refer to theories of systemic and institutional differentiation as well as theories of organizational behaviour. Actors' reactions are discussed by combining arguments from the literature on political opportunity structures and resource mobilization with a variant of value-expectation theory (VET).

## Transformation of the state in education policy

The policy field of education is a prime laboratory for observing if, to what extent and with what consequences a transformation of statehood is taking place. Serving to secure a nation's coherence and wealth through the training of the population in its history, culture, language and tools for a good economic performance, education policy has remained a mainly state-dominated policy field, and for a longer period of time than many other policy fields. Nevertheless, we can observe tremendous dynamics within secondary and higher education over the last decade. The international environment is considered the main stimulus for policy changes (Corbett 2005; Martens et al. 2010; Martens et al. 2007; Verger 2012), and it has triggered domestic reforms of education policy in different ways and with different dynamics. Two processes exemplify the phenomena of internationalization.

The most influential programme in *secondary education* is the PISA Study. Seventy-five participating countries, as diverse as Thailand, Qatar, Tunisia, Uruguay and Belgium, are subject to the same comparative programme. Conceptualized by the Organisation for Economic Co-operation and Development (OECD), PISA is not ideologically unbiased, but rather evaluates education from an economic perspective. Education is regarded as a crucial determinant for the economic performance of a country and the overall standard of living. A low-quality education system is thus equated with risks to overall economic prosperity. PISA focuses on the output of education systems and assesses how students are capable of applying the knowledge and skills learned in school in their future working life and society. The inquiry covers reading, and mathematical and scientific literacy, with a particular emphasis on one of these subjects in each assessment cycle.

The development of educational indicators in the OECD in the mid-1980s was prompted by the political interests of a few countries, particularly the U.S. and France, who pushed the OECD to produce better and more comparable data in education. Both countries, for very different reasons, were concerned about their respective national education systems and the domestic obstacles to reform. The U.S. feared losing the technology race of the Cold War; France's left-wing government was concerned about educational opportunities for socio-economically disadvantaged children. Conceptualized by the OECD secretariat in cooperation with national experts and institutions, the first ideas for PISA arose in the early 1990s. The OECD continued to develop an agenda for conceptualizing and designing outcome indicators in conjunction with member countries and networks of experts (Martens et al. 2007; Martens and Wolf 2009; Normand 2010). Today PISA represents a strong shift towards outcome and performance measures, triggering changes in many participating states.

Unlike previous international processes or evaluation schemes in secondary education, PISA has been widely publicized in participating countries and initiated heated debates about the efficiency and effectiveness of education systems, at least in those countries with lower-than-expected rankings (Martens and Niemann 2013). As a standard international assessment, PISA filters out examples of best practices in highly ranked countries and identifies the weaknesses of low-ranked participants. By doing so, it puts countries under pressure to improve their systems and adapt successful models. Despite criticism, PISA presents one of the most politically acknowledged studies in comparative education statistics.

In *higher education* the most prominent example of internationalization is the Bologna Process. It represents the largest process of structural harmonization of education systems in the world. The number of countries participating in Bologna has grown to a total of 47, ranging from Iceland to Turkey, from Portugal as far as Kazakhstan. Although originally an intergovernmental initiative between participating countries, it has been closely linked to the EU's Lisbon Agenda of making the EU 'the most dynamic and competitive knowledge-based economy in the world' by 2010 (Berlin Communiqué of Ministers 2003). At the recent ministerial conference in Leuven, national education ministers declared their intention to complete the European Higher Education Area (EHEA) by 2020. The participating countries agreed to implement a comparable higher education structure, consisting of a three-cycle bachelor-, master- and doctorate-level degree structure, a Europe-wide structure for quality assurance in higher education and the recognition of foreign degrees and other higher education qualifications (for an overview see Reinalda et al. 2006; Walter 2006).

It was events on the European level that gave rise to the remarkable political dynamics. The starting point for the Bologna project was the Sorbonne Declaration. At the 800th anniversary celebration of the Sorbonne University in 1998, Germany, France, Italy and the United Kingdom signed the project's declaration. Although with different reasons for signing the declaration, these countries agreed on closer cooperation in issues of higher education as well as to vague goals of common reforms in their countries. While the German, French and Italian governments were driven by domestic pressures, the British did not want to miss out on a common initiative between their European partners (Corbett 2005: 169; Witte 2006: 329; Martens and Wolf 2009). One year later, education ministers of 29 countries signed the Bologna Declaration. In the years since, the Bologna Process has been increasingly institutionalized and a number of guidelines have been developed. This has led to fundamental policy changes in most of the participating countries (Crosier et al. 2007).

The Bologna Process triggered wide-ranging reforms in the domestic systems of higher education in many of the participating countries. Since its central aim has been the creation of an EHEA enhancing the comparability and compatibility of higher education structures and degrees in Europe, the Anglo-American understanding of consecutive study structures needed to be implemented within all participating countries. Other basic objectives include the introduction of a three-tier system, a common credit transfer system, the promotion of academic mobility and European cooperation in quality assurance. From this viewpoint, higher education is considered to play a central role in the current transformation into knowledge-based economies as a key element in social or labour market policy. Capable higher education institutions thus are perceived as bearing the potential to increase the competitiveness of the overall economy and further economic growth through research and innovation. In essence, the Bologna Process is considered the greatest reform initiative in higher education of the last decades. By incorporating the Bologna aims into its Lisbon strategy, the EU gained leverage in the field of education policy.

From a more general perspective, the Bologna Process represents shifts in higher education policy towards increasing global competition. This internationalization can be observed at different levels. Countries and their higher education institutions (HEIs) engage in attracting international students or staff and establish bilateral relations with developing regions. In addition, HEIs have started to open so-called 'branch campuses' in other parts of the world. The ways of dealing with these new phenomena differs largely between European countries. In some countries, such as Germany or Austria, the Bologna Process has been dominating domestic discourses and policy reforms. UK higher education policy, in contrast, has traditionally been oriented towards overseas students and its main competitors, in particular the U.S. and Australia. In France, the Bologna Process has triggered domestic reforms, but the main debates in higher education policy-making focus on the global competitiveness of French HEIs.

In sum, education policy today is exercised by a *new constellation* of actors in education policy-making: while the state is still a vibrant shaper and mover of education policy, new actors and institutions are participating in the design, implementation and evaluation of education policy and its outcomes. Particularly, processes and procedures of policy-making at the international level are becoming more important elements that need to be acknowledged when studying education policy. The aforementioned Bologna Process and the PISA Study are the most prominent examples, but they are part of a broader shift in education policy. In this research project, we understand internationalization as a set of processes that are driven by supra- or international organizations, which can be either governmental or non-governmental. These processes substantially change the character of education policy-making, which has become (1) interdependent – that is, multiple levels of authority are involved, (2) competitive – that is, both education institutions and countries compete, and (3) diffuse – that is, new actors participate in policy-making.

## Research in the internationalization of education policy

Education policy as a research subject gained attention predominately within the last decade (for an overview of research on education in political science, see Jakobi et al. 2010; Busemeyer and Trampusch 2011). The fact that the EU has no assigned political competences in education matters has made it previously far less attractive than other policy fields. With the launch of the Bologna Process and the Declaration of Lisbon, the issue has attracted broader scholarly attention. Similarly, research in the area of secondary education was left mainly to education scientists. It was particularly due to PISA that political scientists discovered school politics as a subject of study. The rise of the governance perspective on political processes allowed political scientists to (re)discover education policy as a field of interest in a broader spectrum (Wolf 2010).

Research on *internationalization* in education policy has focused on the emergence of new levels of policy-making beyond the nation state. Over the last 20 years, we can observe new governance structures and organizations in the field of education (Robertson et al. 2012; Martens et al. 2007). The majority of international organizations (IOs) active in the field of education policy are neither democratically legitimized nor do they have formal competences in this policy field. However, organizations such as the European Commission, the OECD, the World Bank or the International Monetary Fund (IMF) have caused policy changes all over Europe (see contributions in Martens et al. 2007).

The Bologna Process has inspired scholars to work with a variety of theoretical approaches in order to understand its emergence and progress. While some authors analyse the Bologna Process from a historical-institutionalist perspective (Walter 2006), others focus on single events, like the so-called Sorbonne Declaration as a 'big bang' in Europeanizing education policy (Toens and Janning 2008). Also, the Bologna Process is conceptualized as a policy network in which the relationships between different political actors are depicted (Nagel 2009; 2010a; b). Owing to its geographic spread and its objective to foster harmonization, the Bologna Process is often selected as a case for testing and further developing convergence theories (Dobbins 2011; Dobbins and Knill 2009). In the case of secondary education, the PISA Study is the most prominent example used for exploring and further developing the potentials of soft governance by international organizations (Martens and Jakobi 2009; Finnemore 1993; Barnett and Finnemore 2004). With PISA, the OECD has become a successful policy entrepreneur and a potential driving force for transformation in the field of education (Nagel et al. 2010: 18; Martens and Jakobi 2010). In the realm of education policy, the OECD relies on its good arguments and persuasion (Marcussen 2004; Grek 2009; Martens and Jakobi 2009). No other international organization is currently as prominent in this policy field as the OECD (Rinne et al. 2004). This is particularly striking since the OECD is not an education organization per se.

Another perspective of research in education policy focuses on the *domestic level*. While the political economy of education has attracted scholars of comparative politics (see for example, Ansell 2010; Busemeyer and Trampusch 2011), changes in both higher and secondary education on the domestic level due to international impulses have only recently become the focus of scholars. In research on the Bologna Process, a large number of publications deal with the practical implication of the Bologna guidelines (Colin et al. 2006; Hagemann 2005; Froment 2006) or the statistical evaluation and its implementation (Teichler 2004; Leszczensky 2005). From a political science perspective, many case studies focus on analysing the degrees of change in higher education, using a set of classic cases such as Germany, France or England, but also more uncommon countries such as New Zealand or Switzerland. Also, the variety of theoretical approaches to find explanations for policy changes ranges from rational choice approaches, such as the veto player approach, to constructivist explanations, including ideationalist approaches (for example, Witte 2006; Martens et al. 2010).

As regards the PISA Study, the research analyses its impact on the national education systems for secondary education. PISA's figures, ratings and rankings have been discussed under the premises of influence on domestic policy-making (Grek 2009, Martens and Niemann 2013). Sociological studies often work with the data generated through PISA and explore topics such as institutional and organizational effects on student performance and social and ethnic inequalities (Dronkers and Levels 2007; Teltemann and Windzio 2011; 2013; Windzio 2013a; 2013b;

Lindemann 2013). PISA also triggered many single or comparative case studies about impact and consequences on national systems (Grek 2009; Knodel et al. 2013; on Germany see Ertl 2006; Niemann 2010; Gruber 2006). In this respect, Finnish education policy and its success in the PISA Study became a prominent issue and triggered analyses on the reasons for the great Finnish results (Rinne et al. 2004; Rautalin 2007).

In sum, after a long period of neglect, education policy has been discovered by social scientists as a fruitful field of research. By now, the international level of education policy-making has been widely explored. Similarly, there are many single and comparative case studies that focus on explaining levels of policy change on the national level. However, the consequences of internationalization have been largely unexplored. This book thus focuses on understanding educational outcomes and actors' reactions.

## Consequences of transformations in education policy

In the following section, we argue that it is useful to distinguish between *outcomes* and actors' *reactions* when analysing the internationalization of education policy. It is clear that these two categories are closely linked, that is, educational outcomes affect the reactions of politically important actors and *vice versa*. In a second step, for analytical purposes, we review them separately and triangulate the findings (see the final chapter by Windzio et al. of this book). The first sections discuss political outcomes of education reforms and their theoretical implications. In a second step, we develop a theoretical framework to understand the reactions of political actors on internationalization.

### Education policies, outcomes and frictions

The outputs of political systems are regulations that should have an effect on actors' situations and behaviours at the micro level. With regard to complex issues, such as the outcome of education, policies aim at changing the conditions of the learning process in educational institutions. Examples of these conditions are, among others, teachers' salaries or the student-teacher ratio. However, it is questionable whether changes in these conditions actually result in the desired *outcome*. At the level of secondary education, there are clear expectations regarding the effect of school resources. Increasing resources should have a positive effect on the outcome. Another change in education policy is the liberalization of the education system with regard to privatization and school choice. Liberalization should increase competition for students and thus could have a positive effect on over-all student performance (for an overview see Teltemann 2013), but it could also increase inequality between students, both in the social reproduction of inequality over generations as well as the ethnic and social segregation across schools.

Regarding the complexity of social systems, even if policy-makers are able to implement programmes in their pure form – which itself is often very difficult in democratic political systems – the desired outcome fails to appear. Hence, we simply follow the notion that decision-makers have only limited capacity to directly create changes in the social world. In our study, we analyse different outcomes of the transformation of education policy for secondary and tertiary education. At the tertiary level we ask whether the employability of graduates has increased in countries that have undergone a fundamental change compared with countries where such a change was not observed, for example, from a one-stage diploma into a two-stage bachelor's and master's (BA/MA) pro-gramme structure. Moreover, we also expect changes in the outcomes with regard to spatial mobility of students between countries. In our design, we compare countries that had a fundamental transformation (for example, Germany, France and Switzerland) with a set of rather static countries (for example, England).

At the secondary level, we analyse whether changes in the conditions of the learning process actually result in changes in the desired outcomes. Here, these outcomes are, among others, overall performance of students, which is expected to increase, as well as inequality, which is supposed to decline. Inequality in student performance can be analysed for differ-ent social classes, or for families with different levels of socio-economic resources, but can also be seen between immigrant and native students, which are, at least to some extent, independent of inequality due to socio-economic resources. Since the expected outcomes of the transformations in education policy are clearly defined, namely an increase in student performance and a reduction in inequality, we present the following theoretical arguments to explain why we expect frictions between the governance of secondary education and its outcomes.

At their best, education policies can change the opportunities and give incentives in choosing specific options (for example, to attend a private school, to study a specific programme or to study abroad), but these opportunities must match the needs and interests of the clients. Moreover, education policies often try to impact society by implement-ing specific measures, but it is not always clear whether a specific meas-ure is an appropriate means to achieve the desired end. Hence, it is by no means clear whether changes in education policies improve the education system towards the desired outcome. We develop our line of argumentation using theories of systemic and institutional differentiation as well as theories of organizational behaviour, as developed in Windzio (2013b). The argument we are making can be summarized as follows: in complex modern societies, social subsystems show a high degree of separation from each other (Luhmann 1998). This separation can be described as distinguishing between codes and programmes. At the code level, the discriminatory power of communication is very high – the code of scientific communication is different from that of political communication. Obviously, scientific truth cannot be established by legal definition. But the subsystem of education is open to the influence of other subsystems at the programme level. Programmes decide the value assignment of a binary code (students being selected or not, or having good or bad grades in education). However, at the programme level, we find an overload with a multiplicity of tasks which the system is expected to accomplish simultaneously. From policy-makers' and educationists' view, the starting point of changing the society in a desired direction is education. Since parenting and early-childhood education predominantly take place in the private sphere of the family, which can be hardly regulated or monitored by authorities, schools are considered important focal points to deal with social problems such as the integration of immigrants, the prevention of intolerance and racism and juvenile delinquency. Hence, educational organizations, especially schools, are places where intervention according to a specific programme occurs in the early stages of the life-course, at a time when pupils and students are still in their formative years.

Educational institutions thus have many functions, such as to groom persons into careers and legitimize social inequality, function as places of general social integration, train pupils' cognitive abilities, integrate and structurally assimilate immigrants, maintain the option of social mobility, teach democracy and proper behaviour, and work to prevent delinquency. Regardless of whether these issues are actually significant or not, once they are declared problems in the public debate, policy-makers or school principals will decide whether measures have to be taken. Educational institutions thus have to deal with this multiplicity of social problems. In a sense, they are 'garbage cans' (Cohen et al. 1972) for issues produced in other subsystems and therefore undergo a permanent reform process. However, numerous studies in organizational science have highlighted the detrimental effects of reforms. Organizational ecology theory and research (Hannan and Freeman 1989) has shown that the short-term effect of reforms is often a 'resetting of the clock' back to zero, or back to the high-level uncertainty similar to the organization's founding period when severe problems arise due to underdeveloped routines (Amburgey et al. 1993: 64).

Moreover, the governance of organizations is a problem in and of itself. In sharp contrast to Max Weber's model of bureaucracy (see Swedberg 2003: 92), Cohen et al. (1972) consider organizations as 'organized anarchies'. Problems originate from both inside and outside the organization: 'they might arise over issues of lifestyle; family; frustrations of work; careers; group relations within the organization; distribution of status, jobs, and money; ideology; or current crises of mankind as interpreted by the mass media or the next-door neighbor. All of these require attention' (Cohen et al. 1972: 3). According to the results of their computer simulation of different types of universities, schools might also consist of at least some anarchic elements due to the fact that their members' concerns and requests are also influenced by the everyday life outside the organization (Cohen et al. 1972: 13). The overall process of problem-solving in the garbage-can model is rather inefficient. Many problems remain unsolved and resources are directed towards tasks that are not part of the organization's technical core. However, organizations are still capable of making decisions, even if they are burdened with conflicts and ambiguous goals (Cohen et al. 1972: 16). In any case, it is hard to imagine that reforms in such 'garbage-can' organizations result only in intended institutional effects on integration and inequality.

Finally, institutional theories of social differentiation as well as ecological theories illustrate that task overloading often impedes the performance of organizations within an institutional field. This assumption can be justified by two arguments from the theory of institutions (Meyer and Rowan 1977; Lepsius 1995). Here, institutionalization means that a criterion of rationality can be established in an action context (which then becomes a *validity context*) and that this criterion of rationality actually determines an actor's behaviour (Lepsius 1995). Successful institutionalization often creates negative externalities, which cannot be handled within the same validity context. Economic profitability, for instance, depends on low labour cost. Firms reduce these costs by dismissing people or moving their production units to regions where labour costs are low. In modern capitalistic societies, a specialized institution, namely the welfare state, has been established in order to deal with these externalities. Here, the guiding idea is solidarity, and one of the most important carrier groups was the labour movement.

The core argument in Lepsius' theory is that institutions often have to defend the validity of their own criteria of rationality within their validity contexts (Lepsius 1995). The operation of an institution will be impeded if it either cannot externalize contingencies or if it has to deal with contingencies created by other institutions. What has this institutional theory to do with educational institutions? Among other things, these institutions have to deal with social problems, such as integrating immigrants or preventing adolescents from engaging in criminal behaviour. Since educational institutions spend a large part of their resources on handling such externalities (Windzio 2013b), their capacity to focus on a specific reform process is limited. It is thus unlikely that reforms designed to improve the outcomes can be implemented without serious friction.

In their groundbreaking paper, Meyer and Rowan (1977) argue that there is a tendency in modern societies to decouple an organization's formal structure and its technical activities. The formal structure reflects myths institutionalized in the organization's environment, and conformity to these myths (for example, isomorphism) increases the legitimacy, and thus the probability of survival, of the organization. In order to gain legitimacy, organizations employ assessment criteria from the environment, which results in the drawback of being controlled by external forces. As Meyer and Rowan (1977: 354) argue, schools strategically redefine the nature of their output in order to meet the criteria of assessment. For instance, universities employ Nobel Prize winners, and the activity of schools can be legitimated by good results in the PISA Study (or similar comparative tests). However, this does not necessarily mean that organizations become inefficient by adopting these external criteria. But if the survival of an organization mainly depends on conformity with institutionalized rules, then conflicts between institutional isomorphism and efficiency become likely: 'organizations often face the dilemma that activities celebrating institutionalized rules, although they count as virtuous ceremonial expenditures, are pure costs from the point of view of efficiency' (Meyer and Rowan 1977: 355). According to Meyer and Rowan, organizations spend a lot of resources on adapting their formal structure to the requirements of the institutional environment. Hence institutions and their organization are not only exposed to social problems, but the institutional environment also imposes institutional rules which prescribe how to deal with these problems, often without regard of actual efficiency.

Taken together, these different theoretical arguments underline an open question of how efficiently reforms can be implemented and the outcomes of the educational system – both at the secondary and tertiary level – can be improved. We expect frictions, that is, policies will be only indirectly transformed into outcomes, if at all.

## Actors' reactions on internationalization

This section outlines a theoretical framework to fully understand the profound changes that are triggered through education policy internationalization. The aim is to study the consequences of a *new constellation of statehood in education* on domestic politics, in particular actors' reactions. We argue that for a comprehensive understanding of the scope of educational transformation, an approach encompassing both the macro and the micro perspective is necessary. In the following section, we set up an analytical framework that takes macro and micro levels into account, combines structural and actor-centred explanatory variables and considers changes over time. In order to explain collective reactions on transformations in education policy, we combine arguments from literature on political opportunity structures and resource mobilization with a variant of value-expectation theory. Figure 1.2 summarizes the theoretical framework.

At a most general level, we are interested in the collective reactions of actors affected by changes in the field of education, for example, stakeholders and interest groups. In order to conceptualize reactions of political actors, that is, our *dependent variable*, we refer to the typology of *loyalty, voice* and *exit* (Hirschman 1970). This typology has recently (re)gained prominence in the social sciences. While the origin of the typology is a discussion about the economic failure of companies, we adapt it for analysing actors' reactions to the internationalization processes in the field of education. In short, Hirschman argues that if a

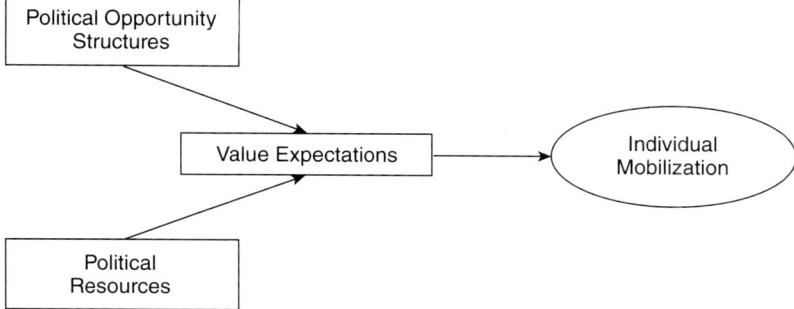

*Figure 1.2*  Overview of the theoretical framework for analysing actors' reactions.

company's performance declines due to increasing competition or mismanagement, clients may show different reactions: They remain loyal (*loyalty*), articulate discontent (*voice*) or stop buying products (*exit*). The starting point of Hirschman's argument is the question of under what conditions these reactions are more likely to occur and which reaction is more efficient. Even though he develops his typology in economics, collective reactions are also relevant for political processes, as identified by Hirschman himself in discussing the implications of his concept for political science in the article 'Exit, Voice, and the State' (1978). The link from economics to politics is quite obvious: in both fields, we have actors who react to new situations by choosing between the different options of *exit, voice* or *loyalty*. In economics these actors are customers; in politics the equivalent are the political actors from a specific policy field. Similarly, new situations in the business realm could be a company's financial mismanagement or failure while new situations in politics can be conceptualized as small adjustments in a policy field or the government's decision to fundamentally reform existing structures. In our study, the new situations are transformations in the field of education policy (Martens et al. 2010).

What are possible reactions of actors to transformations in the policy field of education? First, a *new constellation in education policy-making* may lead to *voice*. At a most general level, *voice* includes different forms of articulating demands and strategies to place problems on the political agenda. In other words, it is about mobilization in order to influence political decisions or stimulate public opinion (Hirschman 1970: 30). The idea of *voice* encompasses a variety of actions (Barnes et al. 1979), ranging from the organization of information events for the public to political violence. Generally speaking, forms of political activity can be closely linked to electoral processes, with voting being one of the most basic forms of democratic participation. However, there are many other forms of participation. For example, engagement in the political discourse through writing statements in newspapers, attending public discussions or joining political organizations also reflect forms of political activity. In addition, other forms include all political action that takes place outside the institutionalized political process, namely strikes, demonstrations and online petitions, but also include more violent opposition, such as the occupation of facilities. For instance, students in Germany and Austria demonstrated and went on strike against the Bologna reform (Irle 2009). Similar patterns of opposition can be observed in the UK where critics raised their *voices* against EU's engagement in higher education (Fearn 2008).

*Loyalty* is closely related to *voice*. The main difference, however, is that claims that are assigned to this category are positive. Even though conditions for actors may change fundamentally and, eventually, in undesired directions, they remain loyal and publicly articulate this. They neither articulate *voice*, nor do they leave the political arena. Yet, we do not understand *loyalty* as an unintentional action. Rather, it is a rational and strategic action driven by 'the expectation that, over a period of time, the right turns will more than balance the wrong ones' (Hirschman 1970: 78). This type of reaction is an intermediate category since a decline of *loyalty* may lead to *voice* and, ultimately, *exit*. Nevertheless, even loyal actors may exert influence by strategically emphasizing the option of *exit*. Hirschman argues that the threat of *exit* will often be made by the most loyal actors, which are members of organizations who really care about the future (Hirschman 1970: 83). In the field of education, organizations can be considered loyal if they remain calm and generally supportive even though transformations may fundamentally reduce their power and influence.

The third possible reaction is *exit*. Generally speaking, this category means that actors migrate elsewhere because of growing discontent. Instead of publicly articulating opposition against new policies or other changes, they simply leave. Individual or collective actors that formerly were active may retreat from the political action. For example, in the field of education policy, cooperation between state and societal actors often takes place in the context of institutionalized and periodical meetings. In order to express discontent about political developments or decisions, some actors may decide to withdraw from these forums of deliberation. Such meetings have existed, in some instances, for a long time and have become part of the policy process. In our cases, *exit* could mean that political actors quit from collective arrangements. For example, the *Diplom* has been for a very long time the degree for engineers in Germany. In the context of the Bologna Process, it was replaced by the two-cycle BA/MA degree. However, recently the German *Bundesland* Mecklenburg-Vorpommern heralded the reintroduction of the *Dipl. Ing.* degree (Kaube 2010). Actors affected by transformations may also refuse to implement new guidelines. German philosophers, for example, have called to boycott the accreditation procedures that have been part of the Bologna guidelines. Thus, *exit* also includes cases where actors respond to transformations by intentionally ignoring them. That is, if organizations are aware of changes and their potential consequences but continue to ignore them, we could interpret such strategies as *exit*. Given that the focus of our analyses is on highly professionalized organizations and interest groups, it can be assumed that these actors are aware of ongoing developments in their respective countries. If actors respond to new situations by choosing the *exit* option, there may be fundamental consequences for democracies, such as political disengagement, demotivation and depoliticization.

According to Hirschman, actors play a key role because of their rational decisions to maintain or dissolve transactional relationships and by being loyal or actively trying to impact their business partners. As we show, assuming bounded rational actors is a fruitful approach to close the epistemic gap between the macro, meso and micro levels. The basic idea is that outcomes at the macro level result from purposeful actions on the micro or meso level. Strictly speaking, meso-level outcomes, such as decisions in organizations, can also be regarded as a result of socially embedded individual decisions (Coleman 1990). This does not imply, however, that actors are always capable of realizing their individual goals. There are logical reasons why this cannot be the case: If two actors have a conflict of interest, it is the exception rather than the rule that both can meet their individual interests. Such arguments have been highlighted during numerous game-theory models (Rapoport 1960). Even the view on the social embeddedness of individual decision-making highlighted the structural determinants of producing outcomes that are not desired by any actor involved in the game (Rapoport 1960: 173).

Well aware of the logic of this micro foundation of meso outcomes, we exclude the level of individual actors for analytical purposes and set the organizational level as the smallest level of analysis. In this study we conceptualize organizations as collective actors following their specific rationalities because we are not able to develop *ex ante* theoretical arguments on the structure of antagonistic or cooperative games of individual actors in each organization. Nevertheless, the theoretical framework is open to the individual level. Depending on the results of the empirical analysis, it provides an avenue for analysing individual actors within the same theoretical framework as it analyses decisions made at the organizational level. However, before discussing why actors choose a specific type of action, we need to understand factors that facilitate political action. Thus, the following section introduces the concepts of political opportunity structures and political resources.

## Political opportunity structures

Social and political action always takes place within certain contexts. The main idea of structural context is that some parts of an environment either constrain or stimulate political activity (Eisinger 1973: 11). Thus, we refer to the concept of *political opportunity structures*. In general, opportunity structures can be distinguished between formal political structures and cultural contexts. Earlier studies particularly focused on institutional characteristics of political systems, such as the degree of openness of local institutions (Eisinger 1973). Kitschelt (1986) argued that the governments' policy-making capacity – as represented by the configuration of resources, institutional settings and historical precedents – affects the dynamics of protest. In addition to earlier variants of this approach, his study argues that specific arrangements of input and output structures explain the strategies collective actors apply. What is more, opportunity structures may also explain the impact of movements on government policies. The more scholars that engaged in studying contentious politics, the more variables were added, for example, political cleavages or coalition building with political elites (for an extensive overview, see Kriesi 2004). Even though the concept has been criticized as being a 'sponge that soaks up every aspect of the social movement environment' (Gamson and Meyer 1996: 275), it is still an important concept when studying political dynamics.

Following a parsimonious approach to political opportunity structures, we take a closer look at the accessibility of a political system and its implementation capacity (Kriesi 2004: 71). *Accessibility* of a political system refers to the formal institutional arrangement of a political system. It is about how political power is distributed. Scholars often distinguish between strong and weak states (Casey 2004; Koopmans and Kriesi 1995; Kriesi et al. 2006). Strong states are relatively closed and have only limited opportunities for non-state actors to engage in the political process. Thus, in a political system where power is centralized, it is difficult to access and actively contribute to decision-making. In addition, governments have a high implementation capacity and are capable of implementing new policies in a strong and effective way without having to consider a large number of actors. Weak states, in contrast, are decentralized, and the political power is distributed between a large number of actors. This implies that various channels to influence decision-making exist, since political processes are inevitably more open. It is more easily manageable for interest groups to approach political elites and convince them of the groups' interests. However, with regards to the implementation of policies, governments in weak states must include many actors at the expense of duration and efficiency. Once a bill is passed, different actors are in charge of implementing it. This carries the risks of inefficient implementation or high levels of contention (Patashnik 2008). Following this distinction with the distribution of power, France would be an example of a strong and centralized state. In contrast, Britain, with its high level of decentralization and various agencies, would be an example of a weak state. This book discusses a number of countries with different opportunity structures.

### Political resources

Nevertheless, there are other dynamics and constellations within states that should be taken into account. Hence, we introduce a second dimension to understand the consequences of internationalization in education policy. Actors' capacities to organize and mobilize are also affected by the ability to access and control *political resources*. Through criticizing literature that explained collective action by societal grievances and mass frustration, scholars developed the so-called resource mobilization approach (McCarthy and Zald 1977). The intellectual framework that was used in this approach follows 'the American political science tradition of interest group theory that viewed politics as a continual contest for influence by groups with different levels of power' (Walder 2009: 398). Following these arguments, a variety of resources are distributed in the political sphere. However, these resources are not equally distributed among the actors (Edwards and McCarthy 2004: 117). Some actors are in a position that enables them to access many resources and, if necessary, use them to influence political processes in a quick and efficient manner. In contrast, other actors are unable to gain control of certain resources and thus are disadvantaged. This unequal distribution of resources is at the core of political action, since politics is about who gets what, when and how (Lasswell 1958). Such patterns of inequality, however, are not carved in stone. In democratic polities there is an ongoing distribution and redistribution of resources (Edwards and McCarthy 2004: 121–4). It is these dynamics that we investigate in this book.

Political resources are multifaceted. Over the last decades, scholars have produced long lists of resources that were strongly dependent on the phenomena under research (Oberschall 1973; McAdam et al. 1988). Cress and Snow (1996) developed a typology of resources in order to establish a more general concept of resource mobilization. Even though they developed these categories in the context of a study on homeless social movement organizations in U.S. cities, their results are more generally applicable. They distinguish between four types of resources: moral, material, informational and human (Cress and Snow 1996: 1095). The first category, *moral resources*, is a non-material resource. It includes support of an organization's goals or actions by external actors. For example, an organization that has a very good reputation and is frequently complimented in the public will less likely be ignored when changes are discussed that might affect its goals. *Material resources* are not only comprised of financial means, such as money for campaigns to make an organization's goals visible, but also a variety of other things, such as office and meeting space. The third category, *informational resources*, refers to the access of an organization to knowledge and information that is of interest. It includes all kinds of strategic or technical support by external experts. With the advent of evidence-based policy-making in the field of education policy, this resource has become more important. Today's education stakeholders, for example, university sector organizations or teachers unions, are keen on producing reports and statistics that underline their agendas. Finally, *human resources* are the people who work for organizations and devote their time to reach a certain goal. For example, it includes individual leaders who speak on behalf of the organization, but also encompasses groups of people and constituencies. This category also includes a relational dimension, namely cooperation with other influential individuals or organizations in the political process. It can be assumed that, for example, the ability to quickly and directly access decision-makers if necessary increases an organization's probability to pursue its interests. To give another example, if an organization has established good relationships with the media, for example, newspapers or TV stations, it might be able to use these networks when necessary for the organization.

To sum up, our analytical framework to analyse reactions to the internationalization of education policy is based on two theoretical arguments. First, we argue that certain characteristics of a country's institutional setting influence the ways in which actors respond to transformations. Such political opportunity structures may either impose constraints on political activity or stimulate it. The empirical chapters that relate to the reactions on the internationalization of education policies will focus especially on the accessibility of political systems and the distinction between strong and weak states. Second, following the concept of resource mobilization, we argue that the availability and accessibility of resources is crucial for actors to mobilize effectively in the political process. The type of resources can vary substantially and includes material and non-material resources.

### Value expectations

In our study, structural context and resources are important for the explanation of reactions since they are assumed to facilitate political action, namely *voice*, *exit* or *loyalty*. However, in the end, it is the (collective) actor who decides on a behavioural alternative. Thus, in this section, we introduce a theoretical approach to actors' reactions that allows for arguments on the micro level. We refer to a rationalist approach to political behaviour to answer the question of why actors use certain strategies to produce political or social outcomes within a given context. Looking at 'what those persons wanted, what they believed, and how they expected their actions to further their goals' (Little 1991: 39) enables us to understand the consequences. The so-called value-expectation theory is a general approach to explain the behaviour of individual and collective actors. Similar to other rational choice approaches, its basic assumption is that actors pursue their goals in a self-interested way. In order to do so, they collect and process information on the environments in which they are operating. Basically, value-expectation theory aims to explain the decision-making rational. According to the level and quality of information actors have access to or are able to process under conditions of bounded rationality, they weigh the subjective value of any alternative with the subjectively expected probability that the expected consequences of the intentional action will actually occur (Gilboa 2010: 55).

We argue that actors' behaviours are rational. According to their interests, values or ideologies, they aim at realizing certain goals. However, the question is how these goals, for example, the intended outcomes of a decision, can be realized. For each behavioural alternative, the actors value the utility it has to realize the outcome. Assuming that they have certain goals, they should be able to identify behavioural alternatives that are appropriate to attain these goals. From this perspective, choosing an alternative is considered as *instrumental* in producing the desired outcome. However, decision-making is not only based on the utility, but also on the subjectively perceived probability that a certain goal can be realized. In order to understand the components of decision-making from a VET perspective, we refer to the utility of a specific alternative $i$ as $U(i)$. Additionally, the degree of uncertainty of realizing a certain outcome by alternative $U(i)$ is described by $p(i)$. This simply means that a specific behavioural alternative becomes more likely the higher the value of utility $U(i)$ and the higher the subjectively assumed probability $p(i)$ of realizing a certain goal is. However, political action is always costly, and these costs can differ between actors and alternatives. The final value of the expected utility of alternative $i$, $EU(i)$, has to also take into account the costs $C(i)$ of choosing this alternative. For reasons of analytical clarity, we distinguish between three behavioural alternatives among which actors can decide: *exit* (e), *voice* (v) and *loyalty* (l). Formally, the expected value of each alternative can be calculated by subtracting the costs of an alternative from its utility multiplied with the assumed probability of reaching a certain goal by choosing it.

$$EU(e) = p(e) \bullet U(e) - C(e)$$
$$EU(v) = p(v) \bullet U(v) - C(v)$$
$$EU(l) = p(l) \bullet U(l) - C(l)$$

In value-expectation theory, it is assumed that the actors make a decision following a simple rule: they chose, for example, alternative v if $EU(v) > EU(l) > EU(e)$. Such a calculation, however, is not easy from the actors' point of view. Of course, they neither compute precise values nor do they explicitly and consciously perform such calculations. Rather, they have vague ideas or even just vague sentiments on utilities, costs and probabilities. As already mentioned, actors' rationality is bounded. Nonetheless, if an action is goal-directed and actors attempt to influence an ongoing political process, these are the basic subjective variables that the decision is based on – even though they cannot be measured and evaluated in a precise way.

### A macro-micro explanation of actors' reactions

The following section combines the theoretical arguments introduced before and integrates them into a general approach in order to understand actors' reactions on internationalization. Figure 1.3 gives an overview of the theoretical framework.

We refer to the so-called *Coleman Bathtub*, suggesting that correlations at the macro level can only be explained by processes at the micro level of individual or collective actors (Coleman 1990). Hence, at the meso and micro level, we focus on the interplay of opportunity structures,

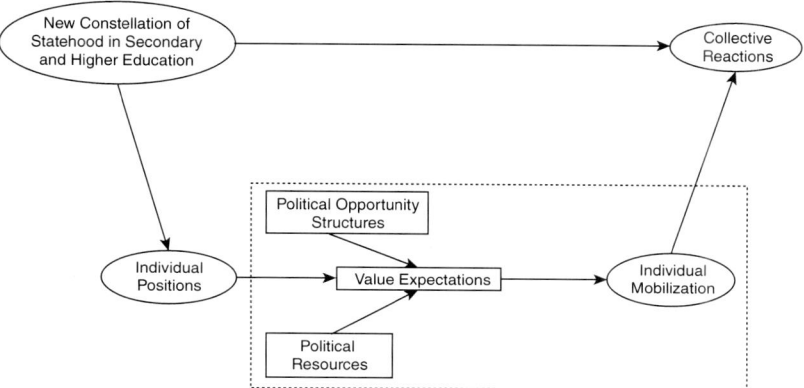

*Figure 1.3*  A macro-micro framework.

the distribution of resources as well as the motives and subjectively perceived situations. As we have argued at the beginning of this chapter, the dependent variable of this study is the reactions of actors to a *new constellation of the state in education* and its consequences. More precisely, the focus is on the consequences of internationalization on secondary and higher education policy in different countries. Two initiatives are of particular interest: the OECD's PISA Study in secondary education and the Bologna Process in higher education. As is argued above, these initiatives are the most prominent examples and are closely linked to other processes of internationalization. In some countries, these processes have triggered substantial policy changes, while other countries were affected rather indirectly. Nevertheless, it can be reasonably argued that the landscape of education policy has changed and a *new constellation of the state in education* has emerged.

We expect that these macro-level processes have effects on domestic politics, for example, the degree of support or conflict of politically relevant actors in our selected countries. As a first step, we reconstruct the so-called *definition of the situation*. Assuming bounded rationality, actors decide on how to respond to the *new constellation* by evaluating their situation. This decision is driven by actors' motives, existing knowledge, values and other components of their frames of reference. The motives are drawn from the ultimate goals of actors. Knowing these motives allows us to understand the utility of certain behavioural alternatives. Such a motive could be relative deprivation due to a considerable worsening of an actor's situation. For example, if actor A is excluded from an important forum of decision-making and, as a consequence of reforms, his or her situation worsens, it is likely that actor A decides to raise *voice* in order to express discontent, or even more drastically, a form of *exit*. On the other hand, however, policy changes in the context of internationalization could also improve an actor's situation. For example, while actor B has not been able to effectively participate in political processes, his or her situation might have improved significantly due to new regulations in education policy-making that are in line with the agenda. Due to this improvement, actor B evaluates the situation positively and expresses *loyalty* with the *new constellation*. Put differently, decisions are mediated by actors' subjective perceptions and definitions of the situation. As argued above, however, the definition of the situation always takes place within certain opportunity structures and is influenced by the availability of resources. It is worth underscoring that every actor perceives opportunity structures and resources subjectively. While some actors prefer centralized institutional settings and the availability of informational resources, others may be in favour of other constellations that allow them to effectively articulate their interests.

In sum, depending on the interplay of these factors – value expectations, opportunity structures and resources – we expect that the reactions of actors to internationalization will fall into one of three categories: *voice, exit* and *loyalty*. By aggregating the findings of the micro level to the macro level, we are able to understand *collective reactions to the new constellation*. Since we analyse various types of actors in a broad set of countries, the aggregated results allow for an interpretation of the current state of political contention in education politics. This study thus contributes to the debate about policy feedback and the effect of policies on politics. It adds to the debate about the question of what happens if formerly well-balanced conflicts are destabilized as a result of policy changes (Gaventa 1980; Patashnik 2008; Pierson 2005; 2011).

## Summary

We now sum up our line of reasoning and give arguments of why our theoretical model provides an *added value* in the explanation of the effects of internationalization of education policies on countries. The starting point of our model comes out of the early stages of our research project when we analysed the *new constellation of statehood in education policy*. The changes in the constellation of statehood come about through the emergence of new political actors, especially of international organizations (Martens et al. 2007). Triggered by a subset of EU countries in the 1990s, the Bologna Process was successful in the field of higher-education policy since most EU member countries adapted their tertiary education to the standards developed at the international level. Regarding secondary education, the relevant international actor was the OECD, who launched the first wave of the PISA Study in the year 2000. In some countries the ranking according to student performance and social inequality triggered fundamental reforms in the secondary education system.

These two transformations – the Bologna Process and the reforms in the wake of the PISA Study – have consequences at the micro level for the clients of education policies, such as students, teachers, employers, but also policy-makers. As we have argued, we expect two main consequences from the internationalization of education policy: first, we expect changes in the outcomes of education policies, both at the secondary and tertiary level. Second, we explain how the relevant political actors perceive these changes and why they either opt for *exit*, *voice* or *loyalty*. The added value of our theoretical model is that it leads to hypotheses on *outcomes* of education policy, while at the same time the model systematically explains the subjective perception of the individual situation by the relevant political actors. Thereby, it allows the derivation of country-specific as well as group-specific hypotheses on *reactions* to be analysed. The subjective perception of the consequences of the internationalization of education policy is expected to result in reactions, especially by those political actors who are affected by these consequences.

We address the following research questions: Can we find indicators of change in the outcomes which are, or not, in line with the intentions of the policy-makers? If not, what are the reasons? Do we observe reactions of political actors who are involved in this process? Why do we observe reactions of specific groups of actors, while we cannot observe the reactions for others?

Regarding education system outcomes, we expect *friction* between the intentions of policy-makers and policies as well as the changes in the outcomes at the micro level, where clients of the education system are affected in one way or another. According to the predefined goals in the Bologna Process, or according to the benchmarking process in secondary education, political actors intend to implement appropriate policy measures (output) in order to reach their goals and improve their situation. The *outcomes* of education policy are indicators of whether the situation of the clients of education policy (at the micro level) is in line with these goals or not. However, the question is whether a policy-output can directly establish the desired outcome at the micro level. In this regard, theories from organization sciences and sociology, such as systems theory, theory of institutional conflicts and the garbage-can model of organizational behaviour, are pessimistic. Our model gives theoretical arguments of why it is unlikely that intentions of policy-makers can be directly transformed into policies and why it is even more unlikely that they establish the desired results at the client or micro level of the educational system. This is what many institutional and organizational theories suggest: collective behaviour is neither organized along highly efficient bureaucracies nor does it produce predictable outcomes. Policies, general social systems and human behaviour are only loosely coupled. For this reason, we do not expect a straightforward causal chain between the internationalization of education policy, adaptations of domestic policies in order to reach the desired goals and desired outcomes at the micro level, namely the clients of education policy at the secondary and tertiary level. Imperfect outcomes, or results that are in contrast to the desired goals, make reactions of interest groups likely.

When explaining actors' *reactions* on internationalization, we based our arguments on *political opportunity structures, political resources* and *value expectations* as preconditions of mobilization of specific interest groups. Political opportunity structures and political resources are context factors which frame the decision process at the individual level of the interest group or the organization. For example, specific actors might perceive a high utility in changing the current state or re-establishing the previous situation in the education system. But at the same time, they might assume that the political opportunity structures are not in favour of their politics. Considering this, actors might not opt for *voice* even though they are highly interested in changing the current state. In the same way, resources are also context factors that result in either a high or low probability of realizing the goals of the organization and make *voice* sometimes unlikely.

Consequently, our theoretical model results in a dynamic view of the interdependence of education policies, outcomes and reactions. We argue that the process of change can only be understood by using a theoretical model that systematically takes the micro level of political actors into account. However, in contrast to many sociological studies, we do not observe individual persons as actors at the micro level, but rather political interest groups or organizations. Nevertheless, we argue that these *collective actors* follow their specific rationales and try to realize their goals. In doing so, they have to take into account political opportunity structures and resources as context factors at time t, namely, opportunities or constraints at the macro level. Regarding the outcome of the decision process on reactions, we expect a specific distribution of actors opting for *voice, exit* or *loyalty*. This distribution leads to an aggregation of all individual decisions to a new structural situation at the macro level at time t + 1. Strictly speaking, however, our qualitative data on actors' situational perceptions and decisions on *exit, voice* or *loyalty* provides only a snapshot of the comprehensive and dynamic process because the structure of collective reactions at the micro level will probably result in new changes to education policies that in turn trigger the next cycle of reactions. But as we will show, in some cases the data allows for predictions about the actors' future behaviour and thus the social foundation of reforms in education policy in the future.

## Outline of the book

Part I deals quantitatively with the internationalization of education and its impact on national education policy in a comparative way. This part focuses on the *outcomes* of education at both the secondary and tertiary levels. The investigation is based on the PISA data for secondary education as well as national individual and household surveys in the respective countries. Multilevel regression models are applied in a trend design, wherein the current average value of each indicator as well as a change score for the respective indicator is used for each time point. This is similar to fixed-effects panel models, and we argue that the change score should be closer to a causal measurement rather than just using the current state in the explanatory variable. For tertiary education, first the trajectory of both outbound and inbound student mobility between the years 2000 and 2010 is traced descriptively. Second, a set of time-series-cross-section analyses is conducted in order to establish which factors account for the overall attractiveness of higher education systems. In addition, a dyadic approach is taken to analyse push and pull factors between pairs of countries.

In chapter 2, *Janna Teltemann* argues that descriptive trend analyses of the four PISA waves lead to a mixed picture. Many OECD countries show changes in educational output factors, such as accountability practices, privatization or stratification, as well as changes in outcomes (competence levels, distributions of competences and associations between competences and individual background factors). However, these changes cannot be described in terms of a common pattern. Whereas Germany, a low performer in PISA 2000, was able to increase performance and decrease the social divide at the same time, Korea, a PISA winner, showed a stronger association between individual social background and competences in the last PISA wave. Although there seems to be some major trends, such as the growing importance of accountability practices and school autonomy, the OECD average values (means and variances) remain rather stable for many indicators. From a longitudinal perspective, hardly any significant associations have been found between changes in educational output variables and changes in outcomes.

In chapter 3, *Timm Fulge and Eva Maria Vögtle* evaluate outcomes of the Bologna Process and find that, while student mobility may have increased in absolute terms between the years 2000 and 2010, it has remained largely unchanged when taking into consideration the overall growth in enrolment. However, outbound mobility rates – defined as the share of students of a given country pursuing their education abroad – have increased moderately in Bologna countries. This relationship is significant and holds when introducing various controls, suggesting that the Bologna Process may have relaxed some of the factors that deterred students from seeking a degree outside their country of origin. Within the EHEA, there are no discernible differences between countries that underwent a high degree of institutional change in implementing Bologna reforms and those that were already in line with the policy prescriptions of the process.

Part II contains the qualitative case studies of Germany, France, England, Spain, Switzerland, U.S. and China. These studies show how actors responded with different *reactions* to the international initiatives in education policy. For the analysis of *reactions* we use expert interviews and document analysis. Most political actors publish documents on their political programmes. For this reason, we use these documents as a first step in understanding the actors' attitudes towards either the Bologna Process or the benchmarking process of the PISA Study. The selected experts represent the most important organizations or interest groups affected by the changes in education policies. Among others, these actors are student organizations, trade unions and employer organizations. All in all, we conducted 75 interviews with senior-level civil servants, governmental agencies, interest groups, think tanks and policy advisors for the seven qualitative country case studies.

For the case of Germany, *Dennis Niemann* shows in chapter 4 that the OECD's PISA Study and the Bologna Process substantially reshaped the national secondary and higher education system in German education policy-making. However, implementation processes and fine-tune adjustments are still ongoing. He analyses how German domestic actors have reacted to the recent reforms and how they act in the *new constellation* of educational policy-making by referring to the decentralized German political opportunity structure with its multiple access points. Niemann highlights that the framework of the new German education system, which is now characterized by output orientation and evidence-based policy-making, is widely accepted. However, some aspects of the 'grand reforms' – like the organization of the BA/MA study structure and economic-based ideas of education – are still objects of political struggle. Basically, in the German environment of semi-corporatism, the main actors argue either for an intensification of the reforms or for a slight rollback. Although the reform implementations are contentious in general, German education politics became business as usual again.

Chapter 5 by *Philipp Knodel* shows that in England responses to internationalization in secondary and higher education are fundamentally different. While PISA has not played an important role, Bologna has become part of a more general discourse about internationalization in English higher education. It is shown that organizations in the higher education sector have widened their agendas and have increasingly turned their attention towards developments beyond the national level. Knodel argues that these changes of actors' strategies are the result of contentions between the government and sector organizations.

In chapter 6, *Michael Dobbins* highlights how tertiary education reforms in reaction to the Bologna Process, combined with France's weak performance in international rankings, have generated not only far-reaching reforms and a new state governance approach, but also a new more polycentric political arena. This includes a new array of reform-friendly centre-right student unions, but also a reinvigorated, reform-sceptic research community with a series of new reactionary organizations. For secondary education, by contrast, he shows that the political process has remained relatively unchanged. Teachers unions repeatedly used strike tactics to prevent significant policy changes and preserve the pre-existing education politics and opportunity structures, which are still characterized by a highly corporatist system of conflictual cooperation between the teaching corps and the state bureaucracy.

In chapter 7, *Marie Popp* describes how the field of education policy in Spain has changed in response to internationalization. In order to meet the international standards, new ways of teaching and learning have been introduced into the Spanish education system. Actors reacted differently to these changes depending on the respective level of education. In higher education, transformations affected the overall structure of the Spanish higher education system: actors participate in new alliances and develop innovative instruments in order to exert influence on education policy-making. In secondary education, the results of the Spanish students in PISA triggered major debates on the quality of Spanish education. In spite of this, education policy-making is still shaped by national factors, especially by the dual logic of the political system (right-wing party vs. left-wing party) and the dual logic of the educational sector (private education vs. public education). The political alliances criticizing or supporting education reforms remained the same before and after PISA.

In chapter 8, *Tonia Bieber* assesses the ramifications of reforms in Switzerland. In the last decade, the OECD's PISA Study and the European Bologna Process have significantly changed domestic education policies and policy-making. As a consequence, output orientation, evidence-based policy-making and economic-based ideas of education have come to the forefront. This chapter analyses how the relevant domestic actors in this political field have reacted to these internationally induced reforms. The reactions of Swiss actors are determined by the domestic political opportunity structure, featuring federal fragmentation of policy-making, direct-democratic principles and consociationalist politics. In particular, consociationalism is reflected in the concerted Swiss-wide undertaking to finalize the implementation of the reforms. Most actors have reacted with general approval and support for the reformed Swiss education system because of long-needed reforms, both to renew teaching processes and to disentangle the complex policy-making structures. Only a few political actors view the recent reforms critically, mostly due to technical problems of implementation.

With the two chapters on the U.S. and China, the book pays tribute to major states and their responses to internationalization processes in education policy. While the U.S. has been participant in the PISA Study from the beginning, China, or rather the Shanghai region, only took part in it from 2009 onwards. Obviously both countries are not members of the European Bologna Process. Nonetheless, both states have to respond to these phenomena in the education process since these processes, at least indirectly, affect their policies.

In chapter 9, *Tonia Bieber*, *Michael Dobbins*, *Timm Fulge* and *Kerstin Martens* look at how the U.S. reacted to PISA and Bologna. Since evidence-based policy-making in education already existed in the U.S. long before PISA, the U.S. has not shown much responsiveness to the OECD's study, despite continual poor ranking. However, because of the good score of Shanghai in the secondary school survey, American policy-makers started to take the PISA Study more seriously, fearing economic problems due to poor schooling. In higher education, only a few policy-makers argued against the European Bologna reform. Rather, the Bologna Process is more prominently discussed by American actors with regards to compatibility with the new European higher education system. Due to the highly decentralized American political opportunity structure, however, reforms are difficult to install.

In chapter 10 on China, *Alexander Akbik*, *Kerstin Martens* and *Chenjian Zhang* explore the impact of international influences on the Chinese educational system, taking into account the Confucian culture of this country. The authors show that the Chinese central authority plays a major role, even in local education discourse, using PISA as a legitimization tool for its reform stance in secondary education and the Bologna Process as an instrument for benchmarking and improving the international competitiveness of its higher education system.

In the concluding chapter 11 by *Michael Windzio, Philipp Knodel* and *Kerstin Martens*, the findings of the individual chapters are summarized and the results of this volume are embedded in the broader context of the relationship between the state, society and education. Based on the studies presented in this volume, the chapter provides a synopsis of the findings.

## References

Amburgey, Terry L., Dawn Kelly and William P. Barnett (1993) 'Resetting the Clock: The Dynamics of Organizational Change and Failure', *Administrative Science Quarterly*, 38(1), 51–73.

Ansell, Ben W. (2010) *From the Ballot to the Blackboard: The Redistributive Political Economy of Education*, Cambridge: Cambridge University Press.

Barnes, Samuel Henry, Max Kaase and Klaus R. Allerbeck (1979) *Political Action: Mass Participation in Five Western Democracies*, London: SAGE.

Barnett, Michael and Martha Finnemore (2004) *Rules for the World: International Organizations in Global Politics*, Ithaca: Cornell University Press.

Berlin Communiqué of Ministers (2003) Realising the European Higher Education Area. Communiqué of the Conference of Ministers responsible for Higher Education in Berlin: http://www.bologna-bergen2005.no/Docs/00-Main_doc/030919Berlin_Communique.PDF, retrieved 2 October 2013.

Busemeyer, Marius R. and Christine Trampusch eds. (2011) *The Comparative Political Economy of Collective Skill Formation Systems*, Oxford: Oxford University Press.

Casey, John (2004) 'Third Sector Participation in the Policy Process: A Framework for Comparative Analysis', *Policy & Politics*, 32(2), 241–57.

Cohen, Michael D., James G. March and Johan P. Olsen (1972) 'A Garbage Can Model of Organizational Choice', *Administrative Science Quarterly*, 17(1), 1–25.

Coleman, James S. (1990) *Foundations of Social Theory*, Cambridge: Harvard University Press.

Colin, Nicole, Joachim Umlauf and Alain Lattard (2006) *Germanistik, eine europäische Wissenschaft?: Der Bologna-Prozess als Herausforderung*, Munich: Ludicium.

Corbett, Anne (2005) *Universities and the Europe of Knowledge: Ideas, Institutions and Policy Entrepreneurship in European Community Higher Education Policy, 1955–2005*, Basingstoke: Palgrave Macmillan.

Cress, Daniel M. and David A. Snow (1996) 'Mobilization at the Margins: Resources, Benefactors, and the Viability of Homeless Social Movement Organizations', *American Sociological Review*, 61(6), 1089–109.

Crosier, David, Lewis Purser and Hanne Smidt (2007) *Trends V: Universities Shaping the European Higher Education Area*, Brussels: European University Association.

Dobbins, Michael (2011) *Higher Education Policies in Central and Eastern Europe: Convergence toward a Common Model?*, Basingstoke: Palgrave Macmillan.

Dobbins, Michael and Christoph Knill (2009) 'Higher Education Policies in Central and Eastern Europe: Convergence toward a Common Model?', *Governance*, 22(3), 397–430.

Dronkers, Jaap and Mark Levels (2007) 'Do School Segregation and School Resources Explain Region-of-Origin Differences in the Mathematics Achievement of Immigrant Students?', *Educational Research and Evaluation*, 13(5), 435–62.

Edwards, Bob and John D. McCarthy (2004) 'Resources and Social Movement Mobilization', in David A. Snow, Sarah A. Soule and Hanspeter Kriesi, eds., *The Blackwell Companion to Social Movements*, Oxford: Blackwell, 116–52.

Eisinger, Peter K. (1973) 'The Conditions of Protest Behavior in American Cities', *The American Political Science Review*, 67(1), 11–28.

Ertl, Hubert (2006) 'Educational Standards and the Changing Discourse on Education: The Reception and Consequences of the PISA Study in Germany', *Oxford Review of Education*, 32(5), 619–34.

Fearn, Hannah (2008) 'A Penny for Your Thoughts', *Times Higher Education*, 28 February 2008, London: TSL Education.

Finnemore, Martha (1993) 'International Organizations as Teachers of Norms: The United Nations Educational, Scientific, and Cutural Organization and Science Policy', *International Organization*, 47(4), 565–97.

Froment, Eric, Jürgen Kohler, Lewis Purser, Lesley Wilson eds. (2006) *EUA Bologna Handbook: Making Bologna Work*, Berlin: Raabe Verlag.

Gamson, William A. and David S. Meyer (1996) 'Framing Political Opportunity', in Doug McAdam, John D. McCarthy and Mayer N. Zald, eds., *Comparative Perspectives on Social Movements: Political Opportunities, Mobilizing Structures, and Cultural Framings*, Cambridge: Cambridge University Press, 273–90.

Gaventa, John (1980) *Power and Powerlessness: Rebellion and Quiescence in an Appalachian Valley*, Urbana: University of Illinois Press.

Gilboa, Itzhak (2010) *Rational Choice*, Cambridge: MIT Press.

Grek, Sotiria (2009) 'Governing by Numbers: The PISA 'Effect' in Europe', *Journal of Education Policy*, 24(1), 23–37.

Gruber, Karl Heinz (2006) 'The German PISA-shock: Some Aspects of the Extraordinary Impact of the OECD's PISA Study on the German Education System', *Oxford Studies in Comparative Education*, 16(1), 195–208.

Hagemann, Susanne (2005) *Translationswissenschaft und der Bologna-Prozess: BA-MA-Studiengänge für Übersetzen und Dolmetschen im internationalen Vergleich*, Cologne: Saxa.

Hannan, Michael T. and John Freeman (1989) *Organizational Ecology*, Cambridge: Harvard University Press.

Hirschman, Albert O. (1970) *Exit, Voice, and Loyalty: Responses to Decline in Firms, Organizations, and States*, Cambridge: Harvard University Press.

Hirschman, Albert O. (1978) 'Exit, Voice, and the State', *World Politics*, 31(1), 90–107.

Irle, Katja (2009) 'Sitzung der Hochschulrektoren. Protestzug nach Leipzig', *Frankfurter Rundschau*, 23 November 2009.

Jakobi, Anja P., Kerstin Martens and Klaus Dieter Wolf eds. (2010) *Education in Political Science: Discovering a Neglected Field*, London: Routledge.

Kaube, Jürgen (2010) 'Der Diplom-Ingenieur kehrt zurück – Die Vernunfttat von Schwerin', *Frankfurter Allgemeine Zeitung*, 16 December 2010.

Kitschelt, Herbert P. (1986) 'Political Opportunity Structures and Political Protest: Anti-Nuclear Movements in Four Democracies', *British Journal of Political Science*, 16(1), 57–85.

Knodel, Philipp, Kerstin Martens, Daniel de Olano and Marie Popp (2010) *Das PISA-Echo. Internationale Reaktionen auf die Bildungsstudie*, Frankfurt: Campus.

Knodel, Philipp, Kerstin Martens and Dennis Niemann (2013) 'PISA as an Ideational Roadmap for Policy Change: Exploring Germany and England in a Comparative Perspective', *Globalisation, Societies and Education*, 11(3), 421–41.

Koopmans, Ruud and Hanspeter Kriesi (1995) *New Social Movements in Western Europe: A Comparative Analysis*, Minneapolis: University of Minnesota Press.

Kriesi, Hanspeter (2004) 'Political Context and Opportunity', in David A. Snow, Sarah A. Soule and Hanspeter Kriesi, eds., *The Blackwell Companion to Social Movements*, London: Wiley-Blackwell, 67–90.

Kriesi, Hanspeter, Silke Adam and Margit Jochum (2006) 'Comparative Analysis of Policy Networks in Western Europe', *Journal of European Public Policy*, 13(3), 341–61.

Lasswell, Harold (1958) *Politics: Who Gets What, When, How*, New York: Meridian Books.

Lepsius, M. Rainer (1995) 'Institutionenanalyse und Institutionenpolitik', in Birgitta Nadelmann, ed., *Politische Institutionen im Wandel*, Opladen: Westdeutscher Verlag, 392–403.

Leszczensky, Michael and Andrä Wolter eds. (2005) *Der Bologna-Prozess im Spiegel der HIS-Hochschulforschung*, Hanover: HIS.

Lindemann, Kristina (2013) 'The School Performance of the Russian-Speaking Minority in Linguistically Divided Educational Systems: A Comparison of Estonia and Latvia', in Michael Windzio, ed., *Integration and Inequality in Educational Institutions*, Dordrecht: Springer, 45–70.

Little, Daniel (1991) *Varieties of Social Explanation: An Introduction to the Philosophy of Social Science*, Boulder: Westview Press.

Luhmann, Niklas (1998) *Die Gesellschaft der Gesellschaft*, Frankfurt: Suhrkamp.

Marcussen, Martin (2004) 'The Organization for Economic Cooperation and Development as Ideational Artist and Arbitrator: Reality or Dream', in Bertjan Verbeek and Bob Reinalda, eds., *Decision Making within International Organisations*, London: Routledge, 90–106.

Martens, Kerstin and Anja P. Jakobi (2009) 'International Organisations as Governance Actors – the OECD in Education Policy', in Irene Dingeldey and Heinz Rothgang, eds., *Governance of Welfare State Reform: A Cross National and Cross Sectoral Comparison of Policy and Politics*, London: Edward Elgar, 90–108.

Martens, Kerstin and Anja P. Jakobi (2010) *Mechanisms of OECD Governance – International Incentives for National Policy Making*, Oxford: Oxford University Press.

Martens, Kerstin and Klaus Dieter Wolf (2009) 'Boomerangs and Trojan Horses: The Internationalization of Education Policy in the EU and the OECD', in Alberto Amaral, Guy Neave, Christine Musselin and Peter Maassen, eds., *European Integration and the Governance of Higher Education and Research*, New York: Springer, 81–107.

Martens, Kerstin and Dennis Niemann (2013) 'When Do Numbers Count? The Differential Impact of Ratings and Rankings on National Education Policy in Germany and the US', *German Politics*, 22(3), 314–32.

Martens, Kerstin, Alessandra Rusconi and Kathrin Leuze eds. (2007) *New Arenas of Education Governance: The Impact of International Organizations and Markets on Educational Policy Making*, Basingstoke: Palgrave Macmillan.

Martens, Kerstin, Alexander-Kenneth Nagel, Michael Windzio and Angsar Weymann eds. (2010) *Transformation of Education Policy*, Basingstoke: Palgrave Macmillan.

McAdam, Doug, John D. McCarthy and Mayer N. Zald (1988) 'Social Movements', in Neil J. Smelser, ed., *Handbook of Sociology*, Beverly Hills: Sage, 695–737.

McCarthy, John D. and Mayer N. Zald (1977) 'Resource Mobilization and Social Movements: A Partial Theory', *American Journal of Sociology*, 82(6), 1212–41.

Meyer, John W. and Brian Rowan (1977) 'Institutionalized Organizations: Formal Structure as Myth and Ceremony', *American Journal of Sociology*, 83(2), 340–63.

Nagel, Alexander-Kenneth (2009) *Politiknetzwerke und politische Steuerung*, Frankfurt: Campus.

Nagel, Alexander-Kenneth (2010a): 'International Networks in Education Politics', in Anja P. Jakobi, Kerstin Martens and Klaus Dieter Wolf, eds., *Education in Political Science – Discovering a Neglected Field*, London: Routledge, 156–74.

Nagel, Alexander-Kenneth (2010b) 'Comparing Education Policy Networks', in Kerstin Martens, Alexander-Kenneth Nagel, Michael Windzio and Angsar Weymann, eds., *Transformation of Education Policy*, Basingstoke: Palgrave Macmillan, 199–226.

Nagel, Alexander-Kenneth, Kerstin Martens and Michael Windzio (2010) 'Introduction – Education Policy in Transformation', in Kerstin Martens, Alexander-Kenneth Nagel, Michael Windzio und Ansgar Weymann, eds., *Transformation of Education Policy*, Basingstoke: Palgrave Macmillan, 3–27.

Niemann, Dennis (2010) 'Turn of the Tide – New Horizons in German Education Policymaking through IO Influence', in Kerstin Martens, Alexander-Kenneth Nagel, Michael Windzio and Angsar Weymann, eds., *Transformation of Education Policy*, Basingstoke: Palgrave Macmillan, 77–104.

Normand, Romuald (2010) 'Expertise, Networks and Indicators: The Construction of the European Strategy in Education', *European Educational Research Journal*, 9(3), 407–21.

Oberschall, Anthony (1973) *Social Conflict and Social Movements*, Englewood Cliffs: Prentice Hall.

Patashnik, Eric M. (2008) *Reforms at Risk: What Happens after Major Policy Changes Are Enacted*, Princeton: Princeton University Press.

Pierson, Paul (2005) 'The Study of Policy Development', *Journal of Policy History*, 17(1), 34–51.

Pierson, Paul (2011) *Politics in Time: History, Institutions, and Social Analysis*, Princeton: Princeton University Press.

Rapoport, Anatol (1960) *Fights, Games and Debates*, Ann Arbor: The University of Michigan Press.

Rautalin, Marjaana (2007) 'The Curse of Success: The Impact of the OECD PISA Study on the Discourses of the Teaching Profession in Finland', *European Educational Research Journal*, 6(4), 348–64.

Reinalda, Bob and Ewa Kulesza-Mietkowski (2006) *The Bologna Process: Harmonizing Europe's Higher Education*, Opladen: Budrich.

Rinne, Risto, Johanna Kallo and Sanna Hokka (2004) 'Too Eager to Comply? OECD Education Policies and the Finnish Response', *European Educational Research Journal*, 3(2), 454–85.

Robertson, Susan, Karen Mundy, Antoni Verger and Francine Menashy eds. (2012) *Public Private Partnerships in Education: New Actors and Modes of Governance in a Globalising World*, Cheltenham: Edward Elgar.

Swedberg, Richard (2003) *Principles of Economic Sociology*, Princeton: Princeton University Press.

Teichler, Ulrich (2004) 'The Changing Debate on Internationalisation of Higher Education', *Higher Education*, 48(1), 5–26.

Teltemann, Janna (2013) *Gleichheit oder Leistung? Wie Bildungssysteme, Wohlfahrtsstaatsregime und Integrationspolitiken die Schulleistungen junger Migranten beeinflussen*, Bremen: PhD Dissertation.

Teltemann, Janna and Michael Windzio (2011) 'Die 'kognitive Exklusion' junger Migranten im Ländervergleich', *Berliner Journal für Soziologie*, 21(3), 335–61.

Teltemann, Janna and Michael Windzio (2013) 'Socio-Structural Effects on Educational Poverty of Young Immigrants – An International Comparative Perspective' in Michael Windzio, ed., *Integration and Inequality in Educational Institutions*, Dordrecht: Springer, 99–122.

Toens, Katrin and Frank Janning (2008) *Zukunft Der Policy-Forschung: Theorien, Methoden, Anwendungen*, Wiesbaden: VS.

Verger, Antoni, Mario Novelli and Hülya Kosar Altinyelken eds. (2012) *Global Education Policy and International Development: An Introductory Framework*, London: Continuum.

Walder, Andrew G. (2009) 'Political Sociology and Social Movements', *Annual Review of Sociology*, 35(1), 393–412.

Walter, Thomas (2006) *Der Bologna-Prozess: Ein Wendepunkt europäischer Hochschulpolitik?*, Wiesbaden: VS.

Windzio, Michael ed. (2013a) *Integration and Inequality in Educational Institutions*, Dordrecht: Springer.

Windzio, Michael (2013b) 'Integration and Inequality in Educational Institutions: An Institutional Perspective', in Michael Windzio, ed., *Integration and Inequality in Educational Institutions*, Dordrecht: Springer, 3–20.

Witte, Johanna Katharina (2006) *Change of Degrees and Degrees of Change: Comparing Adaptations of European Higher Education Systems in the Context of the Bologna Process*, Enschede: CHEPS.

Wolf, Klaus Dieter (2010) 'Normative Dimensions of reforms in Higher Education', in Anja P. Jakobi, Kerstin Martens and Klaus Dieter Wolf, eds., *Education in Political Science – Discovering a Neglected Field*, London: Routledge, 177–90.

# Part I
# Quantitative Analyses

# 2
# Achievement vs. Equality – What Determines PISA Performance?

*Janna Teltemann*

## Introduction

Since the year 2000, the triennial Programme for International Student Assessment (PISA) of the Organisation for Economic Co-operation and Development (OECD) has turned from mere benchmarking into a "backdoor agent" in education policy-making. The study was explicitly administered in order to increase focus and motivation for reform and for the improvement of secondary education (Anderson et al. 2010: 375). Accordingly, the first waves in 2000 and 2003 triggered education policy changes in a number of participating countries that either were unpleasantly surprised by their ranking or that utilized their PISA performance as a pretence for previously intended reforms (Breakspear 2012; Ertl 2006; Egelund 2008; Knodel et al. 2010). In some countries, PISA was not the actual reason for education reform; plans for policy changes had already been developed – a response to increasingly globalized labour markets, growing importance of human capital, and budget shortages. In other countries, the PISA Study and (PISA-independent) education reform took place simultaneously, and policy changes were publicly framed post hoc as direct responses to PISA (Klieme 2011). Either as a direct response to PISA or independently, many countries have changed their education policies during the first decade after PISA 2000.

Although PISA does not formulate explicit policy recommendations, the underlying competitiveness of the study is often associated with implicit policy goals that broadly correspond to "educational efficiency". Efficient education systems promote the creation of social human capital, thereby realizing the prerequisites for economic productivity and active citizenship (van de Werfhorst and Mijs 2010).

Since PISA does not measure performance in terms of goals formulated by national curricula but in terms of a general understanding of "viability" in globalized economies, high performance is perceived as a prerequisite for growth and economic competitiveness. However, a competitive advantage of high-performing countries can only be realized if high performance is distributed evenly. Hence, *high performance* and *equality of opportunity* may be regarded as primary policy goals of PISA. Consequently, the study seeks empirical evidence to prove the kinds of educational institutions that work best in this regard. Correspondingly, policy changes as a response to PISA often come up as a form of "policy borrowing" from successful countries (Phillips and Ochs 2003). This involves high-performing countries (for example, Finland in 2000) to serve as examples for best practices.

Constant with previous empirical findings from educational research, the first PISA results indicated that the classical economic assumption of "competition is good for business" partly works for education too. This means successful education systems are those that set incentives for schools to raise achievement. These incentives commonly involve school autonomy, decentralization, and school choice for parents (Sahlberg 2006: 262; Robert 2010; Wößmann et al. 2012). School autonomy, however, requires policies of *accountability* in order to prevent moral hazard and to secure equal outcomes (see Ball 2009; Lingard and Ozga 2007). Commonly, policies of accountability are implemented according to the degree of *standardization* of education systems (Allmendinger 1989).

As indicated above, not only high achievement but also, at the same time, *equal access* to comprehensive education is an implicit policy goal of PISA. Moreover, providing equality of opportunity is a basic function of modern educational systems as it is a requirement for meritocratic societies (van de Werfhorst and Mijs 2010). However, research has shown that in every modern society achievement is dependent on family background – albeit to different degrees. Equality of opportunity is often related to the *stratification* of education systems (Allmendinger 1989), since tendencies of social closure increase within differentiated ("tracked") educational systems.

Given these roughly sketched associations between education systems and their central *outcomes*, one would expect policy reforms (in response to PISA) in two main *output* dimensions of education systems: *stratification* and *standardization*. The PISA reports regularly provide information about the structure of the education systems in regard to these dimensions. However, as a cross-sectional survey, PISA bears a contradiction: it "explicitly dispenses with causal explanations" (Hartong 2012: 748), leading to severe uncertainty for policy-makers. Several previous studies reported trends of central indicators between the respective PISA waves (OECD 2010a). However, little is known about the consequences of recent changes in education policy. So far, the effects of PISA in relation to education reforms are rarely examined. This is partly due to the fact that changes in outcomes and output are only visible in the long term (Sahlberg 2006: 283), and straight top-down governance in education is not viable (Klieme 2011). Furthermore, reforms may be formalized but impractical to implement, thus would not show any effect on outcomes (see Introduction to this volume).

This chapter asks whether educational reforms are *effective* in fostering achievement and equality at the same time and whether there is a preference for higher achievement at the potential cost of equal opportunities. By drawing on data from four PISA waves (2000, 2003, 2006, and 2009) we examine these questions in three steps: First, changes in the *output* dimension of education policies between 2000 and 2009 are illustrated by looking at indicators of *stratification* and *standardization*. Second, changes in the central outcomes of achievement levels, and the associations between individual social status and achievement, are examined descriptively. Third, we take a *longitudinal* perspective and verify if changes in achievement and social gradients can be traced back to changes in the output dimension. The following section summarizes the theoretical mechanisms behind the association of education systems and educational outcomes and refers to exemplary empirical results. The third section introduces the PISA database and the applied statistical methods. Sections four and five present descriptive analyses of changes in educational output and outcomes; the sixth section is dedicated to the longitudinal analyses.

## How institutions generate educational inequality

In modern education systems, fostering high achievement and providing equal access to education might appear as a contradiction. Students are not equal in terms of their abilities and interests, and labour markets demand a variety of specific skills. In order to handle these basal conditions, most modern education systems are at some stage *stratified*, in that the curriculum is differentiated between specific educational programmes or schools. However, training according to different interests and labour-market demands is not the only rationale behind educational *tracking*. It is assumed that overall achievement can be raised when students are schooled in homogeneous groups because teachers can better adapt their teaching strategies, and it is more conducive to students' motivation if they feel they are among peers with similar abilities (Marsh 1987; Dreeben and Barr 1988; Rumberger and Palardy 2005). This second justification of educational stratification has been intensively discussed as it has been shown that it might result in the aforementioned contradiction between high achievement and educational inequality ("trade-off", for a review see Hattie 2002; Sacerdote 2011; van de Werfhorst and Mijs 2010).

But why does stratification lead to educational inequality? Sociological theories of educational inequality identify several sources for differences in achievement. Apart from genetic dispositions, micro-oriented explanations distinguish two components of inequality, namely differences in *ability* between groups and differences in educational *decisions* between groups (Boudon 1974; Erikson and Jonsson 1996; Esser 1999; Becker 2000). Differences in ability arise from (class) specific patterns of interaction between parents and children. Better-educated parents are able to reinforce their child's achievement, for example, by verbal training or practical help with schoolwork (Erikson and Jonsson 1996: 11). This mechanism is perceived to be relatively stable across Western societies and can hardly be moderated by educational institutions, since interventions would have to start very early in a child's life. Differences in the second component, educational *decisions,* are often examined within the framework of *subjective expected utility theory* (SEU). It is assumed that families make educational decisions depending on their evaluation of benefits, costs, and probabilities of success. To explain differences in educational decision-making between groups, the characteristics of the social situation of a group have to be linked with typical evaluations of costs, probabilities of success, and benefits. If groups differ in terms of their economic resources, it is likely that lower-income families evaluate the costs of education higher than those with more money. If groups differ with regard to their cultural capital, the actual probabilities of success differ accordingly, as parents with better education are able to help their children. The perceived benefits of education vary between groups, since families with a higher status have "more to lose" (for example, by not going to higher education). This mechanism is usually referred to as secondary effect (Boudon 1974), risk aversion (Breen and Goldthorpe 1997), or status-loss motif (Esser 1999).

The class-specific evaluations of costs, benefits, and probabilities of success can be moderated by institutional settings. Erikson and Jonsson (1996: 33) identify five relevant institutional factors: the length of different educational programmes, barriers and opportunities, the overall size of the education system, prevailing principles of transfer between and admission to different programmes, and the significance of "elite" schools. The first factor refers to the stratification of education systems. The fewer differences (in length and number) that exist in a country's educational programmes, the less pronounced the effects of status on educational decisions will be.

Likewise, the second central dimension of education systems, their *standardization*, can produce trade-offs between high achievement and equality of opportunity. Standardization refers to regulations and policies with regard to curriculum, assessments, teacher training, and budget. An education system is considered to be standardized if there is one national curriculum, unitary teacher training, centralized funding regulations, and nationwide assessments (Brint 2006: 42). Standardization might reduce inequality of opportunity, for example, by increasing transparency and comparability of grades. Moreover, it increases the signalling to the labour market if a specific educational qualification is reliably connected with a respective skill level. A stronger signal might reduce discrimination and inequality that evolves at transitions into the labour market. On the other hand, standardization (that is, less school autonomy) might reduce competition among schools and incentives to improve educational efficiency, thereby leading to lower achievement (van de Werfhorst and Mijs 2010: 411). Consequently, education policy-makers should try to combine the advantages of less standardization (more competition) with the necessity of equal outcomes. This is often done by increasing school autonomy accompanied by measures of school accountability, for example, standardized external tests or monitoring and observations.

In their review of the comparative literature on educational inequality, van de Werfhorst and Mijs (2010) find that inequalities are higher in stratified education systems and lower in standardized education systems. They do not find convincing support for a trade-off between equality and achievement with regard to stratification (van de Werfhorst and Mijs 2010: 416). For standardization, there seems to be a contradiction since higher achievement at autonomous schools depends on measures of accountability (van de Werfhorst and Mijs 2010: 420).

Hanushek et al. (2011) find that autonomy influences the competence level in a country, but the size of the effect is heterogeneous depending on the country's stage of development. In line with these findings, Montt (2010) shows that greater homogeneity in teacher equality and the absence of tracking reduces achievement inequality. Likewise, the PISA reports (OECD 2010b: 14) illustrate the features of "successful" school systems: the selection of students and resulting competition for student enrolment, the autonomy of schools in curricula and assessments, the direction of funding, and the existence of standard-based assessments are all decisive factors. The results further show that school systems with lower stratification are more likely to perform above the OECD average.

## Data and methods

The OECD PISA Study is so far the most comprehensive standardized achievement survey at the secondary education level. Its research design is oriented towards international comparability of competences of 15-year-old students and the determinants of these competences. Students that participated in the cognitive tests additionally completed an extensive background questionnaire. Another questionnaire was administered to the heads of the sampled schools. The questionnaires are comprised of a wide range of items in order to assess individual, school, or system determinants of competence production. The resulting data pool is publicly available[1] and has substantive potential for secondary analysis directed towards questions of school efficiency and educational inequality.

The PISA Study assesses individual competences and system performance every three years starting in 2000 with changing focuses of three key competence dimensions: reading, mathematics, and science.

For our analyses of trends in output and outcomes of education systems, we pooled the datasets from four PISA waves: 2000, 2003, 2006, and 2009. One of the main problems for trend analyses within PISA is that many items from the background questionnaires changed between the four years, leading to constrained comparability. School-related items that are available for all rounds are school funding, class size, school autonomy in various areas, and teaching staff qualification. However, even if these questions have been administered in every wave, questions and response categories differ. Other items, such as monitoring practices and ability grouping, are available for two or three cycles.

Our analyses build on several indicators of stratification and standardization as well as on the competence scales and the strength of associations between individual background characteristics and competence. The publicly available datasets only contain information at the individual and school level. Indicators of the education systems (for example, at the country level) can be generated through the aggregation of the individual or school variables and are partly provided in the published documents.

The measuring of competences in PISA relies on the Rasch Model (Rasch 1960), which involves the assignment of every student to five "plausible values" in every competence dimension (reading, science, mathematics). For estimating "representative" country averages, all analyses have to be repeated with these five values with a further adjustment of standard errors (see OECD 2009). For our analyses of *outcomes*, we referred to the reading scales ("achievement"). The strength of the association between individual background characteristics and achievement ("equality of opportunity") is measured as the proportion of variance in achievement that is explained by parental occupational status in a regression model (coefficient of determination). For the descriptive analyses of changes in output and outcomes of education systems, we plot differences in the country averages of a respective indicator between two comparable PISA cycles as well as the absolute values of the latest round (2009).

In order to test the effects of changes in output factors on changes in outcomes we estimated models that included both the difference between two time points of an output variable and the base level of the respective output (resembling a country fixed-effect design). By including the base level we account for the fact that countries with a high value at the beginning of the observed time period are limited in their possible changes as opposed to countries with low starting values ("beta convergence", Jakobi and Teltemann 2011).

The association between changes in the output dimension and changes in achievement can be formalized as:

$$\textit{Reading competence}_{ijk} = \beta_{0ijk} + \beta_1 \textit{Change}_k + \beta_2 \textit{ Base level}_k + \beta_m \textit{Covariates}_{ijk}$$

where

$$\beta_{0ijk} = \beta_0 + \nu_{0k} + u_{0jk} + e_{ijk}.$$

The subscripts denote students ($i$) that are nested in schools ($j$) and countries or country-years ($k$). Changes and base levels of output indicators are measured at the country level. Covariates can be measured at the individual, school, or country level.

In section two, it has been argued that education systems might moderate the secondary effect of individual socioeconomic background (SES) on achievement, thereby increasing or decreasing equality of opportunity. In our model, this mechanism can be included by letting the effect of socioeconomic status vary between countries (*random coefficient*). Since we want to test whether stratification and standardization account for the variance of the random coefficient, an interaction term of socioeconomic background and the respective system indicator has to be included (*cross-level interaction*). The model reads as:

$$Reading\ competence_{ijk} = \beta_{0ijk} + \beta_1 Change_k + \beta_2 Base\ level_k + \beta_{3k}SES_{ijk} + \beta_4 SES_{ijk}*\ Change_k + \beta_m Covariates_{ijk}$$

where

$$\beta_0 = \beta_0 + v_{0k} + u_{0jk} + e_{ijk}$$

$$\beta_{3k}SES_{ijk} = \beta_1 + u_{1jk}.$$

Besides individual socioeconomic background, we included control variables at the individual level – namely gender, migration background (first and second generation, depending on country of birth of a student and their parents), and language.

## Changes in educational output between 2000 and 2009: Stratification and standardization

This section gives an overview of the trends in selected output indicators measuring stratification and standardization. *Stratification* of an education system refers to the number and length of different school tracks (in secondary education), ability-grouping policies, the age of differentiation, as well as the regulations for transition between grades and school tracks. PISA does not provide unambiguous information about the number of different school tracks, but it is possible to assess how schools within a country differ with regard to achievement and if schools have implemented ability grouping and grade repetition.

Figure 2.1a and 2.1b illustrate the degree of ability grouping within a country for some subjects and for all subjects respectively, as well as changes in these values between 2006 and 2009.[2] The bars show the share of 15-year-old students in a country who go to schools where ability grouping is implemented. Apparently, ability grouping for all subjects in a school is less prevalent. There is no clear trend towards decreasing ability grouping; by contrast there seem to be more countries extending this policy with regard to subject-specific ability grouping. On average, the share of students in a country at schools with ability grouping in some subjects increased from about 55 per cent to about 56 per cent. The figures for ability grouping in all subjects decreased: from 16 to 13 per cent. Germany increased subject-specific ability grouping but still ranks within the first quarter of the distribution. Switzerland reduced grouping practices and is also in the lower quarter of the distribution. By contrast, the United Kingdom is among the countries with the highest share of subject-specific ability grouping, although it shows

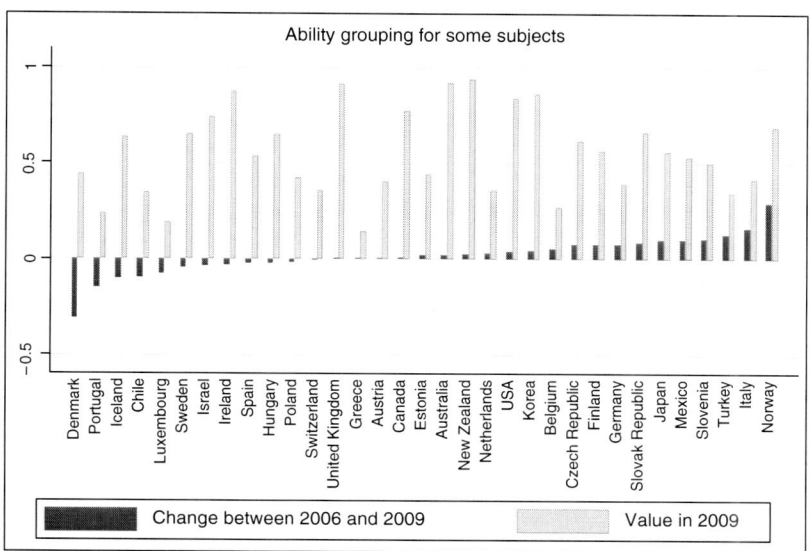

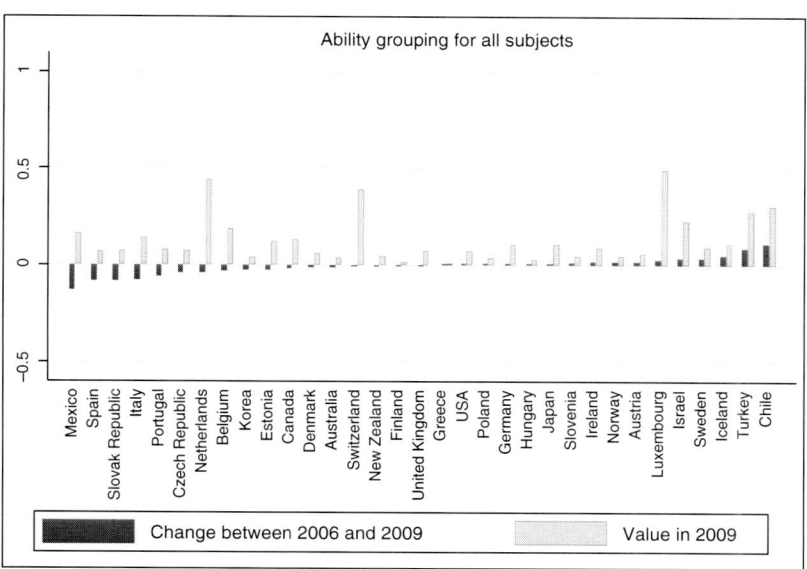

*Figure 2.1a and 2.1b*   Ability grouping for some and for all subjects within a school, PISA 2006, 2009.

*Source:* OECD, PISA 2006, and 2009 databases, own calculations.

slightly declining rates. Greece and Luxembourg are the countries with the lowest levels of subject-specific grouping. Australia, New Zealand, and Denmark are at the other end of the distribution. However, Luxembourg has the highest level of comprehensive tracking, followed by the Netherlands. Again, Greece and Finland show very low levels of tracking in all subjects. Denmark and Portugal show the most pronounced reduction of subject-specific tracking, Italy and Norway the biggest increase. As regards ability grouping for all subjects, Mexico and Spain exhibit remarkable changes towards less tracking. Turkey and Chile, by contrast, show a raise.

A further indicator of stratification is the proportion of variance in achievement between schools (as opposed to variation in achievement within schools). If students in an education system are differentiated according to their ability, this will result in rather homogeneous schools with a larger proportion of between-school variance. If there is no differentiation, most of the variance should be between students within schools. Figure 2.2 shows the share of variance in reading achievement between schools as well as changes within this measure between 2000 and 2009.[3] On average, about one third of the variance in reading achievement is between schools instead of within schools. This figure

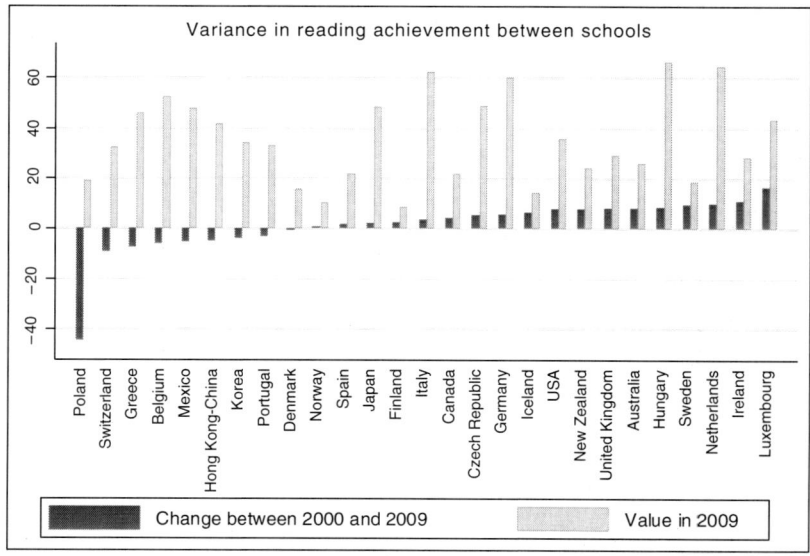

*Figure 2.2*   Variance between schools in 2009, change since 2000.
Source: PISA 2006, Table 4.1d-f, PISA 2009, Table V.4.1, own calculations.

remained stable between 2000 and 2009. Finland and Norway show very low levels of between-school variance; the Netherlands and Hungary, by contrast, exhibit marked differences between schools. Germany is among the four countries with the highest between-school variance (even increasing since 2000), indicating a highly stratified education system. Switzerland was moderately stratified in 2009 after a noticeable reduction of between-school variance. The United States increased variance between schools and rank slightly above the median. Hong Kong decreased stratification slightly. Spain shows stable and rather low achievement heterogeneity between schools. Poland is the country with the most pronounced reduction of between-school variance; Ireland and Luxembourg show figures that rose by more than ten percentage points.

Grade repetition is a further characteristic of stratified education systems (Mons 2007; Park and Sandefur 2010). Figure 2.3 shows that there are substantial differences in the prevalence of grade repetition across education systems.[4] On average, 4 per cent of students repeated a grade during the last year. Compared to 2003, most countries[5] exhibit a decreasing trend. Only Chile and Belgium had higher repetition rates in

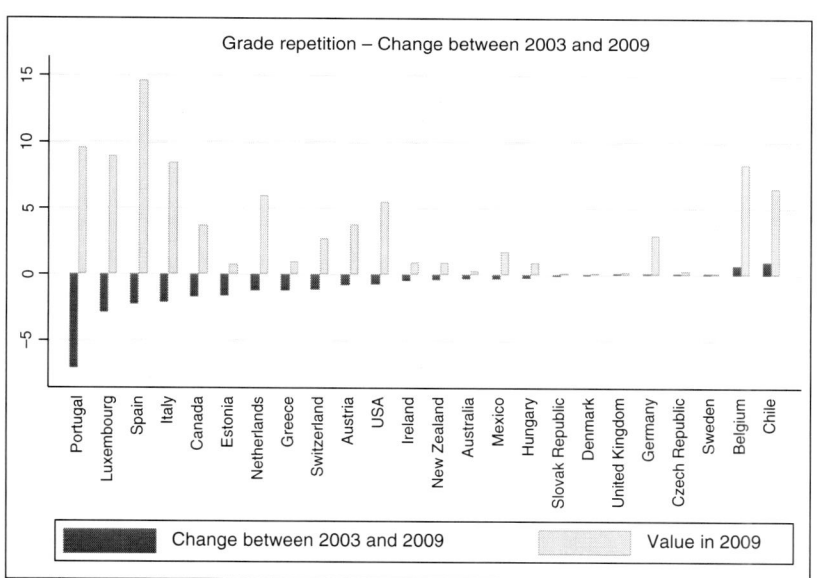

*Figure 2.3* Changes in grade repetition rates, PISA 2003, 2009.
*Source:* OECD, PISA 2003, 2006, and 2009 databases, own calculations.

2009 than in 2003. Portugal almost halved the repetition rate between 2003 and 2009. Germany exhibited a small increase in 2006 but fell back to the base level in 2009. Spain is the country with the highest grade-repetition rates. In the United Kingdom, repeating a grade does not seem to be a common practice.

Overall, the indicators of stratification illustrate that there is considerable variation across countries in regard to tracking practices. Furthermore, there is no clear trend towards less stratification, except for ability grouping for all subjects and for grade-retention practices.

In the next step, we examine the *standardization* of school systems in two dimensions: the autonomy and accountability of schools. Autonomy is measured as the share of 15-year-old students at schools where the principal, teachers, or school governing board have at least some responsibilities in a respective autonomy dimension. We look at three areas of school organization: assessment policies, staff selection, and budgeting.[6] Regarding the first area, assessment autonomy, the PISA results show that there is a large variation across participating countries, from less than 1 per cent to more than 99 per cent of students in autonomous schools per country (results not shown). In more than half of the countries, about two-thirds of 15-year-old students go to schools with at least some responsibility in establishing assessments (median: 0.66). On average in 2009, 67 per cent of students went to autonomous schools. This is about 19 percentage points less than in 2000. On average, countries reduced autonomy in school assessments by almost 20 percentage points. Switzerland, Germany, the USA, and the United Kingdom show moderate reductions in school autonomy. Noticeably, Finland decreased school autonomy by almost 50 per cent.

The picture changes when looking at another autonomy dimension: the responsibility of formulating the school budget. Here, the changes between 2000 and 2009 almost follow a normal distribution: about half of the countries increased budget autonomy, while the other half shows decreasing autonomy in this dimension (results not shown). The average change is slightly negative (–0.8 percentage points). After an increasing trend between 2000 and 2006, budget autonomy decreased; in 2009, an average of 54 per cent of students went to schools with budget autonomy.

In 2009, school autonomy in budgeting was highest in New Zealand and the Netherlands, where more than 95 per cent of students attended autonomous schools. Poland is the only country with less than 10 per cent of students at schools with budget autonomy. Germany shows the second biggest increase (after Portugal) and ranked within the last decentile of the distribution in 2009. While in the United Kingdom autonomy was reduced by about one third, in 2009, the UK was close to the median. Switzerland shows rather stable figures. The USA increased budget autonomy by about 16 percentage points.

Another dimension of autonomy is responsibility for teaching staff. As Figure 2.4 shows, there is no clear trend among the OECD countries in changing this practice. On average, 62 per cent of students go to schools that have at least some autonomy in staffing; the actual figures vary from 2 per cent to 100 per cent. Again, autonomy is highest in the Netherlands and New Zealand. In Italy, Greece, and Turkey, less than 10 per cent of students study at autonomous schools. Changes are not as pronounced as compared with budget autonomy; more than one third of the countries exhibit changes of less than five percentage points. Looking at only those countries that participated in 2000 and 2009, we observe a minimal decrease of 1.6 percentage points. The United Kingdom and Spain show minor negative changes, however at different base levels: in the UK, more than 90 per cent of students are at autonomous schools, whereas the figure corresponds to less than one third in Spain. Germany increased autonomy in staffing but is still in the first quartile of the distribution.

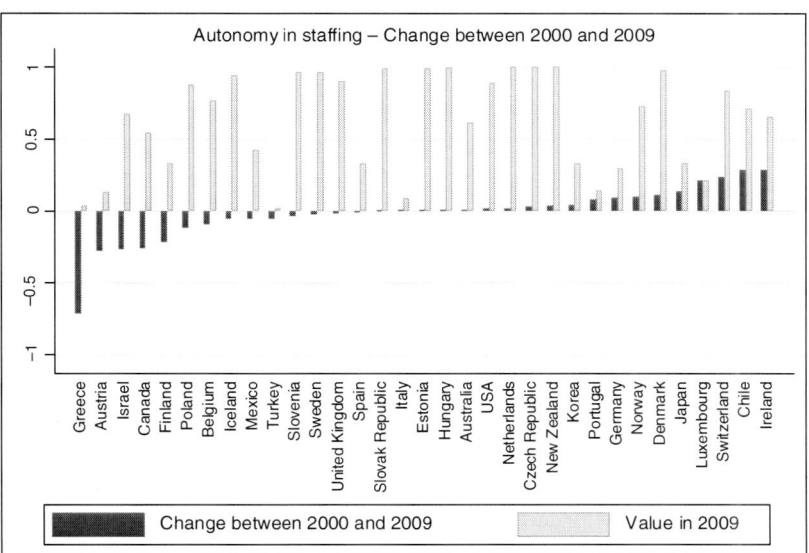

*Figure 2.4*   Autonomy in staffing, PISA 2000–2009.

Source:  OECD, PISA 2000, 2003, 2006, and 2009 databases, own calculations.

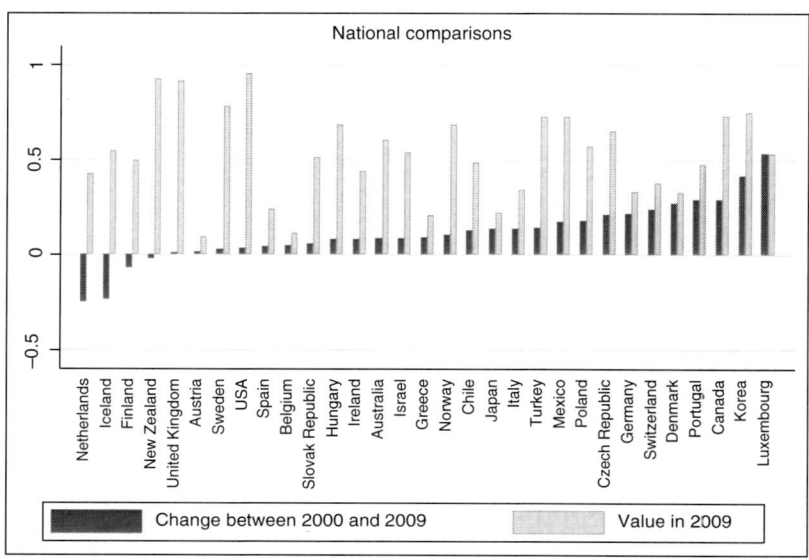

*Figure 2.5*   Use of assessments for comparisons, PISA 2000–2009.
Source: OECD, PISA 2000, 2003, and 2009 databases, own calculations.

The *accountability* of schools is measured as the share of students at schools that use assessments for comparisons with regional or national performance (Figure 2.5).[7] On average, slightly more than half of the students go to schools with this kind of accountability practice – with substantial differences between countries. What is remarkable, however, is the clear trend towards more accountability – only two countries show noticeably decreasing figures. In 2000, on average only 40 per cent of students went to "comparing" schools. The average difference between the values of 2000 and 2009 is 11.4 percentage points. In the UK, the USA, and the Netherlands, more than 90 per cent of all students go to schools that use assessments for comparison.

Germany considerably increased in the number of schools that use comparisons but still remains in the first quarter of the distribution, similar to Switzerland (just above the first quartile in 2009). The USA and Spain exhibit only weak increases but at different base levels. Another measure of accountability is the experience with external monitoring. Figure 2.6 shows the share of students in a country that attend schools where classes have been observed by inspectors or other external evaluators during the last year.[8] The prevalence of this policy is considerably lower than the use of assessments for comparisons; only 28 per cent of students go to schools that experienced observance during the last

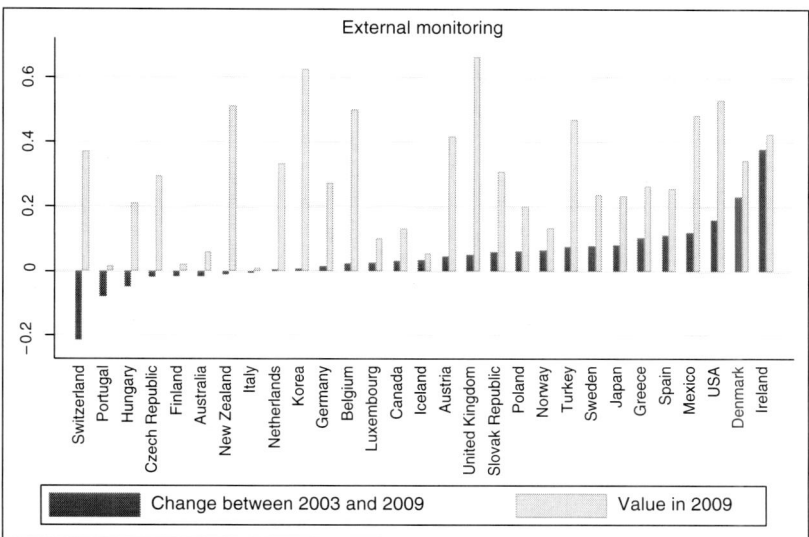

*Figure 2.6* External monitoring of schools, PISA 2003 and 2009.
*Source:* OECD, PISA 2003, and 2009 databases, own calculations.

year. But an increasing trend can be discerned here (average in 2003: 24.5 per cent), though, for example, Switzerland, but also Portugal and Hungary, substantially reduced the external monitoring of schools, the average difference between 2003 and 2009 amounts to 4.5 percentage points. The United Kingdom exhibits the highest share of students at monitored schools, whereas Finland, Italy, and Portugal do not seem to use this practice. The USA, Denmark, and Ireland show the biggest increase.

In summary, it can be said that the two examined dimensions of standardization – autonomy and accountability – show different developments during the decade after the first PISA Study. Whereas accountability practices increased, the different aspects of autonomy developed differently: we observed a strong decrease in the autonomy of schools to establish assessment policies compared with a rather stable setting for budget and staff-related autonomy.

## Changes in the educational outcomes

How do the changes in the central dimensions of education policy-making relate to student performance? This section gives an overview of trends in two central PISA outcomes: *achievement* and *equality*. We look at absolute reading scores, the range of reading scores, and at changes in social gradients.

Figure 2.7 shows that changes in reading achievement are relatively small compared to the overall level of achievement.[9] Not all countries participated in every PISA cycle. Only 23 countries show valid reading competence measures from 2000 until 2009. The graph shows the absolute level in 2009 and the change between PISA 2000 and 2009 for the respective country. The average achievement is 494 points. Chile has the highest increase in reading competence, with a difference of 40 points between 2000 and 2009, corresponding to one year of schooling. By contrast, Ireland depicts the steepest decline in competencies, with 31 points. Other "winners" are Israel, Poland, Portugal, and Germany (13 points). The PISA 2000 high performer, Finland, lost 11 points compared to 2009; Sweden also declined (–19 points). This decline corresponds to almost six months of schooling.[10] The USA and the United Kingdom show stable results between 2000 and 2009. However, there might be pronounced differences between 2000 and 2003 or 2003 and 2009 respectively.

As argued in the beginning of this chapter, institutional settings might induce individual investment decisions that result in a trade-off

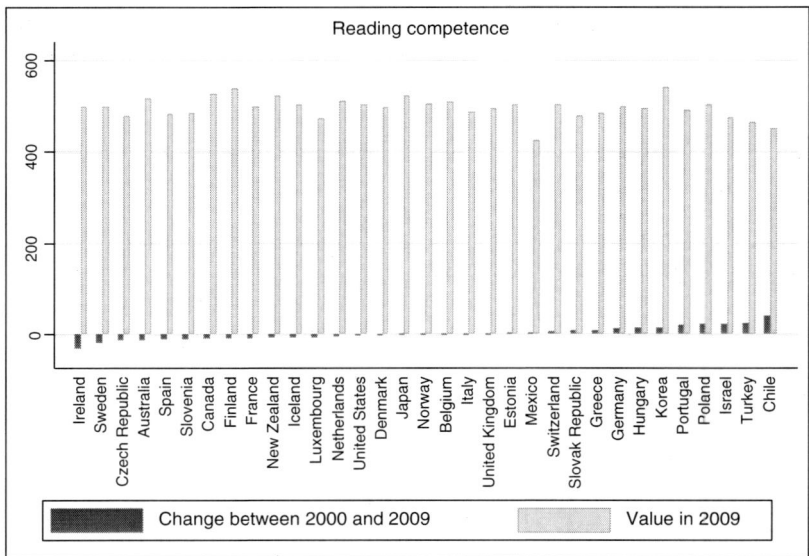

*Figure 2.7*   Reading achievement, PISA 2000–2009.

*Source:* OECD 2011, Annex B1; Table V.2.1, own calculations.

between achievement and equality at the country level. Countries not only need to achieve high average achievement levels, they also depend on equal distributions of achievement as larger low-performing groups might cause high follow-up costs (for example, unemployment benefits). As Figure 2.8 shows, there is no clear trend towards lower ranges (distance between tenth and ninetieth percentile).[11] On average, the distance between the lowest decile of the achievement distribution and the high performers (last decile) amounts to 240 points in 2009 – corresponding to a learning gain of about six years of schooling. On average, countries decreased their reading range by about five points.

Germany was able to reduce the range of reading competence most substantively, from 284 points in 2000 to 248 in 2009. On the other end, Japan, France, and high-performing Korea reported substantively increasing heterogeneity. However, in 2009 Korea was still the country with the smallest reading range.

As laid out in the beginning of this chapter, not only high achievement but also equal distribution of educational opportunities is a goal of educational reform. Figure 2.9 shows that the impact of sociocultural status on achievement varies significantly across countries. The bars indicate

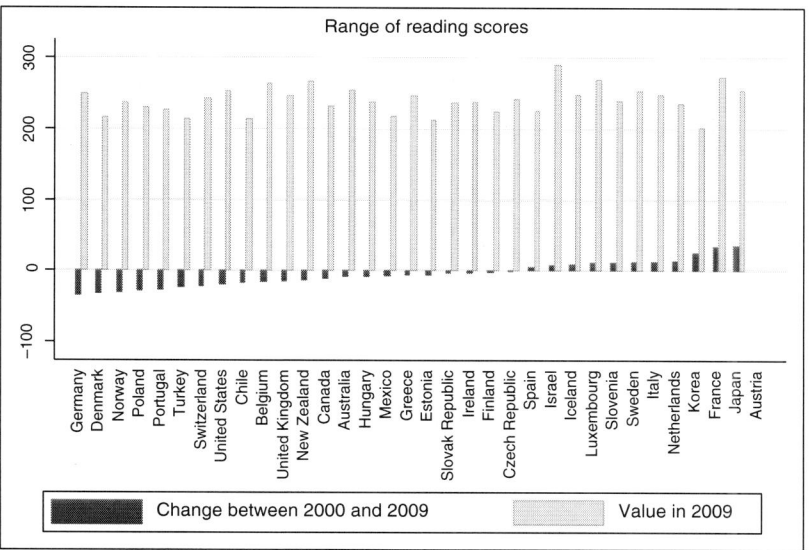

*Figure 2.8*   Range of reading scores.
*Source:* OECD 2011, Annex B1; Table V.2.1, own calculations.

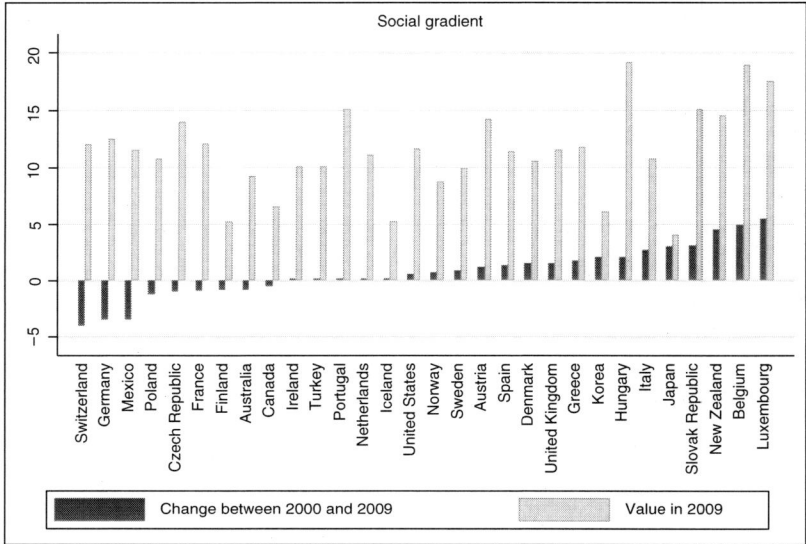

*Figure 2.9*   Association between sociocultural status and reading achievement.
*Source:* OECD 2007: Table 6.5b, PISA 2009 database, own calculations.

the proportion of variance in reading achievement that is explained by the occupational status of parents.[12] On average, about 11 per cent of the variation in reading achievement go back to the differences in occupational status of parents. Overall, there has been an increase in educational inequality, since the differences over time are positive (mean value 0.7 per cent).

Japan, Iceland, and Finland showed the lowest social gradients, whereas in Luxembourg, Belgium, and Hungary, reading achievement is correlated rather strongly to social background. The difference between more equal countries and countries with higher inequality in opportunity amounts to about 15 percentage points of explained variation. Luxembourg is also the country with the biggest increase in inequality.

## Determinants of change in outcomes

Until now, we have examined trends both in output indicators of education systems and in outcome indicators without linking them together. In the next step, we assess how changes in the degrees of standardization and stratification of education systems relate to changes in achievement

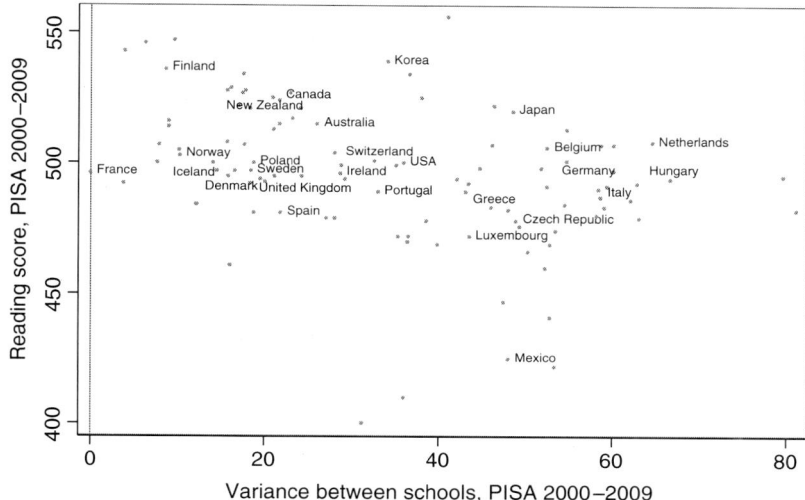

*Figure 2.10*  Association between stratification and achievement, PISA 2000–2009.

*Source:* OECD, PISA 2000, 2003, 2006, and 2009 databases, own calculations.

and equality of opportunity. First, we take a descriptive view on bivariate relationships. Next, we model the effect of institutional changes on achievement and on the effect of individual status, controlling for the composition of the student population.

The scatterplot in Figure 2.10 shows the bivariate association between the *stratification* of education systems, measured as the proportion of variance in achievement between schools and the average reading achievement. The graph includes all values of PISA 2000, 2003, 2006, and 2009 that are available for OECD countries; the labels mark the values of 2009. There seems to be a negative relationship between the two variables: larger between-school variance relates to lower reading scores. The correlation is negative and significant with R = –0.35. Thus, the theoretical hypotheses and empirical findings regarding the impact of stratification on achievement are corroborated with this bivariate approach.

Figure 2.11 depicts the association between the stratification of education systems and inequality of educational opportunity, measured as the share of variance in individual reading achievement that is explained when controlling for the occupational status of parents. Here, as expected from the theory and previous research, the association seems to be positive: in stratified school systems, socioeconomic status of parents has a greater impact on achievement. The correlation is significant

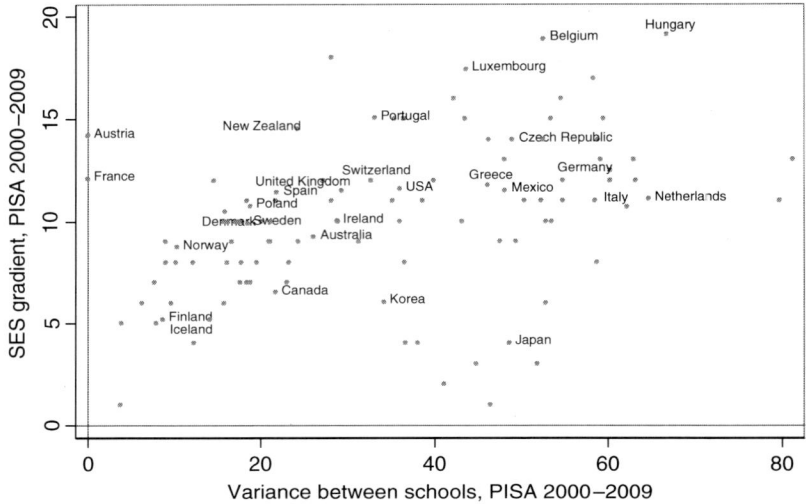

*Figure 2.11*    Association between stratification and educational inequality, PISA 2000–2009.

*Source:* OECD, PISA 2000, 2003, 2006, and 2009 databases, own calculations.

at a moderate level (R = 0.40). Hence, from this first step we could conclude that stratified education systems do not produce trade-offs but rather multiple disadvantages, as they exhibit lower achievement levels and higher inequality.

The next two graphs illustrate the bivariate relationship between an indicator of *standardization*, namely school autonomy in hiring teaching staff, with achievement and equality of opportunity respectively.

Figure 2.12 shows that there is not a clear-cut association between school autonomy and reading achievement. There is a rather weak, but nonetheless significant, positive correlation of 0.19. This means that countries where more schools have at least some opportunity in selecting teaching staff tend to produce higher achievement levels.

Likewise, the picture is not conclusive when looking at the association between school autonomy and inequality of opportunity (Figure 2.13). Here, the correlation is fairly weak (r = 0.05) and not significant. Thus, school autonomy does not seem to moderate the relationship between socioeconomic status of families and achievement.

However, the bivariate associations might be biased by composition effects: if, for example, students in one country have, on average, higher socioeconomic backgrounds than students in another country. Likewise,

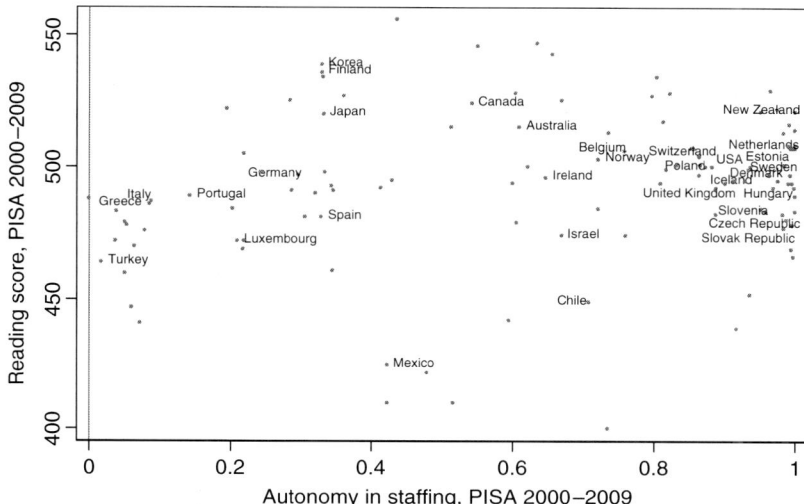

*Figure 2.12* Association between standardization and reading achievement, PISA 2000–2009.

*Source:* OECD, PISA 2000, 2003, 2006, and 2009 databases, own calculations.

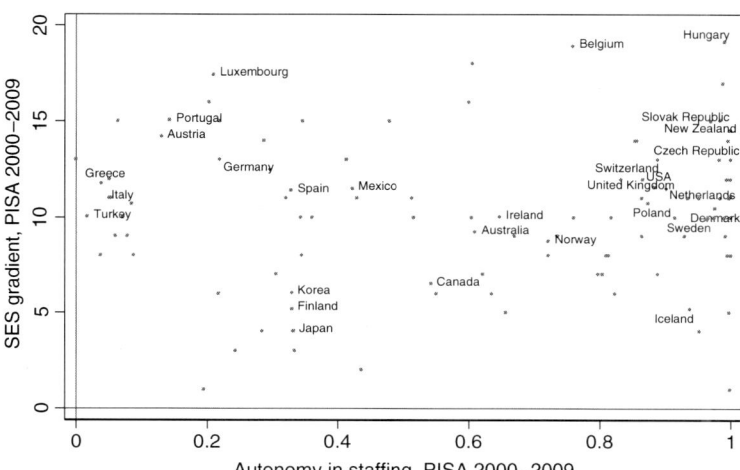

*Figure 2.13* Association between standardization and educational inequality, PISA 2000–2009.

*Source:* OECD, PISA 2000, 2003, 2006, and 2009 databases, own calculations.

*Table 2.1* Multilevel regressions of reading achievement.

| Reading achievement in PISA | Intercept | Model 1[1] | | Model 2[2] | | | Model 3[3] | Model 4[4] | |
|---|---|---|---|---|---|---|---|---|---|
| Indicator | | Base level | Change | Base level | Change | SES | Base* SES | Change* SES | N[5] |
| **Stratification** | | | | | | | | | |
| (1) Ability grouping for some subjects | 491 | 44.00 | 38.33 | 31.88 | 34.10 | 17.47 | 26.75 | -43.82 | 33 |
| (2) Ability grouping for all subjects | 491 | -43.81 | -38.86 | -21.85 | -37.47 | 17.48 | -40.19 | 57.49 | 33 |
| (3) Variance between schools | 496 | -0.51 | -0.212 | -0.35 | -0.169 | 18.85 | -0.352 | -0.07 | 76 |
| (4) Grade repetition | 488 | -0.35 | 1.56 | -0.01 | 1.29 | 17.23 | 0.038 | -0.20 | 47 |
| **Standardization** | | | | | | | | | |
| (5) Autonomy in staffing | 493 | 21.17 | 33.87 | 11.06 | 24.30 | 18.69 | 13.50 | 4.30 | 87 |
| (6) Autonomy in budgeting | 493 | 25.22 | 0.59 | 18.25 | 1.59 | 18.69 | 14.08 | -3.76 | 87 |
| (7) Autonomy in establishing assessments | 494 | 55.23 | 34.26 | 42.58 | 27.80 | 18.69 | 10.81 | -5.18 | 87 |
| (8) Use of assessments for comparison | 496 | 17.44 | -19.56 | 13.15 | -5.68 | 19.65 | 6.96 | -8.30 | 56 |
| (9) External monitoring of schools | 495 | -10.83 | -37.19 | 1.15 | -30.27 | 17.71 | -4.29 | -3.24 | 29 |

*Source:* OECD, PISA 2000, 2003, 2006, and 2009 databases, own calculations.

**Bold: p < 0.05**, upright: p < 0.1, *italic: not significant*

[1] *Included variables: base level and change of respective indicator (in rows).*
[2] *Included variables: base level and change of respective indicator (in rows), migration status, language use, gender, SES.*
[3] *Included variables: base level and change of respective indicator (in rows), migration status, language use, gender, SES, interaction base level\*SES.*
[4] *Included variables: base level and change of respective indicator (in rows), migration status, language use, gender, SES, interaction change \*SES.*
[5] *refers to cases at the country level (country years).*

a country might perform lower because it accommodates a high number of immigrants with language difficulties. These composition effects can be controlled for in hierarchical regression models, as described in section three.

Table 2.1 shows the results of a series of multilevel models, where individual reading achievement is the dependent variable. For illustrative purposes, only selected coefficients are shown. The first greyish block of the table (Model 1, second, third, and fourth column) depicts the intercept and coefficients for a model, where the respective indicator of stratification or standardization (in rows) is included as an independent variable, measured twofold, namely as a *base level* (value of the respective previous PISA Study) and as a *change value* (difference between current and previous study). The second block (Model 2, columns five to seven) depicts the coefficients of a model where both the system indicators and a number of individual student characteristics are included, namely migration status, language use, gender (results of which are not shown), and occupational status of parents (results shown in column seven). The third block (Model 3 and 4, columns eight and nine) depicts coefficients of a model where additional cross-level interaction effects are included separately: in Model 3 an interaction term with the base level of standardization or stratification, and in Model 4 an interaction of SES and the respective change measure. The intercepts for Models 2, 3, and 4 are not shown, nor are the variance (*random*) parts of the model (at the individual, school, and country level).

The first four indicators (rows one to four) describe the stratification of education systems. The coefficients in row one show that ability grouping for some subjects is associated with higher individual achievement (Model 1). Students in countries where subject-related tracking is not implemented lag behind by almost one year of schooling compared to students in countries where ability grouping in some subjects is practiced in every school. Likewise, the estimated coefficient for the change indicator is positive, indicating that an increase in subject-specific tracking practice leads to higher achievement. Yet, the effect is not significant. If individual student characteristics are included (Model 2), the positive effect of the base level of ability grouping remains. As expected, the effect of socioeconomic status is positive and significant. Thus, higher achievement in countries with subject-specific ability grouping is not due to a more favourable composition of the student population in terms of socioeconomic status, migration background, or language use. How are the "moderate" tracking policies related to equality of opportunity? Model 3 shows that the base level of tracking is associated with a steeper SES gradient as the interaction effect of ability grouping and individual socioeconomic status is positive (26.75 points) and significant. This would corroborate the general hypothesis that stratification leads to higher inequality. But this does not hold for the change in tracking practices (Model 4): if countries exhibit a growing number of schools that apply subject-specific ability grouping, the impact of socioeconomic background on achievement decreases significantly (see Figure 2.14).

The picture changes when looking at ability grouping for all subjects (row two): here the association is negative, both for the base level as well as for the change measure. However, the coefficients are not significant. Yet, the interaction effects for socioeconomic status are significant: the base level (Model 3) is related to less steep SES gradients, whereas a trend towards more "complete" tracking enhances the impact of family background on achievement (Model 4). This inverts the previous findings for subject-specific tracking. If we assume that the interaction with the change indicator is more valid in terms of interpreting it as a causal effect, then we could confirm the hypothesis of stratification fostering inequality.

A second measure of stratification, illustrated in the fourth section of this chapter, was the between-school variance in a country. Countries with higher proportions of achievement variance between schools

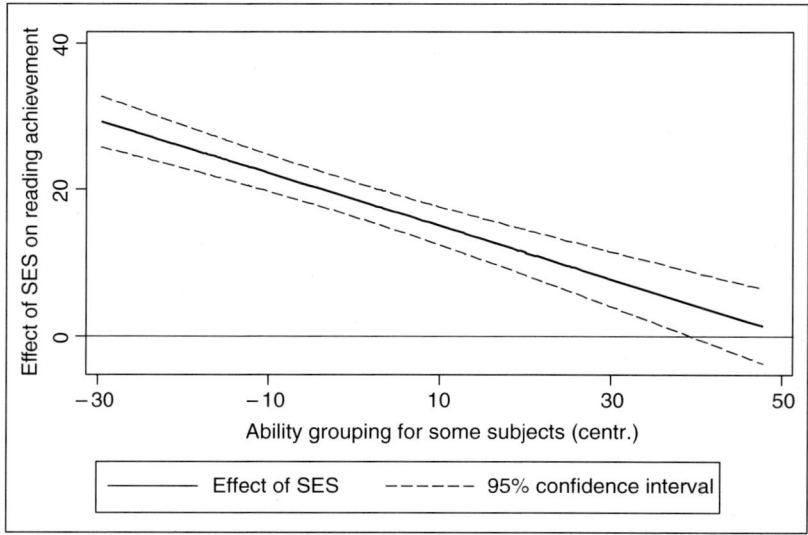

*Figure 2.14*  Effect of socioeconomic status moderated by degree of ability grouping.

are supposed to be more stratified. The coefficients in row three indicate that more variance between schools in a country is associated with lower reading performance (–0.51). However, there is no significant effect of the (negative) change indicator. Again, the moderating effect of stratification on the association between socioeconomic status and achievement contradicts the hypothesis (Model 3): higher levels of between-school variance correspond to weaker associations between socioeconomic status and reading achievement. Yet, this does not hold for the "causal" change indicator. The last indicator of stratification is the share of students that repeated a grade (row four). Here, we do not find any significant effects for the institutional characteristics. Thus, the practice of grade repetition alone apparently is not decisive for achievement or inequality.

Overall, the results for stratification show that policies of ability grouping seem to be most influential and that there is a pronounced difference between the forms of tracking. Whereas subject-specific tracking is related to higher achievement, this does not hold for countries where students are grouped according to their achievement in all subjects. Moreover, countries that show increasing trends of subject-specific tracking exhibit less steep socioeconomic gradients, whereas countries that tend towards more comprehensive tracking exhibit increasing inequality, which confirms the theoretical hypothesis and is in line with previous findings.

The *standardization* of school systems was assessed with indicators of school autonomy and accountability. Rows five to nine in Table 2.1 show how this dimension of education systems is related to achievement and equality of opportunity. A higher proportion of schools with autonomy in selecting teaching staff (row five, Model 1) is related to higher reading competences (21.17 points for countries with full autonomy compared to countries with no autonomy). However, the trend indicator has no significant effect. Again, the interaction effect with individual sociocultural background is positive and significant (Model 3). This corroborates previous findings that show that less-standardized education systems with high school autonomy produce higher inequalities (van de Werfhorst and Mijs 2010). However, a change in autonomy does not mediate the association of socioeconomic status and achievement. Thus it is probably not the level of autonomy itself, but another institutional characteristic that typically is accompanied with autonomy in staffing, which causes higher achievement *and* higher inequality at the same time.

Likewise, school budgetary autonomy (row six in Table 2.1) is associated with better student performance. An increase in the share of autonomous schools of ten percentage points corresponds to an increase of 2.5 points on the reading scale. Again, the change measure is not significant. Moreover, financial autonomy as well as autonomy in staffing go hand in hand with a stronger impact of background characteristics on school achievement. Thus, we might conclude that there is a trade-off between achievement and inequality for school autonomy. Yet, these findings are less valid, since we do not find the effects for the change indicators but rather for the base levels. However, it might be that reforms of these policies may take longer to take effect.

The effects are different when looking at school autonomy in establishing assessment policies (row seven). As with the other autonomy dimensions, the starting values are associated with higher performance, but here the change in autonomy is also significant: an increase in assessment autonomy for schools is related to higher individual reading scores (Model 1, significant at the 10 per cent level). This result is independent of student composition in a country (Model 2). Pertaining to the effect of socioeconomic status, the results show that SES gradients are again steeper in countries with higher assessment autonomy (Model 3), albeit the effect is smaller compared to the other autonomy dimensions. Thus, we might conclude that increasing autonomy in assessment policies is most advantageous (compared to other autonomy dimensions): it increases achievement but is only weakly correlated with inequality of opportunity.

The last two sets of models examine the accountability of education systems. Models 1 and 2 in row eight show that if more schools in a country use assessments for comparison with other schools or overall national achievement, students do perform better. Yet, this does not hold for the change indicator. Moreover, there is no mediating effect on the association between individual background and achievement. This accountability measure thus seems to be rather ineffective.

If there is an increasing trend of external school inspections (row nine) in a country, individual achievement is lower – even if the starting values of inspection practices are controlled for (Model 1), but the effects are not significant. What is apparent, however, is that the SES gradient decreases when there has been a trend towards more external observations of schools in a country (–4.29 points, Model 3, not significant). The results indicate that particularly countries with lower overall achievement (or otherwise adverse results) decided to increase external observation (independent of their initial level of inspections), and that this practice pays off only in the longer run with regard to achievement.

## Conclusion

This chapter provided an overview of changes in two central output dimensions of education systems: standardization and stratification. Further, it showed how the outcome dimension, with regard to the primary policy goals of the OECD PISA Study, *achievement* and *equality of opportunity*, had developed over the years 2000 to 2009. We expected a trend towards less stratification, more standardization in terms of accountability, and less standardization in terms of school autonomy. However, the descriptive analyses did not show clear trends towards less stratification or less centralized educational regulation. It is not surprising that policy recommendations given by an organization without any formal authority are not directly implemented. On the other hand, however, in some countries the dynamics of the reform were striking. Yet, the results indicate that just a subset of countries has interpreted their PISA ranking as an imperative for fundamental reforms. Instead, realized reforms seem to be conceptualized individually, that is, at the national level. Rather than implementing best practices, reforms resemble a kind of "individual coping".

After the descriptive approach, we presented a multivariate longitudinal approach to assess the association between the characteristics of education systems and achievement and inequality. Sociological theory on educational achievement as well as previous empirical findings indicated that more stratification and less standardization of education systems often go hand in hand with higher inequality. We can confirm this hypothesis for one indicator: ability grouping for all subjects. If countries changed their policies during the last years towards more comprehensive ability grouping, the association between individual status and achievement grew stronger. For other changes in output dimensions, we could not find the expected effects on achievement and equality. Yet, according to the theoretical model laid out in the first chapter of this book, those frictions between reform concepts and outcomes are expectable.

The advantage of our approach is in the longitudinal character that allows for the thinking of estimated effects as "causal" effects. However, further research has to examine interactions between the dimensions of education systems and their implications for achievement and inequality. Maybe highly stratified education systems can compensate for their adverse effects on inequality when they are highly standardized.

## Notes

1   http://www.oecd.org/pisa/pisaproducts/, retrieved 22 September 2013.
2   The indicator is generated on the basis of the school-level variable ABGROUP, included in the PISA databases of 2006 and 2009. The variable was recoded in two dummy variables measuring ability grouping for some and for all subjects. In a next step, mean values of these dummy variables were computed for each country.
3   Figures are taken from PISA 2006, Table 4.1d-f; PISA 2009, Table V.4.1.
4   The indicator was generated out of six variables indicating the percentage of repeaters at ISCED 2 and ISCED 3 respectively in the school databases of 2009 (sc07q01 and sc07q02), 2006 (sc05q01 and sc05q02) and 2003 (sc06q01 and sc06q02). For every year, the average of both these variables was calculated at the school level. In a next step, country averages were estimated.
5   Only countries with a repetition rate of more than 1 per cent in 2009 are shown.
6   Indicators of school autonomy were generated by referring to the following questions of the school questionnaires: PISA 2000: SC22, PISA 2003: SC26, PISA 2006: SC11, 2009: SC24. The respective items were recoded into dummy variables taking the value "1" if the school head indicated that the school (head, teachers, or governing board) had at least some responsibility in the respective area. In a next step, the school-level dummy variables were aggregated at the country level.
7   Indicators of school accountability through comparisons were generated by referring to the following questions of the school questionnaires: PISA 2000: SC18q04, PISA 2003: SC13q04, 2009: SC16q04. The respective items were recoded into dummy variables taking the value "1" if the school head indicated that the school used assessments for comparisons to regional or national performance. In the next step, the school-level dummy variables were aggregated at the country level.
8   Indicators of school accountability through external observations were generated by referring to the following questions of the school questionnaires: PISA 2003: SC20Q03, 2009: SC23Q03. The respective items were recoded into dummy variables taking the value "1" if the school head indicated that the classes of the school had been observed by inspectors or other external persons in order to monitor teacher practices. In the next step, the school-level dummy variables were aggregated at the country level.
9   Figures from OECD 2011, Annex B1: Table V.2.1.
10  In PISA, the learning progress of one year of schooling corresponds to about 40 points on the achievement scale.
11  Figures from OECD 2011, Annex B1: Table V.2.3.
12  Figures for 2000, 2003, and 2006 from PISA 2006, Chapter 6 Table T6.5b. Figures for 2009: own calculations with PISA 2009 student database, based on replicated and weighted regressions of reading achievement on highest occupational status of parents (HISEI).

## References

Allmendinger, Jutta (1989) "Educational Systems and Labor Market Outcomes", *European Sociological Review*, 5(3), 231–50.

Anderson, John O., Mei-Hung Chiu and Larry D. Yore (2010) "First Cycle of Pisa (2000–2006) – International Perspectives on Successes and Challenges: Research and Policy Directions", *International Journal of Science and Mathematics Education*, 8(3), 373–88.

Ball, Stephen J. (2009) "Privatising Education, Privatising Education Policy, Privatising Educational Research: Network Governance and the 'Competition State'", *Journal of Education Policy*, 24(1), 83–99.

Becker, Rolf (2000) "Klassenlage und Bildungsentscheidungen. Eine empirische Anwendung der Wert-Erwartungstheorie", *Kölner Zeitschrift für Soziologie und Sozialpsychologie*, 52(3), 450–74.

Boudon, Raymond (1974) *Education, Opportunity, and Social Inequality: Changing Prospects in Western Society*, New York: Wiley & Sons.

Breakspear, Simon (2012) *The Policy Impact of PISA: An Exploration of the Normative Effects of International Benchmarking in School System Performance* (OECD Education Working Paper No. 71).

Breen, Richard and John H. Goldthorpe (1997) "Explaining Educational Differentials: Towards a Formal Rational Action Theory", *Rationality and Society*, 9(3), 275–306.

Brint, Steven G. (2006) *Schools and societies*, Stanford: Stanford University Press.

Dreeben, Robert and Rebecca Barr (1988) "Classroom Composition and the Design of Instruction", *Sociology of Education* 61(3), 129–42.

Egelund, Niels (2008) "The value of international comparative studies of achievement – a Danish perspective", *Assessment in Education: Principles, Policy & Practice*, 15(3), 245–51.

Erikson, Robert and Jan O. Jonsson (1996) "Introduction: Explaining Class Inequality in Education: The Swedish Test Case", in Robert Erikson and Jan O. Jonsson, eds., *Can Education Be Equalized? The Swedish Case in Comparative Perspective*, Boulder: Westview, 1–63.

Ertl, Hubert (2006) "Educational Standards and the Changing Discourse on Education: The Reception and Consequences of the PISA Study in Germany", *Oxford Review of Education*, 32(5), 619–34.

Esser, Hartmut (1999) *Situationslogik und Handeln. Soziologie. Spezielle Grundlagen*, Vol. 1, Frankfurt: Campus.

Hanushek, Eric A., Susanne Link and Ludger Wößmann (2011) *Does School Autonomy Make Sense Everywhere? Panel Estimates from PISA*, Munich: Center for Economic Studies.

Hartong, Sigrid (2012) "Overcoming Resistance to Change: PISA, School Reform in Germany and the Example of Lower Saxony", *Journal of Education Policy*, 27(6), 747–60.

Hattie, John A.C. (2002) "Classroom Composition and Peer Effects", *International Journal of Educational Research*, 37(5), 449–81.

Jakobi, Anja P. and Janna Teltemann (2011) "Convergence in Education Policy? A Quantitative Analysis of Policy Change and Stability in OECD Countries", *Compare*, 41(5), 579–95.

Klieme, Eckhard (2011) "Bildung unter undemokratischem Druck? Anmerkungen zur Kritik der PISA-Studie", in Stefan Aufenanger, ed., *Bildung in der Demokratie*, Opladen: Budrich, 289–303.

Knodel, Philipp, Kerstin Martens, Daniel de Olano and Marie Popp (2010) *Das PISA-Echo. Internationale Reaktionen auf die Bildungsstudie*, Frankfurt: Campus.

Lingard, Bob and Jennifer Ozga (2007) *The RoutledgeFalmer reader in education policy and politics*, London, New York: Routledge.

Marsh, Herbert W. (1987) "The Big-Fish-Little-Pond Effect on Academic Self-Concept", *Journal of Educational Psychology*, 79(3), 280–95.

Mons, Nathalie (2007) *Les nouvelles politiques éducatives. La France fait-elle les bons choix?*, Paris: Presses universitaires de France.

Montt, Guillermo (2010) "Cross-national Differences in Educational Achievement Inequality", *Sociology of Education*, 84(1), 49–68.

OECD (2007) *PISA 2006. Science Competencies for Tomorrow's World. Volume 2 Data*, Paris: OECD.

OECD (2009) *PISA Data Analysis Manual, 2006 Edition*, Paris: OECD.

OECD (2010a) *Changes in student performance since 2000*, Paris: OECD.

OECD (2010b) *What Makes a School Successful? PISA 2009 Results Volume IV*, Paris: OECD.

Park, Hyunjoon and Gary D. Sandefur (2010) "Educational Gaps Between Immigrant and Native Students in Europe: The Role of Grade", in Jaap Dronkers, ed., *Quality and Inequality of Education: Cross-National Perspectives. Assessing the Quality of Education and its Relationships With The Inequality in European and Other Modern Societies*, Berlin: Springer, 113–36.

Phillips, David and Kimberly Ochs (2003) "Processes of Policy Borrowing in Education: Some Explanatory and Analytical Devices", *Comparative Education*, 39(4), 451–61.

Rasch, Georg (1960) *Probabilistic Models for Some Intelligence and Attainment Tests*, Copenhagen: Danmarks pædagogiske Institut.

Robert, Peter (2010) "Social Origin, School Choice, and Student Performance", *Educational Research and Evaluation*, 16(2), 107–30.

Rumberger, Russell W. and Gregory J. Palardy (2005) "Does Segregation Still Matter? The Impact of Student Composition on Academic Achievement in High School", *Teachers College*, 107(9), 1999–2045.

Sacerdote, Bruce (2011) "Peer Effects in Education: How Might They Work, How Big Are They and How Much Do We Know Thus Far?", in Eric A. Hanushek, Stephen Machin and Ludger Wößmann, eds., *Handbook of the Economics of Education*, Amsterdam: Elsevier, 249–77.

Sahlberg, Pasi (2006) "Education Reform for Raising Economic Competitiveness", *Journal of Educational Change*, 7(4), 259–87.

van de Werfhorst, Herman G. and Jonathan J. B. Mijs (2010) "Achievement Inequality and the Institutional Structure of Educational Systems: A Comparative Perspective", *Annual Review Sociology*, 36(1), 407–28.

Wößmann, Ludger, Gabriela Schütz, Elke Lüdemann and Martin R. West (2012) "School Accountability, Autonomy, Choice, and the Equality of Educational Opportunities", in Michael Windzio, ed., *Integration and Inequality in Educational Institutions*, Dodrecht: Springer, 123–52.

# 3
## Sweeping Change – But Does It Matter? The Bologna Process and Determinants of Student Mobility

*Timm Fulge and Eva Maria Vögtle*

## Introduction

As the prime example of the internationalization of higher education policy, the Bologna Process has, despite its voluntary character, induced a remarkable amount of institutional change in many of its 47 participating countries (Dobbins et al. 2011). More expressly, at least three different dimensions of reform efforts associated with the Bologna Process can be identified. First is the adoption of a three-cycle degree structure that distinguishes between undergraduate, graduate and doctoral students. The first degree (*bachelor's*), awarded upon the successful completion of undergraduate studies, in this logic is supposed to both grant access to the second academic cycle (*master's*) and serve as an appropriate qualification to enter the labour market right away (Bologna Declaration 1999). Second, full academic degrees as well as completion of single courses are made compatible and comparable through the adoption of the European Credit Transfer and Accumulation System (ECTS). In this system, mutual recognition of academic records is facilitated by awarding credit points according to specified learning outcomes and student workload in hours. Finally, the Bologna Process aims to enhance the quality of individual higher education institutions by compelling them to adopt systems of quality management and assurance. Taken together, these policy prescriptions represent a desire to achieve policy convergence across participating countries, culminating in one harmonized European Higher Education Area (EHEA).

One of the main goals associated with these harmonization efforts was to foster cross-national student mobility within the EHEA and make it an attractive destination for students from non-EHEA countries as well (Zgaga 2006). In fact, every substantial policy document of the Bologna Process explicitly emphasizes student mobility as both a means to establish the EHEA as well as an indicator to measure its success in terms of competitiveness and compatibility. As a central policy outcome, the trajectory of student mobility can thus be viewed as a benchmark against which to measure the success of Bologna reforms.

Consequently, the question we pose in this chapter is whether the Bologna Process has indeed facilitated student mobility as envisioned by its participants or whether – as theorized in the introduction of this volume – institutional change associated with the Bologna Process has led to frictions hampering its success. In doing so, we investigate degree-seeking international student mobility to and from Bologna and OECD member countries. Utilizing longitudinal data on overall mobility rates as well as student flows between pairs of countries, we employ a two-fold methodological approach. As a first step, we use in- and outbound mobility ratios to illustrate the trajectory of student mobility as Bologna reforms were implemented (2000–10) in a descriptive manner. Subsequently, we run time-series-cross-section (TSCS) models to investigate determinants of student mobility, including Bologna membership as the central independent variable. In a second step, we analyse relational patterns of degree-seeking student mobility between pairs of countries by means of dyadic analysis. Here, we estimate a multilevel Poisson regression model in order to analyse factors shaping the relevance and the balance of dyadic exchange relationships. As a result, we offer a comprehensive analytical framework of student mobility and the Bologna Process's impact on it.

## Theoretical considerations

Conceptually, one can distinguish between degree and credit student mobility. While degree mobility "is a long-term form of mobility which aims at the acquisition of a whole degree or certificate in the country of destination", credit mobility denotes "the acquisition of credits in a foreign institution in the framework of ongoing studies at the home institution" (Eurydice 2012: 153). All of the analyses in this chapter are based exclusively on degree mobility. We will thus not be able to make statements about the impact of the Bologna Process on credit mobility. This choice may be regarded as a serious limitation of our research, but we would argue that it also enhances its analytical clarity because of divergent incentive structures between degree and credit mobility (see, for example, Gonzáles et al. 2011). As a consequence, we define internationally mobile students as individuals who pursue an academic degree in a higher education institution outside of their country of origin. We further distinguish between in- and outbound mobility, denoting country of destination and origin, respectively.

## Determinants of student mobility

In understanding cross-national student mobility flows, it is fruitful to conceptualize prospective students as rational decision-makers. In this line of thought, students pursue their education outside of the country of their origin if anticipated benefits (increased future earnings and employment opportunities) outweigh short-term costs (for example, mobility or housing costs) of studying abroad. The outcome of such a cost-benefit analysis is governed by a set of push and pull factors (Agarwal et al. 2008; Beine et al. 2011; Caruso & De Wit 2013). Push factors determine which countries incur high rates of outbound mobility while pull factors structure which countries promise the highest benefit from studying abroad. Both sets of factors can act either through decreasing the cost of studying abroad or through widening the benefit difference between two countries.

In the (mostly economist) literature about student mobility, at least four broad categories of push and pull factors are identified. These are: condition of the economy, quality of the higher education system, geographic location, and cultural and linguistic ties. Among the economic factors, perhaps the most utilized explanatory variable is GDP per capita. We adopt the reasoning of Dreher and Poutvaara (2005), who assume that it is more attractive for students from a low-GDP country to study abroad because of exorbitantly increased private returns. As a consequence, students from wealthy countries should prefer to stay in their country of origin. Another economic factor suggested to shape mobility flows is economic openness. Here, it is assumed that highly integrated economies lower the cost of both in- and outbound mobility and thus act as a push and pull factor at the same time. The quality of higher education systems, on the other hand, largely determines the benefit attached to pursuing an academic degree in a given country. More expressly, if a country possesses a well-developed higher education sector and good universities, this should be a strong pull factor for international students. On the contrary, students from countries with a low-quality higher education system will be more likely to accept the costs of studying abroad. Geographic location again plays into the cost calculation and can, depending on the method, be conceptualized as the distance between countries (Bessey 2010) or by simply separating countries by continent or region (Tremblay 2001). Whichever approach is used, geographic location empirically seems to play an important role: bordering countries exchange students to a larger extent when compared to distant countries, and countries in remote regions are less likely to attract (or lose) students. As the final push and pull factor, language may counteract the explanatory power possessed by geographic location. In dyadic analyses, for instance, if two countries share the same primary language, they exhibit increased exchange flows (Beine et al. 2011). In comparative studies, it is often assumed that English – as the world's lingua franca – improves the attractiveness of higher education systems to internationally mobile students while countries without widely used primary languages have an in-built disadvantage (Tremblay 2001).

## The impact of the Bologna Process

In our view, the rational-choice framework is well suited to conceptualize and explain cross-national student mobility patterns. As prospective students weigh their decision, a set of push and pull factors determine the utility of studying abroad. How could the Bologna Process and its corresponding policies impact on such cost-benefit analyses? From a programme-theoretical perspective, the goal of the Bologna Process is to increase student mobility by means of harmonizing higher education systems and thus make degrees more comparable and compatible. More expressly, Bologna participants believe that the introduction of certain structural measures (for example, ECTS and modularized programme structures) should – upon widespread implementation of these policies – make it less costly to study abroad. In addition, the Bologna Process should also lead to increased competition between European universities and, ideally, improve the overall quality of the EHEA. As a consequence, studying in Europe would result in greater benefits for international students. If these causal assumptions hold true, Bologna-induced reforms should act as a push and pull factor, fostering both in- and outbound mobility.

As outlined in the introduction of this volume, however, the implementation of policies is seldom a straightforward task and actual policy outcomes can easily be very different from what was initially envisioned by policy-makers. This could be the case for several reasons. For instance, the pronounced heterogeneity of Bologna members may result in uneven implementation of reforms. Implementation success may be context-specific, with higher education systems simply responding differently to new degree structures and increased competition. Moreover, Bologna policy prescriptions may clash with deeply entrenched and path-dependent national traditions, resulting in dysfunctional hybrid regimes. Finally, since Bologna reforms were designed at least partly to circumvent national opposition to institutional change (see Martens and Wolf 2009), the implementation may be contested within national higher education systems.

In conclusion, while programme-theoretical assumptions expect student mobility to increase, there are several factors that could impede or even counteract this goal. In this chapter, we aim to evaluate which is the case by isolating the impact of the Bologna Process from other push and pull factors thought to influence student mobility flows.

## Empirical analyses

In this section, we turn to our empirical analyses of student mobility. We proceed in three steps. First, descriptive data on in- and outbound mobility are presented. We argue that the common practice of conceptualizing (and estimating regressions with) student mobility in terms of absolute numbers is problematic and thus propose an alternative solution – the utilization of so-called mobility ratios. The inspection of these ratios reveals substantial variance both between countries and over time, making an explanatory account a worthwhile undertaking. Therefore, as a second step, we conduct a set of TSCS regressions in order to assess possible determinants of both in- and outbound mobility ratios. Finally, we investigate by means of dyadic analysis which subsample contains the most (im)balanced and relevant student exchange relationships.

Our sample consists of countries that have joined the Bologna Process until 2010 and OECD members who are not part of the Bologna Process. However, we excluded those countries with less than one million inhabitants, countries that did not have a higher education sector at the onset of our investigation (for example, Luxembourg) and countries that changed their statehood status during the period of investigation (for example, Serbia and Montenegro). This leads to a population of 48 countries in total.[1] Additionally, we excluded some of the countries due to too many missing observations on the indicators for the dependent variable, leaving us with 41 (outbound mobility) and 39 (inbound mobility) countries for the TSCS analysis and 41 countries for the dyadic analysis. We draw our student mobility data on student mobility from the *UNESCO Institute for Statistics* (UIS) database.

## The trajectory of student mobility, 2000–10

Virtually all analyses concerned with student mobility and its determinants start with the premise that in light of a globalizing world, more and more students pursue higher education outside of their home country. As we show, these matter-of-fact statements may indeed be reflected in absolute numbers of internationally mobile students. However, they also suffer from a severe underlying misconception. For illustrative purposes, we have aggregated absolute numbers of both total enrolment (ISCED 5a + 6) and international students studying in any of our sample countries. In figure 3.1, the trajectory of both domestic and international enrolment is plotted over time. As can be seen, the number of international students has clearly increased over the past decade. However, a significant increase in absolute numbers appears concurrently in domestic enrolment, suggesting that underlying factors (for example, ongoing deindustrialization processes) may drive growth for both types of students. If the increasing numbers of mobile students were largely a function of growing enrolment worldwide, the conventional wisdom about the trajectory of student mobility as an independent development would thus have to be called into question.

To add to the argument, Table 3.1 displays student numbers more precisely. Again, it becomes apparent that the number of international students has risen sharply: for example, in 2000, a total of 1.58 million students were studying in the countries within the scope of our study;

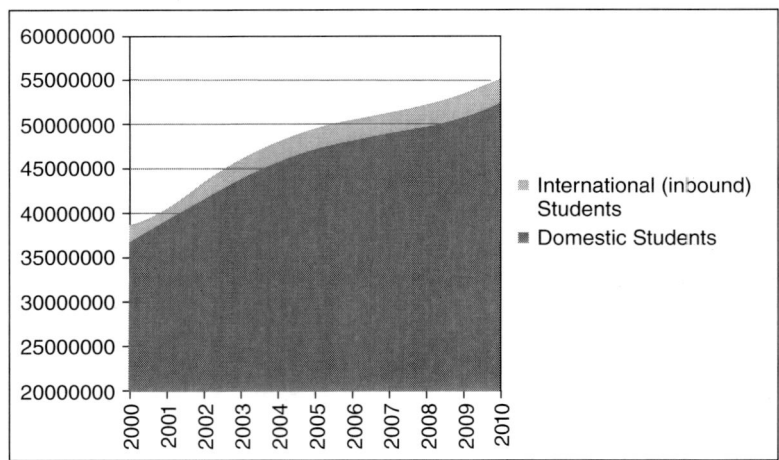

*Figure 3.1*   Growth in enrolment by domestic and international students, 2000–2010.

*Table 3.1* Total enrolment and international students in millions and per year. Δ refers to percentage change in between years 2000 and 2010: included countries are those found in Footnote 1.

| | 2000 | 2001 | 2002 | 2003 | 2004 | 2005 | 2006 | 2007 | 2008 | 2009 | 2010 | Δ |
|---|---|---|---|---|---|---|---|---|---|---|---|---|
| Total Enrolment | 38.65 | 40.54 | 43.60 | 45.94 | 48.12 | 49.58 | 50.59 | 51.53 | 52.18 | 53.57 | 55.24 | 30% |
| International Students | 1.58 | 1.67 | 1.92 | 2.10 | 2.16 | 2.25 | 2.25 | 2.35 | 2.48 | 2.64 | 2.80 | 44% |
| Share of International Students % | 4.08 | 4.11 | 4.40 | 4.57 | 4.48 | 4.54 | 4.45 | 4.58 | 4.76 | 4.92 | 5.07 | 19% |

however, by 2010 this number had grown to 2.80 million – corresponding to an increase of 44 per cent. As figure 3.1 already suggests, total enrolment also grew substantially in the same period – from 38.65 million to 55.24 million, or 30 per cent. The correlation between these variables is exceptionally strong ($r = 0.98$) and again suggests that the rising numbers of internationally mobile students cannot, as is so often done, be treated as exogenous to enrolment.

If one wants to analyse the trajectory of student mobility independently, it is therefore advisable to utilize ratios depicting the share of international students in total enrolment. As is also shown in Table 3.1, calculating such ratios reveals that student mobility has indeed increased over the past decade, but not nearly as profoundly as most of the related literature infers. In the year 2000, the share of international students in total enrolment was 4.08 per cent, and by 2010, this figure increased to 5.09 per cent. This corresponds to a 19 per cent increase in total.[2] In conclusion, it is fair to say that growth in student mobility has only moderately outpaced growth in enrolment. Conceptualizing student mobility in terms of ratios, we would argue, provides a more precise picture of its extent and its trajectory in a descriptive sense. It is also a measure well suited to serve as the dependent variable for analyses investigating determinants of student mobility comparatively, as is done in the next section, because it isolates the phenomenon under question (that is, student mobility) from the confounding influence of enrolment.

As already mentioned, the figures above contain aggregated data from most of our sampled countries. This has been done strictly for illustrative purposes. What they do not tell us, however, is how mobility ratios have developed in individual countries. Since the goal of this paper is to assess student mobility in both a comparative and longitudinal way, we proceed by providing country-level data. In accordance with the argument made above, we utilize mobility ratios rather than absolute numbers of mobile students. Fortunately, the UNESCO provides student mobility ratios for both inbound (referring to foreign students coming in) and outbound mobility (referring to domestic students going out). In both cases, the denominator used to calculate the ratios is the total domestic tertiary enrolment.[3] Isolated missing values have been imputed using cubic interpolation (Cox 2002).[4]

In figure 3.2, both inbound and outbound mobility ratios are plotted for each of the case study countries included in this volume, except for China.[5] Apart from the United States, all of these countries have been members of the Bologna Process since its inception in 1999. No clear patterns emerge from an initial inspection of these graphs. In terms of inbound mobility, one can observe high ratios throughout for France, Germany, Switzerland and the United Kingdom while the proportion of international students is quite low in both Spain and the United States. Tangible increases over the entire time period can only be observed for France and the United Kingdom, with all other countries remaining steady. Interestingly, these increases cannot be attributed to intra-European mobility but are largely a consequence of inflowing

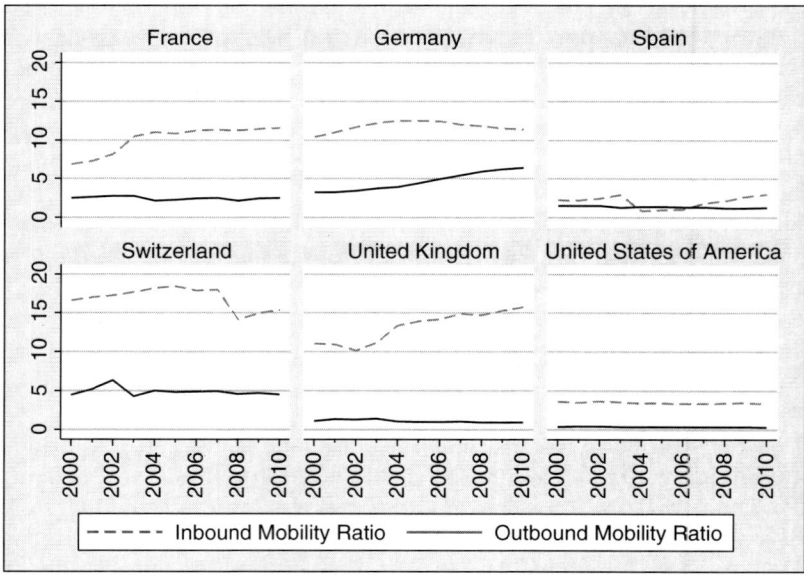

*Figure 3.2*   Mobility ratios of case study countries.

Chinese students. In both cases, the proportion of incoming students of Chinese origin as a portion of the total number of incoming international students increased from less than 3 per cent in 2000 to more than 10 per cent in 2010. When it comes to the outbound mobility ratios, there seems to be little variance over time for most countries. The only country recording a significant change is Germany with an increase of 3.2 per cent, which is mostly due to increasing mobility toward two countries – Austria (+13.4 per cent) and the Netherlands (+12.2 per cent).

While this suggests little to moderate changes in both dimensions of student mobility of our case study countries, the same is not necessarily true for our entire sample. As indicated by the summary statistics in Table 3.2, there is indeed a good bit of variance to explain. Both ratios have on average increased over time. There are also stark differences between sample countries: for some, mobility ratios have increased by nine or ten percentage points, whereas for others, we can even observe a decrease over time. Corresponding standard deviations between countries are 4.82 for inbound mobility and 3.57 for outbound mobility, again denoting considerable variance.

## TSCS analysis

As outlined in the previous section, in- and outbound mobility ratios serve as the dependent variables for our TSCS analysis. As can be inferred from Table 3.2, there are more observations on outbound than on inbound mobility, both in terms of countries included in the sample and average observations per country. This imbalance is due to uneven data availability in the UIS database.

Turning to our independent variables, our central objective is to assess the impact of the Bologna Process on student mobility. Given its goal

*Table 3.2* Summary statistics for inbound and outbound mobility ratios.

| Variable | | Mean | Std. Dev. | Min. | Max. | Obs. |
|---|---|---|---|---|---|---|
| Inbound mobility ratio | Overall | 5.17 | 5.06 | 0.50 | 21.47 | N = 390 |
| | Between | | 4.82 | 0.69 | 17.95 | n = 39 |
| | Within | | 1.37 | –2.67 | 10.35 | $\bar{T}$ = 10 |
| Outbound mobility ratio | Overall | 3.62 | 3.11 | 0.34 | 26.20 | N = 440 |
| | Between | | 3.57 | 0.39 | 20.89 | n = 41 |
| | Within | | 1.07 | –2.87 | 9.71 | $\bar{T}$ = 10.73 |

to increase both in- and outbound mobility in participating countries, we would expect a positive relationship between membership and our dependent variables, *ceteris paribus*. We thus include a dummy variable dubbed *Bologna member*, indicating whether a country was a participant in the Bologna Process in a given year. For founding countries, this variable is set as "1" for all years under consideration, and for countries that joined later in the same decade the indicator varies accordingly. We also include a variable dubbed *Length of membership*, specifying the number of years a country has been participating in the Bologna Process. The rationale for including such a variable is that Bologna Process membership may generate increasing returns over time. As institutional change kicks in and new study-programmes in accordance with the three-cycle degree systems and the ECTS are implemented, the intended effect of the Bologna Process may materialize over time.

We include a plethora of additional variables both to isolate the impact of the Bologna Process (since member countries are highly heterogeneous) and to assess it vis-à-vis other push and pull factors thought to shape mobility flows. We include both time-variant and time-invariant variables in order to comprehensively analyse determinants of student mobility. Starting with time-variant variables, *GDP per capita* is included in our models as a proxy for the economic prosperity in a given country. Taken from the UIS database, it is assumed to exert a positive influence on inbound mobility and a negative one on outbound mobility. *Economic openness*, as taken from the Penn World Table (2012), denotes the degree of a country's integration into the world economy, measured as the sum of exports and imports divided by GDP. Here, the assumption is that the cost of both types of mobility is smaller in highly integrated economies, suggesting a simultaneous push and pull effect. Next, *enrolment ratio* denotes the proportion of students taking on higher education, calculated as enrolment (ISCED 5a + 6) divided by total population in tertiary school age.[6] Data come from the UIS. As a proxy for the size of the higher education sector, it indicates the level of opportunity to study in a given country. A well-developed higher education system, we would expect, acts as a pull factor for prospective international students. At the same time, it should decrease the relative benefit from studying abroad, resulting in lower outbound mobility ratios.

Time-invariant variables include information on the primary language and geographic location of sampled countries, but also a proxy for the quality of their higher education system. For the latter, we rely on the *Shanghai Academic Ranking of World Universities*, in which the top 500 universities worldwide are identified and ranked according to criteria such as number of Nobel laureates and faculty citation counts. The Shanghai Ranking may be a flawed indicator because it does not explicitly address teaching quality and ranks individual institutions rather than national higher education systems, but we would argue that it does relate substantive information about the *perceived* quality of higher education systems for prospective students.[7] Since data from the Shanghai Ranking is only available from 2003–10 and there is little variance between years, we take the average of the available data and treat higher education quality as a time-invariant factor. More expressly, we construct two variables from the Shanghai Ranking. First, due to the fact that a sizable number of countries did not have any universities in the top 500 of the Shanghai Ranking, we include a dummy called *no ranked universities* to absorb variance stemming from the zero-inflated nature of the ranking. We expect a negative relationship with inbound mobility and a positive one with outbound mobility. Second, *quality index* is constructed by dividing the average number of universities ranked in the top 500 by the total population of each country. Obviously, we expect quality to impact positively on inbound mobility and negatively on outbound mobility.

Furthermore, the variable *English* is a dummy indicating whether the official language of a country is English (=1) or not (=0). As it is the world's lingua franca, one would expect English-speaking countries have an in-built advantage in attracting international students. In terms of outbound mobility, the hypothetical relationship is less clear. One could assume, for instance, that the propensity to learn a foreign language is less pronounced in English-speaking countries, and thus the cost of studying in a non-English country is heightened, leading to lower outbound mobility ratios. Geographic location, finally, is taken into account by including a set of dummy variables indicating the region in which a country is situated. The reference category is Central and Eastern Europe (n = 14), and additional groupings include Central Asia (n = 3), East Asia and the Pacific (n = 4), Western Europe (n = 17) and Americas (denoting South, Middle and North America, n = 3). As for hypotheses, one could construct an argument stating that mobility should be low in remote regions (such as East Asia and the Pacific) and that it should be higher in regions that are easily accessible to a bigger fraction of the overall student population (such as Western Europe). However, the purpose of the region variable in this context is rather to absorb regional idiosyncrasies. Since the Bologna Process spans three highly heterogeneous regions, it seems reasonable to evaluate its impact under statistical control of these imbalances.

The structure of our data is longitudinal in that we have multiple observations for each country at different points in time. Within the dataset, we have observed considerable variance both between countries and over time. Since we have a substantial interest in both of these variance types and also want to test for the impact of time-invariant variables (such as English), we have chosen to run hybrid regressions that combine the advantages of fixed-effects (absorbing unit-specific heterogeneity) and random-effects models (inclusion of time-invariant predictors). Formally, the estimation method is a random-effects GLS regression. In order to reproduce fixed-effects coefficient estimates of the time-variant variables (and thus controlling for the fraction of the unobserved heterogeneity that is correlated with those variables), meaned versions of the variables are included in the random-effects model (for detailed discussions, see Allison 2009 or Gießelmann and Windzio 2012). Formally, the regression equation can thus be described as:

$$y_{it} = \beta_1 * x_{it} + \beta_2 * \bar{x} + \beta_2 * z_i + w_{it}$$

In addition to unobserved heterogeneity, TSCS models are also often plagued by serial correlation of their residuals. This is true for our data as well. More specifically, we find autocorrelation of the first order (AR1) in all of our models. We correct for these disturbances following Baltagi and Wu (1999).[8]

Our hybrid regression estimates for both mobility ratios are reported in Table 3.3. In Model 1, only the variables related to the Bologna Process are included. While the dummy indicating Bologna membership does not exert any influence, the length of membership is correlated positively with inbound mobility, with each additional year increasing the ratio by 0.1 percentage points. This effect, however, vanishes as soon as we estimate our full model (Model 2), suggesting Bologna membership does not impact at all on inbound mobility. Three of our predictors do reach significance: *GDP per capita* ($p < 0.1$), *English* ($p < 0.01$) and *quality index* ($p < 0.05$). As hypothesized, all three of these variables exert a positive influence on inbound mobility. Given the mean of the dependent variable (5.26), the effect of *English* is especially pronounced as the mobility ratio of countries with English as the primary language on average is more than four percentage points higher than in countries with other primary languages. Economic openness, enrolment ratios and regional dummies, however, do not seem to shape inbound mobility in either direction.

While the Bologna Process did not have an impact in terms of inbound mobility, the story is quite different for outbound mobility ratios. As

*Table 3.3* Hybrid regression estimates for mobility ratios[+].

| Variables | Model 1 Inbound Mobility | Model 2 Inbound Mobility | Model 3 Outbound Mobility | Model 4 Outbound Mobility |
|---|---|---|---|---|
| Bologna member | −0.00619 (0.389) | −0.110 (0.394) | 1.054*** (0.313) | 1.103*** (0.308) |
| Length of membership | 0.101*** (0.0359) | 0.0379 (0.0431) | 0.00235 (0.0291) | 0.0890*** (0.0344) |
| GDP per capita | | 0.000135* (0.0000) | | −0.000117** (0.0000) |
| Openness | | −0.0120 (0.00770) | | 0.00921 (0.00620) |
| Enrolment Ratio | | 2.369 (1.533) | | −4.470*** (1.177) |
| Central Asia[++] | | 0.285 (2.303) | | −5.854*** (1.642) |
| East Asia & Pacific | | 4.602 (3.963) | | −5.126* (2.972) |
| Western Europe | | 2.086 (1.937) | | 0.598 (1.580) |
| Americas | | −2.305 (4.131) | | −6.188** (2.962) |
| English | | 4.146*** (1.572) | | 0.309 (1.278) |
| No Ranked Universities | | 0.203 (1.508) | | 2.558* (1.328) |
| Quality Index | | 28.485*** (8.935) | | −12.577* (7.095) |
| Constant | 4.857*** (1.740) | 5.212 (3.921) | 1.966** (0.926) | 5.414* (3.078) |
| Observations | 390 | 390 | 440 | 440 |
| Number of Countries | 39 | 39 | 41 | 41 |
| $R^2$ Within | 0.041 | 0.094 | 0.042 | 0.100 |
| $R^2$ Between | 0.003 | 0.682 | 0.274 | 0.566 |
| $R^2$ Overall | 0.017 | 0.631 | 0.172 | 0.426 |
| Chi$^2$ | 8.16 | 96.03*** | 29.84*** | 92.09*** |

*Notes:* Standard errors in parentheses; ***$p < 0.01$, **$p < 0.05$, *$p < 0.1$; + Meaned variables are included in all models, but not reported; ++ reference category is *Eastern Europe*.

shown in Models 3 and 4, the coefficient for the membership in the Bologna Process is consistently significant and positive (p < 0.01). In other words, once a country joins the Bologna Process, its outbound mobility ratio increases by more than 1.1 percentage points, *ceteris paribus*. This effect is substantial since the dependent variable has a mean of only 3.62. Interestingly, while the coefficient for length of membership is not significant in the simple model, it becomes highly significant (p < 0.01) in the full model. Once other factors are controlled for, each year of membership adds a mere 0.09 percentage points to outbound mobility, suggesting a positive but small effect. As regards the time-variant variables, economic openness again fails to reach significance, but *GDP per capita* and *enrolment ratio* both significantly decrease outbound mobility. As hypothesized, therefore, low GDP and underdeveloped higher education sectors act as push factors for students to study abroad. Geographic location also plays a role in explaining outbound mobility. Compared to Eastern European countries, countries from central Asia (p < 0.01), East Asia and the Pacific (p < 0.1) and the Americas (p < 0.01) have significantly lower outbound mobility ratios. Finally, the quality of the higher education systems is very important. Countries without ranked universities on average had an outbound mobility ratio 2.6 percentage points higher than those who did (p < 0.1), while an increase in the quality index corresponds to a decrease in the proportion of students pursuing their degree in a different country (p < 0.1).

In sum, we find no evidence for an impact of the Bologna Process on inbound mobility ratios, but a robustly positive relationship with membership and outbound mobility. While official Bologna Process documents are vague in specifying what type of mobility should increase, the notion of a highly competitive Europe of knowledge would suggest that policy-makers were primarily interested in growing inbound mobility. Rather, the propensity to study in a higher education system outside of the country of origin seems to have been fostered by the Bologna Process. It is unclear whether this could be qualified as a programmatic policy success. On the one hand, the Bologna Process is explicit in stating that increasing outbound mobility is desirable so long as it occurs within the EHEA. On the other hand, the analysis above does not take into account the destination countries for outbound flows. This is done, however, in the following dyadic analysis of country-pairs.

### Dyadic analysis

This part of our analysis rests on a comparison of country pairs, so-called *dyads*. In general, the dyadic approach allows scholars to study exchange patterns directly between all pairs of states. It has been widely used in the international relations literature, where often the dependent variable does not measure attributes of countries but rather of pairs of countries: "The advantage of the dyadic approach is that observable relationships of theoretical interest, such as geographic proximity or similarities in socio-economic structures, can be included easily into the analysis" (Gilardi and Füglister 2008: 418). The pair approach can "more accurately measure peer relationship between each pair of states" (Boehmke 2009: 1125). In the directed approach, each state can function as potential "receiver" and "sender" whereby independent variables capture the characteristics of both "receivers" and "senders", as well as their relationships. These models have the following general form:

$$y_{ijt} = \alpha + x_{ijt}\beta + \beta + \varepsilon_{ijt}$$

where $i$, $j$ and $t$ indexes are, respectively, "receivers", "senders" and time, $y_{ijt}$ is a vector of relational outcomes, $x_{ijt}$ is a matrix of measures for the characteristics of the dyad and $\beta$ is a vector of coefficients to be estimated (Gilardi and Füglister 2008: 416).

Utilizing a dyadic approach in investigating student mobility has several important advantages. First, it makes it possible to model relational student exchange flows between pairs of countries, including relevancy of the relationship and whether it is balanced. Second, it allows us to test the programme-theoretical assumptions behind the Bologna Process. Since the main mechanism thought to facilitate student mobility is the principle of comparability and compatibility, an estimation testing this proposition should incorporate information on whether higher education systems have indeed become more alike with regard to their study structures.

The data used for the construction of our dependent variables was gathered by referring to the UIS online database. It is micro data, counting every student seeking a degree abroad. We collected data for the period 2000 to 2010 and analysed it cross-sectionally across time periods (in 2000, 2003, 2006 and 2009). These numbers are then used to construct our two dependent variables, *relevance* and *balanced*. The variable *relevance* measures the magnitude of cross-national student exchanges. It includes the number of students one country receives from another and divides it by the number of outbound mobile students of the sending country. We thus calculate the proportion of outbound mobile students from one country choosing a specific country as their study destination. The variable *balanced* measures whether exchange relationships between countries are symmetrical. We first compared the number of students exchanged between two countries constituting a dyad while controlling for the size of the higher education sectors of both countries. We then subtracted the lower value from the higher one and divided these values by the total amount of internationally mobile students of both countries. As a consequence, a high value for this variable indicates an imbalanced exchange relationship.[9]

On part of the independent variables, membership status in the Bologna Process was coded into three subcategories: the group of nonmember countries (=0), used as reference category in the analyses; a group called mixed dyads (=1), where one country is a Bologna EU member and the other is not; and common membership in the Bologna Process, coded (=2). The same coding procedure was applied for EU membership, as the freedom of mobility within the EU may lower mobility cost. Information on stage of implementation of ECTS or a comparable system was gathered by means of the Stocktaking as well as the National Reports of the Bologna Process, by reference to secondary academic literature (Westerheijden et al. 2010; Knill et al. 2012) and extensive document analysis of national higher education regulations. The reference category is the "yellow" category of the 2005 Stocktaking Report scorecard, which indicates whether a "national system for credit transfer and accumulation is in place, which is compatible with ECTS, or [whether] the national credit transfer and accumulation system is being gradually integrated with ECTS" (Stocktaking Report 2005: 21). The logic for coding the stage of implementation of ECTS in the dyadic approach follows the same as for Bologna and EU membership.

Additionally, we include information about study programme structures in the analyses. We thus refer to the percentage of students enrolled in any kind of two-cycle degree system to assess the extent to which this policy is implemented. To do so, we referred to Stocktaking and National Reports of the Bologna Process as well as OECD Education at a Glance reports. We used the scorecard of the Stocktaking Reports as benchmarks, level of student enrolment, light green and up, from 2009 on yellow and up, as reference category, thus if "51–80 [or more] of students are enrolled in the two-cycle system" (Stocktaking Report 2005: 19) respectively if "50–69 [or more] of all students are enrolled in a two-cycle degree system that is in accordance with the Bologna principles" (Stocktaking Report 2009: 31). Dyads with approximately the same level of student enrolment in two-tier degree systems were coded with 1, otherwise with 0.

Besides assessing the effects of common higher education policies, we include factors mentioned in the literature as impacting cross-national student migration, namely language commonalities, geographical proximity and economic performance – measured in GDP per capita. To assess language commonalities, we refer to common official language(s) used (=1); otherwise (=0), as indicated in the CIA World Fact Book. Common borders were coded with reference to the online resource NationMaster; the coding scheme resembles the one for common official language. Data on GDP per capita was taken from UIS online resources, and similarity was assessed by calculating the absolute difference in GDP per capita between two countries forming a dyad.

The dependent variables of our study can be regarded as count data since they account for 1) the absolute number of degree-seeking students going from one country to another and 2) the absolute difference in student exchange between two countries. The dataset for our analysis has a macro-panel structure, since we observe a large number of units over a small number of "waves". Merely pooling observations across time in addition to space is problematic, since the data has an explicit structure that should be modelled (cf. Shor et al. 2007: 166). Due to the dyadic coding of our data as well as the resulting lack of independence between the units of analysis, it is not advisable to conduct standard regression analysis (Rabe-Hesketh and Skrondal 2008: 185), and thus, we refer to multilevel models, whereas the countries constituting the observations (dyads) are introduced as second level. We refer to multilevel Poisson regression, wherein coefficients are interpreted as the difference between the log of expected counts and can thus be written as

$$\beta = \log (\mu_{x+1}) - \log (\mu_x),$$

where $\beta$ is the regression coefficient, $\mu$ is the expected count and the subscripts represent where the predictor variable is evaluated at $x$ and $x+1$. Since the difference of two logs is equal to the log of their quotient, or

$$\log (\mu_{x+1}) - \log (\mu_x) = \log (\mu_{x+1} / \mu_x),$$

we can interpret the parameter estimate as the log of the ratio of expected count or a rate. By definition a rate is the number of events per time (or space), for which our response variable qualifies. In our case, the number of events is simply the number of students from one country studying in another country in a given year.

Table 3.4 depicts the results for the two dependent variables. We begin with the results for *relevance*. To our surprise, taking the group of non-Bologna participants as reference category, participation in the Bologna Process has a significantly negative impact on the magnitude of student exchanges. Pooled over the whole period of investigation, membership

*Table 3.4*   Pooled Poisson multilevel model of factors impacting on dyadic student exchange patterns.

| Variables | Model 5 Relevance | Model 6 Balanced |
|---|---|---|
| Bologna-membership | | |
| 1 | −0.617(.034)*** | −1.269(.065)*** |
| 2 | −0.177(.043)*** | −1.086(.085)*** |
| EU-membership | | |
| 1 | −0.469(.030)*** | 0.104(.052)** |
| 2 | −0.451(.038)*** | 0.606(.069)*** |
| ECTS | | |
| 1 | −0.359(.041)*** | −0.357(.082)*** |
| 2 | −0.258(.041)*** | 0.200(.083)** |
| TC | 0.138(.033)*** | −0.291(.064)*** |
| Language | 0.136(.027)*** | −0.144(.061)** |
| Borders | 1.380(.023)*** | 1.630(.047)*** |
| GDP per capita | −.001(0.000)*** | −0.001(0.000)*** |
| Constant | 0.608(.250)** | 0.424(.162)** |
| Random intercept standard deviation | 1.563(.178) | 0.846(.103) |
| Log-likelihood | −14026.987 | −5223.389 |
| N (dyads) | 6560 | 3280 |
| N (groups) | 41 | 41 |
| Test vs. Poisson regression | .000 | .000 |

of one or both countries of a dyad influences the probability for an increase in *relevance*. Hence, the strongest exchange ties can be found in the group of non-Bologna members. Looking at the results for EU membership, the results can be interpreted analogously. Thus, non-EU member countries have the strongest exchange ties.

Common implementation of ECTS or a comparable system does not impact the relevance of the exchange relationship. Rather, the most relevant exchange patterns can be found among countries at different stages of implementation. In contrast, dyads in which both countries had a two-tier study system implemented to a comparable degree have the most relevant relationships. Besides structural higher education policy similarity, a common official language and geographical proximity account for the magnitude of cross-national student exchanges. A highly influential factor is geographical proximity, whereas similarity in GDP per capita exerts a significant negative influence, although the strength of the effect is negligible. Thus, the most relevant exchange relationships are between countries with comparable GDP per capita.

Turning to the second dependent variable, we find the most balanced relationships within the group of mixed Bologna dyads. The most imbalanced relationships are among the non-participants, followed by the Bologna participants. The starkest difference can be found between EU members, although this effect is rather small. The most balanced patterns can be found in the group of countries with mixed stages of implementation of ECTS or comparable systems. A common stage of enrolment in a two-cycle study system decreases the imbalance in exchange relationships; therefore, the most balanced student exchange patterns are among countries which both have a two-cycle system in place with comparable enrolment levels. Likewise, if two countries have the same official language, their student exchange relationships are more balanced; however, this does not hold for bordering countries. Rather, common borders have a strong and significant impact on increasing the imbalance of exchange relationships. For commonalities in socioeconomic factors, an increase in difference in GDP per capita decreases imbalance. Thus, the more similar the countries are in their economic performance, the more balanced their student exchanges are.

In conclusion, the highest imbalance can be found in dyads where countries neither participate in the Bologna Process nor are members of the EU. Moreover, the most relevant exchange relationships can be found in the group of non-Bologna members. With regard to structural similarities between higher education systems, imbalances in exchanges are smallest if both countries have approximately the same stage of implementation of a two-cycle degree system. Likewise, language similarities reduce imbalances in exchanges. If two countries have a common official language, their student exchange patterns are more balanced compared to countries with dissimilar official languages. Contrastingly, bordering countries have the most relevant, and yet most imbalanced, student exchanges.

## Comparative conclusions

In this chapter, we analysed the impact of the Bologna Process on degree-seeking student mobility flows. We defined programmatic success as an increase in both inbound and outbound mobility and whether exchange relationships between Bologna member countries were balanced. In order to isolate the impact of the Bologna Process, we derived a set of push and pull factors thought to drive student mobility flows from a rational-choice framework. We tested the explanatory power of these factors and Bologna membership by estimating TSCS and pooled Poisson regression models.

Overall, we find that international student mobility has increased between 2000 and 2010, albeit to a much lesser extent than previous studies would suggest. Bologna membership did not have a positive impact on inbound mobility but increased outbound mobility ratios moderately. As programme-theoretical assumptions of the policy instruments associated with the Bologna Process clearly state, hurdles to studying in foreign countries should be lowered due to the harmonized degree cycles and system of transferable degrees. Thus, increasing outbound mobility ratios can be interpreted as a programmatic success.

With regard to mobility flows between country-pairs, we find that the most relevant exchange relationships are those between non-members. In contrast to the programme-theoretical assumptions of the Bologna Process, mutual implementation of modularized degree structures does not impact the magnitude of exchange relationships. Likewise, the most balanced exchange relationships cannot be found in Bologna-dyads, suggesting programmatic failure.

## Notes

1  Bologna members in our sample thus are: Albania, Armenia, Austria, Belgium, Croatia, Czech Republic, Denmark, Estonia, Finland, France, Georgia, Germany, Greece, Hungary, Ireland, Italy, Kazakhstan, Latvia, Lithuania, the Netherlands, Norway, Poland, Portugal, Romania, Russia, the Slovak Republic, Slovenia, Spain, Sweden, Switzerland, Turkey, Ukraine and the United Kingdom. Additional OECD members include Australia, Chile, Japan, Korea, New Zealand and the United States.
2  Compare this figure to the 9 per cent *annual* increase Beine, Noel et al. (2011) found in between 2000–08 utilizing absolute numbers only.
3  Because students are always counted in the country in which they are enrolled, there is an important difference between inbound and outbound mobility ratios. In the case of inbound mobility, the measure yields the share of international students in total enrolment. In the case of outbound mobility, it is the number of outgoing students compared to total enrolment.
4  Isolated (and thus imputable) missings are defined as having at least two non-missing observations in the two years before and after the missing value.
5  Inbound mobility ratios for Germany and outbound mobility ratios for the United States were missing in the UIS data. We therefore supplemented our original dataset with data provided by the statistical offices of both countries.
6  Tertiary school age is defined as the "total population of the five-year age group following on from secondary school leaving" (Unesco Institute for Statistics 2013).
7  For a detailed discussion on indicators measuring the quality of higher education systems, see Van Bouwel and Veugelers (2013).
8  This method is also robust for estimating regression coefficients with unbalanced and unevenly spaced underlying data, as is the case with ours.

9   Since *balanced* is coded in a non-directed way, the total amount of observations is half of the value for *relevance*.

# References

Agarwal, Pawan, Mohsen Said, Molathegi Sehoole, Muhammad Sirozi and Hans De Wit (2008) "The Dynamics of International Student Circulation in a Global Context: Summary, Conclusions and Recommendations", in Hans De Wit, Pawan Agarwal, Muhammad Said, Molathegi Sehoole and Muhammad Sirozi, eds., *The Dynamics of International Student Circulation in a Global Context*, Rotterdam: Sense Publishers, 233–62.

Allison, Paul D. (2009) *Fixed Effects Regression Models*, Thousand Oaks: SAGE.

Baltagi, Badi H. and Ping X. Wu (1999) "Unequally spaced panel data regressions with AR(1) disturbances", *Econometric Theory*, 15(6), 814–23.

Beine, Michael, Romain Noel and Lionel Ragot (2011) "The determinants of international mobility of students", *CESifo Working Paper Series* No. 3498.

Bessey, Donata (2010) "International student migration to Germany", *Empirical Economics*, 42(1), 345–61.

Boehmke, Frederick J. (2009) "Policy Emulation or Policy Convergence? Potential Ambiguities in the Dyadic Event History Approach to State Policy Emulation", *The Journal of Politics*, 71(3), 1125–40.

Bologna Declaration (1999) *The Bologna Declaration of 19 June 1999 – Conference of European Ministers Responsible for Higher Education*: http://www.ehea.info/Uploads/Declarations/BOLOGNA_ DECLARATION1.pdf, retrieved 3 May 2013.

Bologna Follow Up Group (2005) *Stocktaking Report 2005 – Bologna Process Stocktaking*: http://www.ehea.info/article-details.aspx?ArticleId=73, retrieved 1 July 2013.

Bologna Follow Up Group (2007) *Stocktaking Report 2007 – Bologna Process Stocktaking*: http://www.ehea.info/article-details.aspx?ArticleId=73, retrieved 1 July 2013.

Bologna Follow Up Group (2009) *Stocktaking Report 2009 – Bologna Process Stocktaking*: http://www.ehea.info/article-details.aspx?ArticleId=73, retrieved 1 July 2013.

Caruso, Raul and Hans de Wit (2013) *Determinants of Mobility of Students in Europe: a preliminary quantitative study*, Catholic University of the Sacred Heart, Centre for Higher Education Internationalisation (CHEI).

Cox, Nicholas J. (2002) *CIPOLATE: Stata module for cubic interpolation*, Boston College: Department of Economics.

Eurydice (2012) *The European Higher Education Area in 2012: Bologna Process Implementation Report*, Brussels: http://eacea.ec.europa.eu/education/eurydice/documents/thematic_reports/138EN.pdf, retrieved 23 November 2013.

Dobbins, Michael, Christoph Knill and Eva Maria Vögtle (2011) "An analytical framework for the cross-country comparison of higher education governance", *Higher Education*, 62(5), 665–83.

Dreher, Axel and Panu Poutvaara (2005) "Student flows and migration: an empirical analysis", *CESifo working papers*, No. 1490.

Giesselmann, Marco and Michael Windzio (2012) *Regressionsmodelle zur Analyse von Paneldaten*, Wiesbaden: VS.

Gilardi, Fabrizio and Katharina Füglister (2008) "Empirical Modeling of Policy Diffusion in Federal States: The Dyadic Approach", *Swiss Political Science Review*, 14(3), 413–50.

González, Carlos Rodríguez, Ricardo Bustillo Mesanza and Petr Mariel (2011) "The determinants of international student mobility flows: An empirical study on the Erasmus programme", *Higher Education*, 62(4), 413–30.

Heston, Alan, Robert Summers and Bettina Aten (2012) *Penn World Table Version 7.1*, Center for International Comparisons of Production, Income and Prices at the University of Pennsylvania.

Knill, Christoph, Eva Maria Vögtle and Michael Dobbins (2012) *Hochschulpolitische Reformen im Zuge des Bologna-Prozesses: Eine vergleichende Analyse von Konvergenzdynamiken im OECD-Raum*, Wiesbaden: VS.

Martens, Kerstin and Klaus Dieter Wolf (2009) "Boomerangs and Trojan Horses. The Unintended Consequences of Internationalizing Education Policy Through the EU and the OECD", in Alberto Amaral, Guy Neave, Christine Musselin and Peter Maassen, eds., *European Integration and the Governance of Higher Education and Research*. Dordrecht: Springer, 81–108.

NationMaster (2013) *World Statistics, Country Comparisons*: http://www.nationmaster.com/index.php, retrieved 1 July 2013.

Rabe-Hesketh, Sophia and Anders Skrondal (2008) *Multilevel and longitudinal modeling using Stata*, College Station: Stata Press.

Shanghai Academic Ranking of World Universities (2003–10): http://www.shanghairanking.com/index.html, retrieved 18 November 2013.

Shor, Boris, Joseph Bafumi, Luke Keele and David Park (2007) "A Bayesian Multilevel Modeling Approach to Time-Series Cross-Sectional Data", *Political Analysis*, 15(2), 165–81.

Tremblay, Karine (2001) "Student mobility between and towards OECD countries: A comparative analysis", *OECD Trends in International Migration (Annual Report)*.

UNESCO Institute for Statistics (2013) *UIS online database*: http://www.uis.unesco.org/Pages/default.aspx, retrieved 1 July 2013.

Van Bouwel, Linda and Reinhilde Veugelers (2013) "The determinants of student mobility in Europe: the quality dimension", *European Journal of Higher Education*, 3(2), 172–90.

Westerheijden, Don. F., Eric Beerkens, Leon Remonini et al. (2010) "The first decade of working on the European Higher Education Area", *Bologna Process independent assessment volume 1: Main report*, Enschede: CHEPS.

Zgaga, Pavel (2006) *Looking Out: The Bologna Process in a Global Setting. On the 'External Dimension' of the Bologna Process*: http://www.madrid.org/eees/acap/historia/Bologna_Global_final_report.pdf, retrieved 3 May 2013.

# Part II
# Case Studies

# 4
## After the Big Bang – German Education Policy in the Wake of the PISA Study and the Bologna Process

*Dennis Niemann*

## Introduction

The expansion of the education policy universe to the international space affected Germany and its constellation of education policy, politics, polity, and ideas substantially. Recent reforms in German education policy could not be assessed without referring to two international institutions that were particularly important for Germany: the Programme for International Student Assessment (PISA) by the Organisation for Economic Co-operation and Development (OECD) in secondary education and the Bologna Process in higher education. Both projects were set up on the international level and incorporated no binding commitments. However, the actual effects of the internationalization of education policy on Germany were neither foreseeable nor universally intended; both PISA and the Bologna Process successively generated severe repercussions for domestic education policy-making. Since encompassing education reforms in the late 1960s and early 1970s, education policy in Germany has been characterized by a backlog of reforms (for secondary education, see Baumert et al. 2003; Ertl 2006; for higher education, see Teichler 2005). Although some minor adjustments were enacted and agendas were set for further core reforms, no groundbreaking reforms were conducted.

PISA and the Bologna Process led to a reorganization and reorientation of the German education sector (Niemann 2010). Hence, almost all relevant stakeholders were faced with new education policies. Interest groups and corporate actors in German education policy represent different points of view on education and they aim to influence the policy-making processes. Consequently, in order to pursue their interests and beliefs, they were assumed to develop their own positions and claims in response to recent developments in the field of education. In this regard, it has to be asked how the relevant German education policy actors reacted to the changes and how they evaluated the new constellation. Did they raise their *voices*, decide to *exit*, or show *loyalty* to the changes?

This chapter assesses how German policy actors evaluated the reforms conducted in secondary and higher education and how they tried to achieve their goals by influencing the policy process. Generally, it shows that nearly all the actors appreciated the reform intentions. However, the implementation of the reforms was criticized. I proceed in the following steps. First, Germany's system of education policy-making is elaborated, explaining the background of its political opportunity structure (POS) and available resources of actors for mobilization and participation. Additionally, the key features of the German education polity are described. Since education policy-making in Germany is *qua* Basic Law of the Federal Republic of Germany a matter of the federal states (the *Länder*), two of them are more closely considered in this chapter: North Rhine-Westphalia (NRW) and Bavaria.[1] In the next part, the reactions to recent reforms in secondary education are analysed. By highlighting the multiple changes in German secondary education due to PISA, it is shown that the reactions were surprisingly moderate. The reactions of relevant actors to the *new constellation* of higher education are described in the following part. The effects of the Bologna Process resulted in various reactions of mainly *voice* and *loyalty*.

## Education policy-making in Germany

The reactions towards reforms conducted depend on the domestic POS. In short, the institutional setup and the perpetual political interactions strongly determine the reactions of relevant actors by granting many or few strong or weak opportunities for political participation. According to the theoretical approach of this book, the institutional POS setting of a state defines, on the one hand, the openness of access for collective actors and, on the other hand, the state's capacity to act autonomously, reflecting the strength of the state (Kriesi 2004). Decentralized states are characterized by a multiplicity of access points since actors can approach several levels of decision-making (see Dowding and John 2008). Decentralization is a core feature of German education policy-making because of the exclusive authority of the 16 German *Länder* and the very limited formal competences of the federal government and its ministry, the Federal Ministry of Education and Research (BMBF). Furthermore, since Germany's education system is a matter of the *Länder,* and each of the *Länder* has exclusive jurisdiction over education policy,[2] coherent reform endeavours were generally difficult to implement. However, the factual autonomy of the *Länder* has not resulted in the establishment of 16 different education systems. Although some minor differences between the *Länder* prevail, the overall education system is coherent across Germany. In this regard, the second basic feature of German federalism comes into play: the pursuit for uniform living conditions. As a consequence, too much deviation is not tolerated (Wolf 2008). To put it differently, the diversified polity is contrasted by a homogenous population that calls for uniform policy structures (Katzenstein 1987). In sum, the German education policy-making process is characterized by coherent decisions that consult all relevant actors.[3] It is important to note that coordinating institutions in education policy-making exist, providing places for exchange, coordination, and unified approaches to perceived problems. First and foremost, the Standing Conference of the Ministers of Education and Cultural Affairs (KMK) is the primary coordination committee between the *Länder* in matters of education. Thereby, the KMK represents the interests of the *Länder* and has to argue on behalf of their interests while also representing an overarching German view.

Due to the federated structure, there are several points where domestic stakeholders can access the decision-making process for German secondary and higher education policy. Actors can approach the administration, parliament and commissions, parties, courts, or the public sphere (including the media) in each of the 16 *Länder* or at the federal level. Furthermore, Germany can be regarded as a corporatist political system that features a "high degree of centralization in the organization of societal interests" (Zürn 2005: 24). Proportional representation makes Germany a consensual democracy with strong tendencies for coalition governments (also on the *Länder* level). Hence, political stakeholders have many opportunities to formally access the political process to realize their positions. This is also true in the case of education. German actors can gain leverage by approaching certain factions of decision-makers and by participating in several informal coordinating committees, roundtables, and consultations established on the *Länder* and federal level. Usually, this cooperation has a more *ad hoc* characteristic than a binding institutionalized cooperation.

Taken together, education policy in Germany is essentially characterized by the decentralized structure of 16 *Länder*, with autonomous
decision-making authority and a comparatively weak federal authority
which only has very restricted formal governance capabilities. German
education policy-making features the opportunity for a high degree of
influence by actors. The POS in German education policy enables groups
of actors to access the decision-making process at several points to influence policies. This makes Germany a weak state in education policy-
making. Hence, consensus is expected to be favoured when making
decisions in order to avoid massive opposition. It can be assumed that
because of the diverse access points, actors choose to influence education policies by accessing the official political arena, making use of coe-
qual bargaining processes rather than external or extra-parliamentary
channels of influence.

Within this environment of the German POS, rational actors are
expected to use their available resources for political participation, mobilization, and organization to foster their interests (see Introduction in
this volume by Knodel et al.). In this context, the available resources of
German education policy actors are pivotal to determine their chances
for successful participation.

## Consequences of secondary education reforms in Germany

The first PISA Study revealed that, contrary to expectations, the German
secondary education system produced only mediocre outcomes. Compared to its peers, the performance of German pupils was below average (Deutsches PISA-Konsortium 2001). While performance improved
successively in the following PISA Study (Prenzel et al. 2005; Prenzel et
al. 2007; Klieme et al. 2010; Prenzel et al. 2013), some substantial criticism remained. In particular, the high variation of performance between
pupils from different socio-economic backgrounds continued to be
problematic. Essentially, pupils from low-income families have less of
a chance to succeed in school (Prenzel 2007) and thus, social exclusion
became another topic of the German post-PISA discourse (Allmendinger
and Leibfried 2003). Once again the latest PISA Study of 2012 recently
affirmed that the performance of German pupils further improved and,
hence, that the German secondary education system responded well to
the introduced reforms.

Unaware of Germany's status as an education laggard, the public and
policy-makers were shocked when the first PISA report was published
in 2001. Formerly, the German self-perception in education was the

opposite: a leading world economy with a long and successful tradition in research and innovation was also expected to be a leader in education. Contrasted with the empirical evidence of PISA, this fuzzy self-perception collapsed and the poor results were translated into fear of overall economic decline (Martens and Niemann 2013). In order to (re) gain education excellence, a huge demand for reforms developed, and the entire PISA era was accompanied by an extensive public discourse.

## Changes in German secondary education

While the German secondary education system has been quite resistant to encompassing changes since the mid-1970s, the last decade saw the introduction of multiple reform measures (Rürup 2007; Baumert et al. 2003). This development was strongly linked to the PISA Study, which pinpointed significant weaknesses and provided best-practice examples for problem-solving. The German secondary education system was substantially reformed, and the reforms introduced strongly correlate with the policies promoted by the OECD's PISA (Niemann 2010). The comprehensive reform endeavour affected almost all areas of the German secondary education system. Immediately after PISA was publicized in 2001, the KMK introduced an action plan to address the main deficits of the domestic education system. Seven spheres of activity were identified where changes were required (and comparatively easy to conduct). The main emphasis was placed on early education in order to create a better academic basis and counterweigh the effect of socio-economic backgrounds. Furthermore, the statement included the advancement of underprivileged pupils, particularly in the PISA competencies (reading, mathematics, and scientific literacy) and the expansion of quality assurance, improvements in the skills of teachers, and the extension of all-day services (KMK 2011). In this context, already existing and less controversial educational reform concepts were linked to the issues brought up by PISA (Tillmann et al. 2008).

The traditional German focus on input-oriented education was identified as a blind spot that prevented the implementation of appropriate reactions to problems. Education politics mainly relied on budget allocation according to teacher/pupil ratio, structured education plans, which were set up centrally, and the like. In response, a shift to output-oriented governance was introduced in the course of PISA. By looking at performance outcomes more systematically, German policy-makers decided to act in accordance with what was necessary to achieve certain outcomes. Accordingly, education standards were introduced in Germany that define the skills pupils should have at certain points in their school career irrespective of the detailed curricula (Klieme et al. 2003).[4] Testing schemes were developed and institutionalized to monitor the accomplishment of the education standards. According to this "empirical turn" external (academic) expertise started to play a more important role in German education policy-making since it identifies education-related problems and provides empirical-based solutions.

The new secondary education constellation in Germany entailed a fundamental change of the education idea within the context of the PISA-induced reforms. Since OECD's PISA was not ideologically neutral, but rather analysed education policy from an economic perspective of usability and employability (Grek 2009), the conducted reforms were consequentially also seen in an economic light (Münch 2009; Niemann 2010). Taken together, the emergence of PISA was a decisive watershed in German secondary education policy and encompassing reforms have since been introduced. Thus, education policy actors were faced with a new constellation in the field of German secondary education policy and had to find their own position, evaluation, and course of action in the face of changed statuses.

### Reactions of relevant actors in secondary education in Germany

In general, the overall reactions by the relevant actors in secondary education to the reforms initiated in the wake of PISA are in decline and mitigated. Basically, the remaining cleavage was between advocators of an economy-centred education approach and those who argued for a more holistic, traditional approach in German education. Additionally, the aspect of how performance should be measured was part of the discourse as well as the question of how much empirical research and testing should be part of the policy-making process. In sum, the described reactions mainly addressed issues of quality assurance, output orientation, and underlying education ideas. In this regard, it became obvious that secondary education reforms were not discussed under the label of PISA but rather the discourse focused on single reform aspects or the general orientations in the "new age of secondary education". Overall, the performance of pupils successively improved in the subsequent rounds of the PISA Study. In turn, the reform measures and the new education path in Germany gained more legitimacy since it appeared to be successful in improving the outcomes of the secondary education system.

The most extreme reaction to the new secondary education policy in Germany came with the manifestation of the dissatisfaction of German pupils with the education system, culminating in the participation in the "education strike" in 2009. The pupils *voiced* massive criticism regarding perceived cuts in education, the increased workload, and the resulting pressure. In general, pupils were not among the most relevant actors in German education politics. Although pupil bodies exist at the local or regional level and have the right to represent their interests, their participation in political decision-making is rather restricted to issues of concrete school management (Hepp 2011: 72–3). Representation also takes place through parent advisory boards, which are also organized on the *Länder* and federal level. Accordingly, parents are more concerned with local school issues than with general education policy and politics (Hepp 2011: 75).

The Trade Union for Education and Science (GEW) is one of the main actors when it comes to the representation of teachers' interests.[5] Before PISA, the GEW was critical towards the German education system and pushed for encompassing reforms. Finally, when reforms were initiated in the course of PISA, the GEW was not able to *voice* too strongly against them. Overall, the GEW was one of the relevant actors in Germany who brought forward the most criticism of the recent reforms. However, some reform aspects were evaluated as positive, such as the orientation towards all-day schooling and the intensified political discourse regarding equal opportunities. Since PISA has shown that strong performance variations were determined by the socio-economic background of pupils, it broke the previous German taboo and triggered an intensive discourse on this issue (Interview GER 01). The GEW supported output orientation as long as the evaluation was equally accompanied by measures to actively support schools and teachers in acting according to the evaluation results in terms of further training for teachers (Interview GER 01).

Nevertheless, the GEW was overall critical towards the changes in German education policy and saw the "empirical turn" as widely ineffective. Although academic performances were assessed comprehensively by various tests, the actual improvement was, according to the GEW, more or less superficial. The main issue for the GEW was that the implementation of reforms was rather poorly done and there was not enough support given to teachers to cope with the new challenges and tasks. A lack of personnel and financial resources made concrete implementations on the school level difficult.

In the context of PISA-related reform undertakings and in contrast to French unions (see Dobbins in this volume), the GEW only had limited political resources for fostering its interests and beliefs. Primarily with classical lobbying, information gathering, and publishing position papers and empirical studies on the impact of the reform, the

GEW aimed to influence the education policy-making process.[6] Furthermore, to pursue its interests, the GEW cooperated with other actors and applied a strategy of intensive lobbying and sought to join with other unions and student/parent representatives in order to increase its lobbying power. In education policy the union's power to call for strike is limited since the majority of German teachers (about 75 per cent) are employed as civil servants and they are not entitled to go on strike – but at least they can organize and demonstrate. Until now there has not been a substantial *voice*, such as boycotts or strikes, as a direct reaction to the test. However, these actions were discussed as means of last resort (Interview GER 01). Additionally, public relations is one of the activities of the teachers union. Thus, the GEW attempts to frame topics in the media according to its position ("the first headline frames the whole debate", Interview GER 01).

Representatives of German employers and industry are organized in the Confederation of German Employers' Associations (BDA) whose "central mission is actively to represent business interests in the field of social policy".[7] The resources of the BDA provide funding for conducting research, initiating epistemic community networks, and promoting their interests through lobbying political stakeholders and the public. Since its formal influence on German education policy-making is limited, the BDA's informal activities generated the capacity through its strong position as the main representative of German employers.

Overall, the BDA appreciated the introduced secondary education reforms and welcomed the PISA Study (Interview GER 02). Consequently, the BDA recommended continued German participation in PISA in order to ensure an internationally comparable perspective of education; also, inner-German comparisons should be sustained and expanded (Interview GER 02). Drawing from the idea of human capital, the BDA supported the reforms regarding quality assurance since this was seen as a keystone for educational success. Particularly, assessable education standards were emphasized as a central measure to secure education quality. In this regard, the employers' representative organization demanded a continuation of the introduced reforms.

The primary interest of the BDA was to prepare pupils for the challenges in the labour market and ensure the relevancy of knowledge in terms of its applicability in the economy (Interview GER 02). Although the BDA did not actively advocate a one-sided application of education, it nevertheless lobbied for the expansion of support for the so-called MINT subjects (mathematics, informatics, natural sciences, and technology) because they are highly demanded by employers. The BDA (with others) launched information and supported campaigns through its secondary education network organization, advertising that improving the education system will also benefit the whole (welfare) state. Additionally, the BDA pursued its interests in education policy through highlighting best practices, for instance by co-awarding a prize to schools which performed well according to innovative concepts. *Voice* reaction of the BDA was present when it came to schools, school structure, and teachers' roles. On the one hand, the BDA criticized that some schools and some German teachers were not committed to the reforms. The BDA supported a further expansion for school autonomy and, accordingly, reduced state governance (Interview GER 02). In this context, the BDA also offered support and advice in an active *loyal* fashion by pointing out businesses for support.[8] On the other hand, the BDA requested state authorities to provide more funding for disadvantaged pupils and more assistance for teachers' training and schools' organization structures (Interview GER 02).

Overall, the employers' organization, BDA, made use of traditional lobby instruments in pursuing its interests and beliefs. It initiated lobby campaigns, networking with its partners from politics, economics, and civil society, and conducted its own empirical research to support its arguments. The BDA cooperated closely with (economy-oriented) foundations as well as with other corporate actors, such as the umbrella organization German Federation of Trade Unions (DGB). Being a lobby organization, the BDA put pressure on decision-makers from its external position and sought to access the ministries at the *Länder* level to gain influence and promote its positions on education (Interview GER 02). Hence, the BDA made use of the German POS in education to participate in the decision-making process.

German state actors supported the introduced secondary education reforms with great *loyalty*. Both the federal government and the *Länder* widely accepted that after PISA, reforms were necessary, also the direction of reforms was set: evidence-based policy-making with increased output orientation. This is now common sense (Interview GER 03) and the *Länder* bow to the quality assessments of the OECD (Interview GER 04).

However, while the *Länder* were puzzled about the implementation and further reform steps, the federal government was more concerned with informally influencing the general reform discourse in secondary education. The BMBF embraced the international comparison of domestic education performances, supported the output orientation (Interview GER 03), and underscored the importance of PISA for improving the German education system. Accordingly, the BMBF demanded an intensification of reforms, particularly focusing on the advancement of poor-performing pupils. Additionally, the BMBF, in cooperation with the KMK, issued a joint education report (biennially) to evaluate the reform effects and to influence the discussion for future aims and measures. The BMBF operated in consultation with the *Länder* and acted carefully not to intervene directly in the *Länder*'s responsibilities (Interview GER 03). Some reactions of *voice* came from the *Länder*, claiming that the reforms went too far, limiting their original governance capacity since too much is determined by empirical expertise rather than by political debate (Interview GER 04).

## Summary

Taking the extreme changes in the German secondary education system into consideration, the reactions to the reforms were not that severe. The relevant corporate actors tended to be loyal to secondary education reforms; the urgency for reforms was pervasive. The *loyalty* of almost all actors indicates that the reforms were seen as appropriate to counteract the perceived weaknesses in the German secondary education system. In turn, the *voice* against the reforms might have been interpreted as advocating for the *status quo ante*, which was proven to produce negative educational outcomes, and none of the actors wanted to be blamed for blocking the (necessary) reform process. However, some criticism was *voiced* by unions (for example, GEW) due to the increased focus on the economic interpretation of education and the deficiency in the support for teachers and schools to implement the changes. On the other hand, some actors (BDA and BMBF) pushed for further intensified reforms. From the rational actors' perspective, the obvious need for reforms, as well as the explicit *loyalty* from the BMBF and research, increased the costs of *voice* enormously, even though others (for example, GEW) disagreed with the economic view on education.

German POS and the availability of resources of the actors can explain the reactions. Germany can be considered a weak state in secondary education policy due to its decentralized structure and its consensual political system. Hence, corporate actors can easily access the decision-making process and participate politically, and it was not surprising that reactions were put forward in cooperative committees, using active lobbying and information dissemination. Thereby, actors with sufficient resources campaigned strongly for their interests and beliefs using their own information initiatives and media activity. It was important for most actors with low legislative power (particularly for the BMBF, GEW, and BDA) to be able to frame the public discourse according to their own respective perspectives.

## Consequences of higher education reforms in Germany

German higher education was substantially reformed through the Bologna Process and further internationalization processes. After a boom of reforms during the 1960s and 1970s, German higher education policy was largely characterized by a period of stagnation (Teichler 2005: 32–3). Against this background, the recent enthusiasm for reform was surprising. The traditional supremacy of the *Länder* in matters of education makes encompassing, unitary reforms also in higher education especially difficult. In addition, the traditional German *Humboldt* university model of unity in research and teaching was quite different to the Bologna Process model, which refers to the demand-driven, market-oriented nature of higher education.

### Changes in German higher education

First, the Bologna Process effectuated profound changes in higher education driven by the aim of establishing the European Higher Education Area (EHEA) and fostering mobility and comparability. Since the Bologna Process aimed to introduce a consecutive-study model[9] and Germany's traditional study programmes were one-tracked, comprehensive efforts have been undertaken to realize the objectives of the bachelor's and master's (BA/MA) study programmes. Furthermore, the diploma supplement and the European Credit Transfer and Accumulation System (ECTS) were introduced in the German higher-education system through the Bologna Process. Additionally, the Bologna Process also led to the establishment of an accreditation system of individual study programmes to ensure that defined standard requirements were met (Blossfeld et al. 2013).

Furthermore, German policy-makers responded to internationalization by reforming the higher-education institutions in terms of further decentralization, according more autonomy to universities, and minimizing the details of state governance. However, these changes in higher education cannot be linked to the Bologna Process alone. Additionally, the changes regarding (higher) education cooperation between the federal government and the *Länder* were rooted in the federalism reform of 2006, which addressed the decartelization of competences in order to create a more effective administration. In short, the German *Länder* gained full autonomy while the federal government lost its already limited governance competences in education (Scharpf 2007; Kamm and Köller 2010). As a by-product, universities became more autonomous from the *Länder* administrations by being granted more freedom for budgeting, planning, and study programmes.

Against this background, and closely related to the federalism reform, the aspect of competition and diversification between German universities was politically fostered. In this context, the competences of the federal government were relevant in matters of research funding. First and foremost, the German Excellence Initiative became synonymous for the diversification of the German higher education landscape. In 2005, the federal government announced its project to create elite universities by supporting select universities. After a successful application, the selected universities together would receive a total amount of 1.9 billion euros in funding over a four-year period. The initiative provided additional funding for the few universities that were successful in their application (Hartmann 2006). Overall, the Excellence Initiative created an awareness of the competitive system that German universities find themselves in; it also provoked some criticism, since the initiative is a substantial drift from the traditional German idea of the *de jure* equal status of universities (Münch 2009).

The perceived need to be internationally competitive, the provisions of the federalism reform, and the Excellence Initiative implied the release of German universities from detailed state control and granted them more autonomy by abolishing the state's competence to pass detailed legislation. In reference to New Public Management, the *Länder* increasingly govern through target agreements, financial means, and framework contracts (see Lanzendorf and Pasternack 2008: 52–5). However, the actual level of the universities' autonomy varies between the *Länder*. In NRW, universities were enabled to operate almost completely autonomously without being affected by the *Land*'s administration (Kamm and Köller 2010: 668). In a similar vein, Bavaria also expanded the autonomy of higher education institutions – but not to the extent of NRW. The influence of the Bavarian administration in higher education was basically limited to aspects of fundamental interests and financial elements; universities have to arrange target agreements with the state administration in order to receive public funding.

To conclude, the Bologna Process, along with other reforms, have had a great impact on the German higher education system. Perceived internationalization processes were seen as a strong impetus for the decentralization of higher education policy-making (Niemann et al. 2013). In this regard, the changes reflected a deeper recognition of the international aspects of higher education whereby the Bologna Process only indirectly caused these changes. Generally, the implementation of the Bologna Process and the federalism reform signalized a parallel trend that can be considered a phenomenon in the context of globalization

(Toens 2009: 254). Overall, the introduced reforms have had some important consequences for the relevant political actors since they were faced with new circumstances and shifted policy-making roles, functions, and institutions.

## Reactions of relevant actors in German higher education

The Bologna Process (plus other higher education reforms in the course of internationalization) evoked comprehensive reactions from the relevant German actors. Despite the diversity of actors – ranging from students and university administrations to economic representatives and state actors – the positions and patterns of reactions were surprisingly similar. The aim of the Bologna Process, to create the EHEA, was unanimously welcomed. In addition, fostering international mobility and making German higher education more competitive met the interests of almost all actors. However, the effects of the reforms and their actual implementation were subject to a critical discourse of mainly *voice* and *loyalty*. All the relevant actors acknowledged that reforms in higher education were necessary; the actual direction and range of reforms was disputed.

The reforms were seen as controversial by many student groups, since they perceived a negative alteration of their status. Overall, German student representative bodies are often included in decision-making procedures at the university level and in informal administrative committees; this varies from *Land* to *Land* and from university to university (KMK 2011). The central and largest umbrella organization for student groups in Germany is the National Union of Students in Germany (fzs)[10], which lobbies for students' interests by organizing public discussions, demonstrations, campaigns, and even protests.

Generally, student representatives did not criticize the underlying ideas of the reforms but partially *voiced* severe opposition to the implementation of the Bologna Process in Germany. They criticized the strict provisions for study programmes that reduced flexibility in study (self-) organization, the increased workload, and the restricted access to and selective admission procedures for the master's programmes. The fzs' essential demands were free admission to master's programmes, fewer compulsory study hours, and more flexibility for individual study management.[11] Moreover, the fzs heavily criticized the underlying reform ideas as being too centred on market mechanisms and employability. Additionally, the fzs blamed the new study structures for a decline in extracurricular activities – such as democratic participation, additional job qualifications, and social commitments.

In order to advocate their interests and beliefs, the fzs teamed up with like-minded organizations (like unions) and lobbied for its position. In advocating free access to master's programmes, the fzs also issued a joint declaration with a leftist and liberal student organization. The critique of the fzs was supplemented by their co-edited empirical study "Bologna with Student Eyes", which showed the insufficiencies of the German reform implementation from the students' perspective. Furthermore, when arguing and lobbying for a revision of the conducted reforms did not pay off, student organizations co-initiated large education protests in 2009. This "strike" was an encompassing, coordinated series of demonstrations across Germany and created a lot of publicity. Two main addressees of the students' *voice* reaction were present: the state and the institutions of higher education. The state authorities were requested to counteract the negative reform consequences by granting more flexibility and less detailed prescriptions. University administrations were called upon to allow for better accessibility to master's programmes and to introduce less strict study curricula.

Providers of education can be separated into two groups: representatives of universities' administration and representatives of universities' teaching and research staff (through unions and professors' associations). Although both groups varied regarding their reactions to the introduced higher education reforms, the fundamental ideas are evaluated as positive. Dissent between the groups of education providers takes place, once again, regarding implementation.

The German Rectors' Conference (HRK) reflects the organized opinions of the administrations of universities and also intends to represent all German universities as a whole (Interview GER 05). Hence, its amalgamated weight makes it an influential actor in higher-education politics. The HRK showed general *loyalty* to the introduced reforms by highlighting the strengthened status of German universities and the acquired potential of each institution to specialize and foster its individual profile. Although the HRK strongly supported the reform aims, it admitted that the conversion of old study programmes and degrees into the BA/MA-system was not always optimal because the curricula were sometimes overburdened (Interview GER 05). Furthermore, the HRK called for a shift from a teaching- to a student-centred learning approach, which was not fully established yet in most German universities (Interview GER 05). The HRK also advocated for more financial resources to be channelled for the implementation of the BA/MA structure, since decision-makers did not take the increased need for financial support into account when they agreed on the introduction of the tiered system (Interview GER 05).

In disseminating their positions on higher education, the HRK basically relied on two resources: first, it networked with other actors like student representatives, employer representatives, and state actors. Second, the HRK made use of its status as an expert organization to give advice on good implementation drawing from best-practice examples and its own empirical assessments.[12] Against this background, the HRK established a Bologna Center to provide assistance to universities in implementing the reforms, individually acting as a consultant. Taken together, the HRK's reaction can be characterized as active *loyalty* towards the higher education reforms.

Considering employees, the GEW also has a stake in higher education politics through the representation of a part of universities' staff (and students). The GEW is seen as an important social partner and, for instance, is member of the German Bologna Working Group,[13] which has consultative status and also takes part in the Bologna Follow-Up conferences.

The idea of the EHEA was loyally supported as well as the issue of study orientation towards profession which, in contrast to employability, was seen as a more holistic concept concentrating on the employees' interests and not on the employers' needs (Interview GER 08). Once again, the reform implementation and the prominent focal points were criticized and the GEW reacted with *voice* calling for a re-reform in German higher education. The position of the GEW was close to the students' demands: unrestricted access to master's programmes for all students, reduced workload (also for the teaching staff), and (partial) revision of the new study structure and curricula. The bureaucratic expenditures for accreditation were also seen as counterproductive. Additionally, the GEW called for a stronger recognition of the social dimension of the Bologna Process in Germany and, in order to represent the entire society, the union demanded a stronger incorporation of stakeholders (including unions) in the higher education decision-making process (Interview GER 08).

The GEW had no formal stake in the higher education decision-making process and its main resource was networking with other actors and the bundling of political claims (Interview GER 08). To foster its interests and beliefs, the GEW worked in higher education mostly through lobbying, conducting studies, and broadcasting information. Additionally, the GEW frequently cooperated with like-minded actors, in particular student representative organizations like the fzs. The participation of the GEW in the German Bologna Working Group was seen as a semiformal influence channel because the latter had just a consultative, nonbinding status. Hence, the GEW was rather sceptical if the results of the Working Group were recognized by relevant policy-makers (Interview GER 08). Ultimately, the GEW supported the "education strike" of students in 2009 and in this context organized several demonstrations.

Furthermore, the German Association of University Professors and Lecturers (DHV), with more than 25,000 members, plays a crucial role in German higher education by actively contributing to university and education politics. The DHV acts in the political, legal, and business interests of professors in opposition to the state and society. Hence, their *voice* is seen as important in supporting or blocking reform efforts.

Since the DHV strongly emphasizes the *Humboldtian* principle of unity in teaching and research and the autonomy of research in Germany is strongly linked to the role of full professors (who are heads of independent university departments) the DHV was highly doubtful of the reform implementations introduced by the Bologna Process. The DHV championed impartial academia in a liberal constitutional state and advocated the freedom and indivisibility of research and teaching. In this regard, the DHV supported the aims of the reform but criticized the failure of their implementation in Germany; central aspects of the reforms were just rudimentarily implemented. The DHV called for massive corrections: MA degrees as a standard certificate, MA quotas of 80 per cent, reintroduction of the well-respected label *Dipl.-Ing.*, and support programmes for more mobility. To foster its interests, the DHV lobbied and published position papers such as the "Blackbook Bologna" (Scholz and Stein 2009). However, the opportunities of German professors for *voice* was limited since they were employed as civil servants and, hence, not entitled to take collective actions. Overall, the DHV was the antipole to the state and its progressive higher education reform policy.

Like in secondary education, the formal competences of the BDA in higher education were absent. However, through its membership in the Bologna Follow-Up Group and its participation in Business Europe, the European institution for employer representation, the BDA is a consulting member of the Bologna Process and can lobby directly on the international level. Through its memberships, the BDA also affects future developments and influences domestic German policy-making by implementing the Bologna Process.

The BDA's reaction to the German higher education reforms was overall (active) *loyalty*. The employer organization appreciated the emphasis on better employability, shorter study duration through consecutive cycles, and international comparability (Interview GER 09). In sum, the reforms were interpreted as the appropriate step to prepare the German higher education system for the coming challenges. Also, the limited access to master's programmes was not seen as problematic as long as the access is awarded according to students' BA performances and not by quotas. Besides *loyalty*, the BDA also reacted with *voice* and criticized some reform aspects. First and foremost, the BDA did not criticize the Bologna Process but rather the universities (and professors) for insufficiently implementing the reforms and acting contradictory to the spirit of employability. Reforms should be focused more on the practical approach of job orientation in study programmes and student-centred learning (Interview GER 09). The already enhanced autonomy of universities should be expanded even more in order to stimulate competition. Part of the explanation for why the BDA showed *loyalty* was that the German higher education reforms reflected the basic positions and interests of employers, and the new constellation guaranteed more influence capabilities for the BDA, since the economic-centred shift also provided more argumentative leverage for employers.

To advocate its interests and beliefs, the BDA launched information and support initiatives to increase acceptance of the new German higher education policies in general and the bachelor's degree in particular. In this regard, the BDA issued the "bachelors welcome" campaign, organized several events assessing the feedback on the labour market, and propagated information. Furthermore, by providing consultation and best-practice examples, employers offered some assistance to universities in implementing the reforms.

Additionally, the reactions of state actors (*Länder* and federal government) have to be taken into account. In NRW, the Ministry of Innovation, Science, Research, and Technology defended the introduced higher education reforms as necessary steps for making German universities more competitive globally. This *loyalty* was accompanied by some scepticism regarding the side effects of the Bologna Process and other higher education reforms – namely some changes in higher education politics and a marginalization of the *Länder*. However, the Act on Freedom of Higher Education Institutions (of 2006), unique to NRW, granted universities much more freedom than any other German *Land*. In consequence, it became increasingly difficult for NRW's policy-makers to govern its universities (Interview GER 06). Moreover, the NRW state actors primarily criticized the universities for problems in implementing the reforms appropriately (Interview GER 06). In this regard, even the state authorities show some form of *voice* reaction towards universities. Bavaria was more cautious in implementing higher education reforms. Although the Bavarian State Ministry of Science, Research and the Arts was a proponent of the Bologna Process, it was more reluctant towards external initiatives, trends, and severe changes. First and foremost, Bavaria reformed its higher education system because everybody around it was doing it (Interview GER 07). Overall, the higher education reforms were seen as a success. Like in NRW, the Bavarian State Ministry identified problems in the Bologna reforms as a result of insufficient implementation efforts at the university level – some professors were criticized for blocking the reform process (Interview GER 07). In Bavaria a close consultation between the *Land*'s administration and stakeholders from the economic, scientific, and other communities took place. However, due to past experiences, unions were not widely considered (Interview GER 07). Furthermore, the Bavarian ministry used the media as an important resource in fostering its interests and promoting its policy positions.

The strategies of both *Länder* in advocating their interests and beliefs were quite similar. Besides their legislative competences, which was by far the most powerful policy tool, both *Länder* were active in campaigning for the reforms by initiating their own assessments and publicizing informational reports.

Although the *Länder* are exclusively responsible for education policy in Germany, the federal government comes into play in the context of the arrangement of international cooperation. The federal government strongly supported the efforts made through the Bologna Process in Germany. Through all the different changes in the governance constellations, the opinions of the Bologna Process were relatively coherent. This means that across all major parties there was broad consensus that the reforms were necessary and it was worthwhile to progressively follow the chosen path. The BMBF introduced various means to strengthen acceptance for the higher education reforms but, under the pressure of student protests, it was willing to agree on the revision of some parts of the reform. It was critically *voiced* that due to too detailed regulations, some positive effects were prevented (Interview GER 10). The BMBF provided some extra funding for higher education (*Hochschulpakt 2020*) and research on reforms (*AG Hochschulforschung*), organized symposia, headed national and international roundtables with stakeholders, and so on. In sum, the BMBF played a strong coordination role in the aftermath of the higher education reforms and mainly through its discursive weight the BMBF unfolds its capabilities to influence.

## Summary

All relevant German actors welcomed the general intentions of the reforms; like in Switzerland (see Bieber in this volume) *loyalty* to the aims was consensual. Nevertheless, the actual implementation of the reforms was critically viewed. Almost all actors *voiced* resistance to various reform aspects. Students and unions both criticized the restricted access to master's programmes, the increased (perceived) workload, and insufficient participation of stakeholders in the reform process. Representatives of employers (BDA) and university administrations (HRK) were generally more loyal to the implemented reforms; they supported the changes and pushed for further acceptance. Furthermore, the new direction in German higher education also fostered the influence of both actor groups: the economic view is identical to the desires of the BDA and the increased autonomy of universities means more power for the HRK, since universities can act on their own. Hence, the interests and beliefs of the BDA and HRK were reflected in the reforms. Both groups of actors *voiced* minor criticisms and argued for selected revisions but insisted that the cornerstones of the reforms should be preserved. The German state authorities showed almost the same reactions. The federal government and the *Länder* strongly defended the reforms in terms of *loyalty* but also blamed the universities for insufficient implementation.

The actors' reactions can be analysed by considering the German POS in combination with the distribution of actors' resources. The weak German state in higher education opened the window of opportunity for actors' *voice*. The premise holds true that many access points also provided a great possibility to participate in the decision-making process in "normal" ways. Actors joined consultation roundtables and engaged in lobbying. Only when some actors felt that they were not heard and no consensus was reached did they choose to publicly reclaim their interests and beliefs through demonstrations and protests. In sum, the consensus-oriented policy-making process in German higher education enabled all relevant actors to negotiate their interests and beliefs in official forums.

In addition, the effects of available resources of German higher education actors can be summarized as follows: actors with strong financial resources (state and employers' representatives) actively lobbied for their policy positions through publishing information, campaigning, and working with like-minded organized networks. Actors with limited resources and who were also less organized (students and unions) relied particularly on strategies of coalition building in order to have a stronger political *voice*. Nevertheless, there were massive student protests. Contrary to the common view that protest results from blocked opportunity structures, in this case protest is rational because most German universities have institutionalized the incorporation of student representatives in their decision-making processes. In addition, the mobilization of students on campuses is low cost. Political decision-makers – either at the local, federal, or national level – who support the BA/MA structure are highly interested in optimizing implementation and are thus rather responsive towards *voice*. Especially under these circumstances, it is rational to *voice* against defects in the implementation process in order to emphasize that the vast majority of students were affected by these defects.

## Conclusion

After eventful years of many reforms in German education policy, a normalization of education policy-making becomes apparent. Although the reforms were severe and changed almost all major aspects of the German education system, the reactions of relevant actors were not that severe. Basically, this means that reactions took place in the usual well-known political arenas and were not extreme in terms of mass *exit* or intense *voice*. In contrast to France (see Dobbins in this volume) the isolated events of the "education strike" in 2009 show that *voice* reactions outside the decision-making negotiation system (extra-parliamentary) were unusual. However, this outburst also indicated that some interests and beliefs of those affected by education reforms were not sufficiently incorporated into the education reform processes. To summarize, the overall reaction patterns in Germany have some important implications. While the implementation of the Bologna reforms in higher education were highly debated across the different relevant groups of actors, the PISA reforms were not seen as that controversial; like in Switzerland (see Bieber in this volume), the need for secondary education reforms was accepted as common sense. What seems to be characteristic of the reactions in the new German constellation of education policy is that the underlying new paradigm of market-oriented education policy is addressed as problematic, undesired, and controversial while the consequences of this new paradigm – output orientation, evidence-based policy-making, and so on – were widely accepted as appropriate to advance the German secondary and higher education system. On the larger scale, it can be concluded that the new constellation did not enforce critical rifts across relevant actors in the policy-making process.

Against the theoretical background in education policy, Germany is a weak state and, hence, offers many access points for actors to participate in the policy-making process. Accordingly, the POS assumptions hold true. Since many political access points are available, German actors primarily try to influence the education reforms via usual arenas and through day-to-day politics. As theoretically assumed, open protests occur very seldom. It was rational for actors to make use of the well-institutionalized decision-making structures and access points to the political process since this approach minimized transaction costs. Accordingly, the available resources to actors were important for the mobilization and dissemination of their beliefs and interests within the decision-making process. The simple formula is: the more resources available, the more individual actors can do to foster their interests and beliefs. Actors use their resources to support their position by arguing. In this regard, they usually try to put forward claims backed by evidence and legitimacy. Hence, influencing the public discourse is pivotal for almost all actors. If actors do not have many resource capacities available, they tend to pool their scarce resources with like-minded organizations and increase their clout.

## Notes

1 Both *Länder* are suitable for further analysis because they feature almost equal (population) size and similar distribution of rural and metropolitan areas. However, they differ substantially with regards to their political tradition – NRW being social democratic, Bavaria being conservative – and recent economic strength – NRW is weaker than Bavaria.

2 After the federalism reform in 2006, the federal government retained some competence in regards to admission regulations and degrees in higher education, vocational training, research funding, and international comparative education studies.

3 Until the federalism reform, German education politics was an example of "joint decision-making" (Scharpf 1985).

4 Education standards were successively expanded (http://www.iqb.hu-berlin .de/bista/subject, retrieved 11 September 2013).

5 Other relevant teachers unions are organized through the German Association of Civil Servants (DBB), http://www.dbb.de/fileadmin/pdfs/themen/ Bildungspolitik_2007.pdf, retrieved 11 September 2013.

6 See, for example: http://www.gew.de/Binaries/Binary82535/2011_12_02_ Zehn%20Jahre%20PISA-Trauma%20%20Demmer-Text.pdf, retrieved 11 September 2013.

7 http://www.arbeitgeber.de/www/arbeitgeber.nsf/id/EN_Missions_of_BDA, retrieved 11 September 2013.

8 http://www.schulewirtschaft.de/www/schulewirtschaft.nsf/id/EN_Home? open, retrieved 11 September 2013.

9 The model comprised of two main cycles (undergraduate/graduate). A third cycle, doctoral programs, was added in 2005.

10  Although the fzs is perceived to represent rather leftist student groups (Hepp 2011: 74), it is accepted as the representative for student interests and, hence, participates in many roundtables, working groups, and so on.
11  http://www.fzs.de/themen/studienreform/index_2009.html, retrieved 16 September 2013.
12  http://www.hrk-nexus.de/projekt-nexus/, retrieved 16 September 2013.
13  The Joint Federal Government-*Länder* Working Group on the "Continuation of the Bologna Process" (http://www.bmbf.de/en/7007.php, retrieved 16 September 2013).

## References

Allmendinger, Jutta and Stephan Leibfried (2003) "Education and the Welfare State: The Four Worlds of Competence Production", *Journal of European Social Policy*, 13(1), 63–81.
Baumert, Jürgen, Kai S. Cortina and Achim Leschinsky (2003) "Grundlegende Entwicklungen und Strukturprobleme im allgemein bildenden Schulwesen. Strukturen und Entwicklungen im Überblick", in Kai S. Cortina, Jürgen Baumert, Achim Leschinsky, Karl Ulrich Mayer and Luitgard Trommer, eds., *Das Bildungswesen in der Bundesrepublik Deutschland. Strukturen und Entwicklungen im Überblick*, Reinbek: Rowohlt, 52–147.
Blossfeld, Hans-Peter, Wilfried Bos, Hans-Dieter Daniel, Bettina Hannover, Dieter Lenzen, Manfred Prenzel, Hans-Günther Roßbach, Rudolf Tippelt and Ludger Wößmann (2013) *Qualitätssicherung an Hochschulen: von der Akkreditierung zur Auditierung*, Münster: Vereinigung der Bayerischen Wirtschaft e.V.
Deutsches PISA-Konsortium (2001) *PISA 2000. Basiskompetenzen von Schülerinnen und Schülern im internationalen Vergleich*, Opladen: Leske + Budrich.
Dowding, Keith and Peter John (2008) "The Three Exit, Three Voice and Loyalty Framework: a Test with Survey Data on Local Services", *Political Studies*, 56(2), 288–311.
Ertl, Hubert (2006) "Educational Standards and the Changing Discourse on Education: The Reception and Consequences of the PISA Study in Germany", *Oxford Review of Education*, 32(5), 619–34.
Grek, Sotiria (2009) "Governing by Numbers: the PISA 'Effect' in Europe", *Journal of Education Policy*, 24(1), 23–37.
Hartmann, Michael (2006) "Die Exzellenzinitiative – ein Paradigmenwechsel in der deutschen Hochschulpolitik", *Leviathan*, 34(4), 447–65.
Hepp, Gerd F. (2011) *Bildungspolitik in Deutschland. Eine Einführung*, Wiesbaden: VS.
Kamm, Ruth and Michaela Köller (2010) "Hochschulsteuerung im deutschen Bildungsföderalismus", *Swiss Political Science Review*, 16(4), 649–86.
Katzenstein, Peter (1987) *Policy and Politics in West Germany. The Growth of a Semi-sovereign State*, Philadelphia: Temple University Press.
Klieme, Eckhard, Cordula Artelt, Johannes Hartig, Nina Jude, Olaf Köller, Manfred Prenzel, Wolfgang Schneider and Petra Stanat (2010) *PISA 2009. Bilanz nach einem Jahrzehnt*, Münster: Waxmann.
Klieme, Eckhard, Hermann Avenarius, Werner Blum, Peter Döbrich, Hans Gruber, Manfred Prenzel, Kristina Reiss, Kurt Riquarts, Jürgen Rost, Heinz-Elmar Tenorth and Helmut J. Vollmer (2003) *Zur Entwicklung nationaler Bildungsstandards. Eine Expertise*, Bonn: BMBF.

KMK (2011) *The Education System in the Federal Republic of Germany 2010/2011*, Bonn: KMK.

Kriesi, Hanspeter (2004) "Political Context and Opportunity", in David A. Snow, Sarah A. Soule and Hanspeter Kriesi, eds., *The Blackwell Companion to Social Movements*, Oxford: Blackwell, 67–90.

Lanzendorf, Ute and Peer Pasternack (2008) "Landeshochschulpolitiken", in Achim Hildebrandt and Frieder Wolf, eds., *Die Politik der Bundesländer. Staatstätigkeit im Vergleich*, Wiesbaden: VS, 43–66.

Martens, Kerstin and Dennis Niemann (2013) "When Do Numbers Count? The Differential Impact of Ratings and Rankings on National Education Policy in Germany and the US", *German Politics*, 22(3), 314–32.

Münch, Richard (2009) *Globale Eliten, lokale Autoritäten. Bildung und Wissenschaft unter dem Regime von PISA, McKinsey & Co.*, Frankfurt: Suhrkamp.

Niemann, Dennis (2010) "Turn of the Tide – New Horizons in German Education Policymaking through IO Influence", in Kerstin Martens, Alexander-Kenneth Nagel, Michael Windzio and Ansgar Weymann, eds., *Transformation of Education Policy*, Basingstoke: Palgrave Macmillan, 77–104.

Niemann, Dennis, Tonia Bieber and Kerstin Martens (2013) "Contre toutes attentes – L'influence européenne sur les politiques d'enseignement supérieur en Allemagne et en Suisse", *Revue Éducation Comparée*, 8, 65–99.

Prenzel, Manfred (2007) "PISA 2006: Die wichtigsten Ergebnisse im Überblick", in Manfred Prenzel, Cordula Artelt, Jürgen Baumert, Werner Blum, Marcus Hammann, Eckhard Klieme and Reinhard Pekrun, eds., *PISA 2006. Die Ergebnisse der dritten internationalen Vergleichsstudie*, Münster: Waxmann, 13–30.

Prenzel, Manfred, Cordula Artelt, Jürgen Baumert, Werner Blum, Marcus Hammann, Eckhardt Klieme and Reinhard Pekrun eds. (2007) *Pisa 2006. Die Ergebnisse der dritten internationalen Vergleichsstudie*, Münster: Waxmann.

Prenzel, Manfred, Jürgen Baumert, Werner Blum, Rainer Lehmann, Detlev Leutner, Michael Neubrand, Reinhard Pekrun, Jürgen Rost and Ulrich Schiefele eds. (2005) *PISA 2003. Der zweite Vergleich der Länder in Deutschland – Was wissen und können Jugendliche?*, Münster: Waxmann.

Prenzel, Manfred, Christiane Sälzer, Eckhard Klieme, Olaf Köller eds. (2013) *PISA 2012. Fortschritte und Herausforderungen in Deutschland*, Münster: Waxmann.

Rürup, Matthias (2007) *Innovationswege im deutschen Bildungssystem. Die Verbreitung der Idee "Schulautonomie" im Ländervergleich*, Wiesbaden: VS.

Scharpf, Fritz W. (1985) "Die Politikverflechtungs-Falle: Europäische Integration und deutscher Föderalismus im Vergleich", *Politische Vierteljahresschrift*, 26(4), 323–56.

Scharpf, Fritz W. (2007) "Nicht genutzte Chancen der Föderalismusreform", in Christoph Egle and Reimut Zohlnhöfer, eds., *Ende des rot-grünen Projektes. Eine Bilanz der Regierung Schröder 2002–2005*, Wiesbaden: VS, 197–214.

Scholz, Christian and Volker Stein eds. (2009) *Bologna-Schwarzbuch*, Bonn: Deutscher Hochschulverband.

Teichler, Ulrich (2005) *Hochschulstrukturen im Umbruch. Eine Bilanz der Reformdynamik seit vier Jahrzehnten*, Frankfurt: Campus.

Tillmann, Klaus-Jürgen, Kathrin Dedering, Daniel Kneuper, Christian Kuhlmann and Isa Nessel (2008) *PISA als bildungspolitisches Ereignis. Fallstudien in vier Bundesländern*, Wiesbaden: VS.

Toens, Katrin (2009) "The Bologna Process in German Educational Federalism. State Strategies, Policy Fragmentation and Interest Mediation", *German Politics*, 18(2), 246–64.

Wolf, Frieder (2008) "Die Schulpolitik – Kernbestand der Kulturhoheit", in Achim Hildebrandt and Frieder Wolf, eds., *Die Politik der Bundesländer. Staatstätigkeit im Vergleich*, Wiesbaden: VS, 21–41.

Zürn, Michael (2005) "Globalizing Interests – an Introduction", in Gregor Walter and Michael Zürn, eds., *Globalizing Interests. Pressure Groups and Denationalization*, Albany: State University of New York Press, 1–37.

# 5
# French Education Politics after PISA and Bologna – *Rupture* or *Continuité*?

*Michael Dobbins*

## Introduction

Around the world, education policy-making has changed significantly over the past ten years. France is no exception in this regard. Its education system has recently embraced new strategies to promote access and equality, while also redefining the relationship between the state and education providers. In the academic literature, there is a consensus that internationalization has substantially contributed to the new modes of governance in higher education, in addition to a major overhaul of existing study structures (Musselin and Paradeise 2009; Dobbins 2012; Dobbins and Martens 2012). France's lacklustre results in the Programme for International Student Assessment (PISA) increased the already strong problem pressure and provided additional ammunition for reform efforts by the Sarkozy government. References to PISA top performers have justified new education policies which link the goals of the French left (for example, the promotion of equality) and conservatives (for example, pedagogical autonomy) (Robert 2008; Baudelot and Establet 2009; Dobbins and Martens 2012).

Instead of focusing on policy output, I analyse how new education policies have impacted the *political process* in French education. In doing so, I look at three main aspects: actors' subjective perceptions of reforms, reactions of affected actors to policy changes, and emerging political opportunity structures. How have actors reacted to the changing role of the state? Do they perceive themselves at a disadvantage, or are the new policy frameworks widely accepted? Have policy actors embarked on new strategies of action and forged new alliances?

As hinted at already, France stands out as a crucial case due to various peculiarities. Firstly, the country still has a highly centralized public education system. This has led to a strong attachment to state-centred policies, putting the institutional legacies of French education at odds with current trends towards marketization, institutional autonomy, and decentralization. Secondly, the deeply entrenched principle of education equality (*égalité*) has frequently translated into a strong aversion to institutional competition and differentiation. Historically, the central government has been regarded as the guarantor of social equality and justice, which results in a reflexive resistance to policies perceived as neo-liberal or excessively market-oriented. Thirdly, the French public sector stands out with its tradition of strikes and political activism. The reform capacity of the state is frequently diminished by the rapid mobilization of reform adversaries. Thus, education reform in France has previously proven to be a daunting minefield, often resulting in ideological clashes, mass protests, and at times even violence.

This chapter provides a preliminary stocktaking of the effects of internationalization on French education politics. The *new forms of state provision and regulation of secondary and tertiary education* are treated as the independent variable, while the *newly emerging arena of education politics and the reactions of the affected actors* are the dependent variable. These reactions will be assessed on the basis of Hirschman's typology, which classifies actors' reactions according to the concepts of *voice, exit,* and *loyalty* (Hirschman 1970) (see Introduction by Knodel et al. in this volume; see Gurr 1970; Walker and Smith 2002).

## Secondary education in France

French secondary education finds itself in a phase marked by both institutional continuity and adaptation. On the one hand, the state-centred system has been undergoing reforms for several decades, as reflected in various efforts at decentralization (for example, *lois de décentralisation*; Loi n° 82–213, 1982; Loi n° 83–8 1983), eliminating inequalities and promoting inclusion (for example, with *zones d'éducation prioritaires*; see Meuret 1994; Moisan and Simon 1997), and the expansion of the Ministry's monitoring authority. On the other hand, the fundamental pillars of the system have remained in place (Cole 2001), most notably strong centralization, institutional and pedagogical uniformity, and high public expenditure. Yet, it is precisely these aspects that have recently come under fire. The pressures on French secondary education culminated with the PISA Study, which shed light on three major weaknesses: financial inefficiencies, high educational inequality, and pedagogical weaknesses. Essentially, France spends more on education than the average in the Organisation for Economic Co-operation and Development (OECD), but performs worse in international comparisons (OECD 2007; OECD 2001; Grenet 2008; OECD 2002: 392; Meuret 2003).[1] Along these lines, France continues to maintain a very large teaching corps despite continuously decreasing numbers of pupils (Institut Thomas More 2012). In addition, the strong impact of social background on performance shows that the French system does not live up to its main guiding principle of educational equality (Meuret and Morlaix 2006; Duru-Bellat et al. 2004). Finally, the results point to weaknesses in the pedagogical approach, which is characterized by a lack of individualized teaching and learning methods (see Rémond 2006: 79; Grenet 2008; Baudelot and Establet 2009: 26–7). Consequently, French policy-makers have directed increased attention to the "PISA winners", above all Finland and Canada (Thélot 2005; Robert 2008; Jacob 2008; Bruneel 2008), which demonstrate more effective strategies for reducing the disparity between the best and worst performing pupils[2] and guaranteeing teachers a high level of pedagogical autonomy (Baudelot and Establet 2009: 38–44).

Recently, moderate policy changes aimed at remedying these deficits have occurred. Despite numerous failed reform attempts and political setbacks (see below), the government passed a reform package known as *Lycée pour tous* (upper secondary school for all) in 2009. Similarly to the purported Finnish recipe for success (Robert 2008), the reform provides for personalized special lessons, support for youth with learning difficulties, the expansion of integrated class lessons (*enseignements communs*), and additional lessons during vacation if requested (MEN 2010b; 2010c).[3] Also in line with the Finnish approach, the reforms institutionalized a new teacher training procedure, requiring them to acquire a master's degree from an *Institut de Formation de Maîtres*. This policy, known as *masterisation*, accounts for fewer, but better trained and paid teachers. Altogether, there has been a shift away from extreme centralization and uniformity towards more "tailor-made", pedagogically flexible education. Simultaneously, individual schools have gained slightly more autonomy, while the state has maintained its traditionally strong role in performance evaluation with the DEPP (*Direction de l'évaluation, de la prospective et de la performance*).

## Political opportunity structures and relevant actors in secondary education in France

French secondary education is frequently described as centralistic and dirigistic (Corbett 1996). Contrary to decentralized systems, for example, the USA or Germany, education content is centrally defined by the National Ministry of Education (*Ministère de l'Éducation Nationale* – MEN). Moreover, the school system is almost exclusively publicly financed and all primary and secondary school teachers are employed by the central government, making the Ministry of Education the country's largest employer (MEN 2010a). However, these institutional arrangements do not necessarily result in unfettered state autonomy and vertical control. Teachers unions are strongly incorporated into decision-making processes; therefore, the policy-making mode can be best described as "statist-corporatist". For much of the post-war era, education policy-making was strongly influenced by the *Fédération de l'éducation nationale* (FEN), a conglomeration of over 50 factions representing different (primarily leftist) ideological tendencies and employees of different segments of the education system (primary schools, *lycées*, *collèges*, higher education) (Mouriaux 1996). The main union operating outside the federation structure was the initially left-leaning *Syndicat Général de l'Éducation Nationale* (SGEN), which since the 1980s has primarily viewed itself as a force for reform and pedagogical innovation (Geay 2005). Due to internal strife, the FEN was dismantled during the 1990s, giving rise to the *Union nationale des syndicats autonomes* (UNSA) and *Fédération Syndicale Unitaire* (FSU), whose major secondary school faction is known as *Syndicat National de l'Enseignement Secondaire* (SNES). At the same time, *Solidaires, Unitaires, Démocratiques* (SUD Education) was formed in the 1990s as a conglomeration of adamantly leftist teachers and students who oppose educational deregulation, privatization, and liberalization.

Despite the organizational reshuffling in the 1990s, teacher unionization in France remains high, and the previous policy-making logic from the FEN era continues to apply (Geay 2005; Moriaux 1996). The strong presence of public teachers unions is also accompanied by the active interest in education by the French labour unions (for example, *Confédération française démocratique du travail* – CFDT, *Force Ouvrière*), which engage in fluctuating alliances with education-specific unions.

Due to their strong integration into governmental decision-making, the above-mentioned interest groups find themselves in a state of conflictual collaboration, both with the Ministry as well as among themselves. Teachers unions have extensive delegated powers and dominate ministerial committees that decide on personnel matters (for example, staff transfers, promotions, and so on) (Cole 2001: 714). Thus, they not only engage in the co-management of education policy (Fowler 1992: 29), but are also subsidized by the Ministry, who seeks their support for policy implementation. As each group strives for privileged access to the state apparatus, fierce competition exists between the education unions. The competitive nature of policy-making is compounded by the ideological cleavages within the federated unions, as centre, left-, and far-left forces compete for control of the overarching federations.

These constellations have numerous implications for the opportunity structures of teachers associations and other stakeholders. There are many incentives for teachers to uphold the present centralized system. Not only are they directly involved in policy-making and have secured numerous privileges (for example, tenure, seniority-based promotions, health care, and so on) (Fowler 1992), but they are also shielded from school headmasters and local authorities. Moreover, teachers unions often strategically legitimize their strong influence over policy-making by referring to the historical guiding principle of education as a protected national sphere, in which the central state – via co-management with teachers unions – is the guardian of the public interest and buffer against local (religious and economic) interests. Thus, it can be viewed as rational for French academics to strike against greater local institutional autonomy, for such measures would likely undermine their privileged status and proximity to the decision-making apparatus. Along these lines, van Zanten (2002: 294) speaks of an alliance between the "educational state" and "republic of teachers", often to the exclusion of other actors. For example, parents have only played a very small role in the French education system when compared to other countries such as the United States and the United Kingdom. The largest parent organization (*Fédération des Conseils de Parents d'Élèves* – FCPE) was essentially created by the *Syndicat National des Instituteurs* (SNI), a teachers union, in 1951 in an effort to bolster its own position by allying with parents. Thus, the FCPE has been strongly linked to teacher unionism. The main actors generally hold key functions within both the FCPE and SNI, which – as noted above – is incorporated into the federation structure (Gombert 2008). The main venue for integrating pupils and parents into policy-making, the *Haut Conseil de l'éducation* (High Council of Education), is also characterized by the strong presence of teachers unions and, importantly, the exclusion of employer representatives. Moreover, the main secondary-education student union, the *Union Nationale Lycéenne*, was only established in 1994 and generally operates outside the policy-making apparatus by organizing strikes. In this context, the government frequently accuses teachers' organizations of encouraging pupils to engage in strikes to undermine its autonomy (Darcos 2009).

The frequency and intensity of education strikes can also be traced back to institutionalized patterns of conflictual cooperation between the state and teachers. Union factions reflexively oppose policies that threaten their professional interests and ideological convictions, that is, education as a protected national space. They are in a position to resist policy proposals that might benefit rival inner-union and inter-union interest groups. Thus, unions often pursue a seemingly counterintuitive rational strategy: they frequently raise objections to government plans that they ideologically support, because they compete with each other for members and resources (Baumgartner and Walker 1989). Along these lines, strikes frequently serve to increase their presence and visibility *vis-à-vis* other unions. Due to large ideological divisions, French teachers unions also strike when reform proposals do not go far enough. This applies, in particular, to the reformist SGEN (Interview FR 03). If it refused to participate in a strike involving leftist unions, the leftist forces would likely be able to pull the reform outcome in their desired direction.

Furthermore, the strikes are often driven by social desirability. Observers have referred to the organizational precision, breadth, and impact of strikes as important reputational criteria for union leaders within the inner-union competition (Frajerman 2008). Strikes often serve to reinforce inter-union ties (Frajermann 2008: 544–5) and increase their collective bargaining position later. This makes it difficult for the government to strategically exploit divisions between rival unions (Cole and John 2001). Subsequently, there are stronger incentives for key educational actors to *voice* opposition to governmental reforms rather than to demonstrate *loyalty*. These underlying opportunity structures place strong limits on the state's autonomy and capacity for policy change.

### Reactions of relevant actors in secondary education

At the beginning of the 2000s, the education ministry and its Evaluation Department (DEPP) initially attempted to conceal the poor PISA results from the public. Faced with high youth unemployment and a burgeoning discourse on the crisis of education, the Ministry initially triggered a debate on "ideal" education policy and governance (*gouvernance idéale*), which did not result in concrete reforms. However, the continual deterioration of the PISA results and an increasing focus on the economic utility of education quickly resulted in new education policy activism, which has largely been characterized by "trial and error" and the paradoxical reactions of affected actors. As presumed above, coordinated strikes have posed a major challenge to the government's capacity for reform. Proposed in 2004 with specific reference to the PISA results (Mons and Pons 2009; Pons 2011), the so-called Fillon reform[4] intended to reduce the number of drop-outs, increase the number of *baccalauréat* (bac) graduates from low-income families, enhance teacher training, and promote greater participation in scientific and technical tracks (*filières*). However, a central component of the reform – the decentralization of the *baccalauréat* procedure – was retracted after enduring student and teacher strikes. The reform prescribed that part of the final result be based on performance during the last three years of school, and not only the examination results. This drew heavy resistance from student representatives who expressed fears that teachers would not be able to objectively judge students' performance without reference to their social background. At the same time, the planned decentralization of the procedure was regarded by teachers unions and student groups as an "attack against the public service" and a "slippery slope" towards the "denationalization" of education (SUD Education 2006; Bronner 2004: 7). Hence, the seemingly benevolent reforms (that is, enhanced teacher training, local school autonomy, and support for weak performers) were framed as an attack against the principle of equality and undermining the social contract.

Amid the deterioration of the French PISA results between 2001 and 2006, the new education minister, Xavier Darcos, soon proposed a new package of secondary education reforms "with a Finnish touch" (Jacob 2008). The reforms aimed to empower schools to pursue their own strategies and pedagogical approaches, while granting them more financial autonomy. In addition, the *carte scolaire*, which geographically assigns pupils to schools, was to be liberalized to promote school choice. The reforms also promoted the principle of social diversity (*mixité sociale*), which is increasingly regarded as a recipe for success in view of the Canadian and Finnish PISA results (Bruneel 2008; Sarkozy 2007; Duru-Bellat and Marin 2010), and allocated additional teaching staff to "problem" schools. According to the slogan *lycée à la carte*, the reforms allowed for more elective subjects and special measures for slow learners, while economics was to become an obligatory subject.[5] However, the rational-tactical actions of teachers unions again helped bury the reform package. Here, students and teachers engaged in intense strikes over the feared "denationalization" of the *baccalauréat* procedure and the looming elimination of 13,500 teaching positions as part of overarching public sector reforms (Pech and Sérès 2008; Chayet and Court 2005). Further-more, the teachers argued that the planned additional special lessons would be too large of a burden and contradict the ideal of equal educational opportunities (that is equal attention to all pupils) (Cody 2009). The linkage of job losses with a greater commitment on behalf of the teaching corps pitted students and teachers against the state, leading to intense rotating strikes. Here students argued that the state was attempting to introduce a *"baccalauréat light"* and hence undermine the equivalence of national degrees.

### A new orientation in French education politics?

However, a third reform surge under the label *lycée pour tous* ("upper secondary education for all") has moderately altered the political process. Firstly, intense resistance to the first two proposals forced the state to retune its strategy and engage in stronger public consultation efforts with students, teachers, and parents regarding the future of education (Pech 2009). Thus, the political process has become somewhat more multilateral and dialogue-oriented. Secondly, two major weaknesses revealed by PISA – a lack of pedagogical autonomy and persistent inequality – and efforts to remedy them have actually eased tensions between leftist and centrist-reformist unions. Specifically, the increasing sense of urgency created new possibilities for issue-linkages between right-wing and left-wing political forces, the former of which aims above all to boost performance, accountability, and pedagogical autonomy, while the latter aims to reduce social inequalities. In particular, the leftist UNSA has recently drawn on the PISA results while pressing for greater education equality and increased support for weak-performers (UNSA 2010), while the reformist SGEN has pushed to design classes in a more flexible and individual manner (Interview FR 03).

However, the resulting *lycée pour tous* law (2009)[6] has triggered seemingly paradoxical reactions among the core education stakeholders. The main pupil association, the *Union Nationale Lycéenne* (UNL), has shown a relatively positive tenor towards the law, but has officially rejected it in an internal vote. The organization argues that the reforms will not sufficiently reduce inequalities and are not linked with adequate further investments in education. Thus, in line with the French tradition, the UNL argues that the state must undertake more to decrease educational inequalities.

UNSA and SNES-FSU have more forcefully *voiced* opposition, claiming that the Ministry is forcing teaching staff to "do more with less", thus impoverishing the education sector while simultaneously demanding improved performance (UNSA 2011a; 2010; Radio France Internationale 2010). Both organizations have also fiercely resisted the decentralization of teacher recruitment procedures (UNSA 2011b). Despite their support for some reform components (equality-promoting measures and pedagogical diversity), teachers and labour unions have reacted with anger and discontent to recent education reforms on the whole. In this regard, internationalization has arguably reduced the room of the state to manoeuvre *vis-à-vis* the education policy community. The reason for this lies in the very weaknesses of the French secondary education system that was brought to light by international comparisons: structural inefficiencies, educational inequality, and pedagogical shortcomings. High educational expenditures and decreasing teacher-to-pupil ratios, combined with a crippling budget deficit, left the previous centre-right government no other viable option than to downsize teaching staff. The dissatisfaction with these measures among powerful teachers unions has thus significantly hindered the government's efforts to reach the PISA-inspired objectives of greater pedagogical flexibility and reducing the equality gap, as such measures require a greater commitment on behalf of precisely those actors potentially affected by job losses. Despite the strong argumentative "ammunition" for governmental reform coalitions, the *window of opportunity* for the state to effectuate policy change has actually narrowed due to this linkage of objectives, that is public-sector downsizing and increased pedagogical flexibility (Interview FR 03).

This reality sheds light on a cause-and-effect problem in this analysis: it is difficult to disentangle the reactions to reforms inspired by internationalization from broader public-sector reforms. In other words, the new pedagogical approaches "*à la finlandaise*" were reflexively rejected because of overarching public sector reforms. What is noticeable, however, is the decreasing intensity of the negative reactions between the original Fillon proposals and the ultimately passed *lycée pour tous* law (Sérès 2008). This can be explained by the fact that the government gradually eliminated all reform components that would have structurally altered the *politics of education* and undermined the opportunity structures for powerful teachers unions. Specifically, all initial efforts to decentralize education (for example, decentralization of the *baccalauréat* procedure, abolition of the *carte scolaire*, greater financial autonomy) or which could be interpreted as potentially "denationalizing" education were consistently dropped after intense strikes. Thus, the government was forced to accommodate the concerns of those pursuing the *voice* tactic. As a result, the final reform package is entirely restricted to pedagogical aspects that do not infringe upon the relationship between the "education state" and the "republic of teachers". Hence, the PISA-inspired reforms are essentially limited to pedagogical diversity, despite the elimination of some teaching posts. In other words, the fluctuating alliances of teachers unions, labour unions, and students succeeded in preserving the existing opportunity structures in which teachers unions are tightly interlocked with the ministerial apparatus and purportedly act in the public interest.

## Summary

Referring back to our classification of stakeholder reactions – *voice*, *exit*, and *loyalty* – French secondary education presents a special case. Due to the specific nature of French education politics, *voice* is very frequently an automatic and rational reaction to policy change – even among reform "loyalists". This has to do, on the one hand, with the internal tensions and competition among and within teachers unions, which often result in strikes, and on the other hand, the simultaneity of education reform and public-sector downsizing that pitted teachers against the government, making *loyalty* an unlikely prospect, even though numerous teachers unions (for example, SGEN) supported the various reform components (Interview FR 03). At the same time, *exit* also remains an unlikely option, as there is no significantly large private-school sector for affected stakeholders to flee to.

Finally, the historical context must not be overlooked. Historically, French schools have been regarded as neutral venues, isolated from their socio-economic environment, in order to ensure justice, equal opportunity, and national cohesion (Cole 2001: 709–10). This in turn has led to a different understanding of educational autonomy, according to which the central government – and the powerful teachers unions that interlock with the state bureaucracy – is supposed to uphold the principles of secularism, equality, and republicanism. This explains the resistance to any reform that can be remotely interpreted as a step towards privatization, decentralization, and marketization. Firstly, such measures would contradict the historical references of French educators and purportedly undermine educational neutrality and equality. Secondly, they would arguably weaken the bargaining power of the powerful teaching corps. Therefore, teachers unions repeatedly used the tactic of *voice* by means of strikes to prevent significant policy change (regardless of some pedagogical and content-related matters) and preserve the existing character of education *politics*.

## Higher education in France

Internationalization, Europeanization, and concerns over global competitiveness have also provided a significant additional impetus to higher education reforms. In a state of gradual change since the mid-1980s (Dobbins 2012; Musselin 2001; Kaiser 2007), French higher education has recently been transformed on four main fronts: diploma structures, university management, quality assurance, and the role of research in universities. While engaging more closely with European counterparts, the Ministry aimed to simplify the – at least for outsiders – highly confusing diploma structures.[7] With certain exceptions, this resulted in a three-cycle structure ("LMD" = *licence, master, doctorat*), which was to be implemented as part of contractual agreements with the Ministry (Kaiser 2007; Witte 2006).

Much more contentious, however, are the recent governance-related reforms. The poor performance of French universities in international rankings, in particular the widely acknowledged Shanghai ranking, triggered a shock. Thus, the main reform catalyst was not so much the Bologna Process, but rather the problem pressure stimulated by the performance in international rankings. The below-average international standing of French universities (Dalsheimer and Déspreaux 2008: 2), combined with a reform discourse focusing on global competitiveness (Aghion and Cohen 2004), have resulted in numerous changes.

Previously incorporated into the MEN, the Ministry of Higher Education and Research (*Ministère de l'enseignement supérieur*, MESR) was re-established in 2007, and the newly appointed Minister Valérie Pécresse was explicitly called on by President Sarkozy to increase the performance of French universities in international comparisons. The reform activism led to a series of still highly contentious changes to the governance system. Three existing evaluation bodies[8] were merged into the *Agence de l'évaluation de la recherche et de l'enseignement supérieur* (AERES), which evaluates universities and research performance with bibliometric data (that is journal-impact factors). The *Agence Nationale de la Recherche* (ANR), which was established in 2004,[9] also expanded its operations. The agency manages public funds for research projects, which are to be funded on a selective basis, while also promoting public–private research partnerships. To increase the international visibility of French higher education, the MESR has also supported so-called *pôles de recherche et d'enseignement supérieur* (PRES), which are local groups of universities, *grandes écoles*, and research institutes that bundle research and teaching activities.

The 2007 law regarding the liberties and responsibilities of universities (*Loi relative aux libertés et responsabilités des universités;* also LRU and *Loi Pécresse*) constitutes the most significant turning point. The law aims to instil entrepreneurialism in university governance by enhancing decision-making autonomy. For example, universities now manage their own global budgets, and the size of the administrative council (*conseil d'administration*) has been reduced from 60 to 20–30 members, including economic and regional stakeholders and students (LRU 2007: Article 7). Importantly, the powers of university presidents have been strengthened and various academic, personnel, and administrative decision-making matters have been transferred to university management, much like in Anglo-American systems (Dobbins and Knill 2009). Particularly striking is the concentration of power in the hands of university presidents, who are now not only responsible for the implementation of the four-year contracts (*contrats quadrienniaux*) and the monitoring of finances, but they are also authorized to employ staff on a temporary or unlimited basis and are in charge of pay performance bonuses (LRU 2007: Article 19).

Breaking with the previous bureaucratic traditions, the state is also taking a more performance-oriented and selective approach and has become increasingly involved in the evaluation of research output. Nevertheless, France has not entirely refuted the principle of *égalité*, as funding remains state-centred without tuition fees, and underfunded universities receive additional state support.

## Political opportunity structures in French higher education

Historically, French higher education policy-making has been characterized by the parallelism of central steering and structural fragmentation. Like in secondary education, strong centralization was reflected by the previous uniformity of degrees and study content (Kaiser 2007) as well as the uniform legal framework. Structural fragmentation, by contrast, was reflected by the absence of multidisciplinary universities for over one century. Research activities were concentrated in the *grands établissements*, while the compartmentalized *facultés* were overshadowed by the financially privileged *grandes écoles*.

In view of the institutional weakness of universities (Musselin 2001), the Ministry has been the main policy-making venue and decided on matters such as staff recruitment, programme content, and budget (Kaiser 2007). However, like in secondary education, the academic community has traditionally played a significant role in governance through strong interlinkages with the Ministry (Musselin and Paradeise 2009: 22–3).

However, French higher education policy-making is less corporatist and less dominated by public unions than secondary education. This is due to the institutional fragmentation into universities, *grandes écoles,* and research centres as well as the fact that the MEN (since 2007 MESR) is not responsible for various institutional types, for example, *grandes écoles* and *grands établissements.*[10]

Besides the MESR, it is useful to pinpoint the other crucial actors in the French higher education system. The university-based academic profession, known in French as *universitaires,* consists of teaching-researchers (*enseignants-chercheurs*) and teaching-only academic staff, the latter of which are frequently transferred from secondary schools to universities. Thanks to their incorporation into the public sector, the *universitaires* enjoy high individual autonomy and employment security; up to 80 per cent of university academic staff are tenured public servants (Chevaillier 2001). A further notable feature of French higher education is the traditional separation of teaching and research. In addition to the teaching-oriented university sector, France maintains a large system of publically funded research centres which are organized by special research agencies, most notably the *Centre national de la recherche scientifique* (CNRS) with approximately 26,000 employees holding public-service status (*chercheurs*). Although institutionally distinct from universities, the research agencies are increasingly integrated into universities in the form of jointly operated "mixed research units" (*unités mixtes*). This leads to frequent multiple institutional affiliations of researchers, who are usually employed by national research agencies like the CNRS, even though they work in university laboratories or institutes (Chevaillier 2001).

Altogether, higher education governance can be regarded as more multilateral than secondary education and marked by increasing institutional self-determination and individuality. The new "polycentric" opportunity structures (Aust and Crespy 2009) can initially be traced back to the expansion of the *contractualisation* procedure, which provided for four-year negotiated contracts with development plans. Previously, universities and faculties were widely buffered off from their local socio-economic environment, while so-called *recteurs* acted as the state's on-site hand in higher education governance (Kaiser 2007). The *contractualisation* strategy, however, resulted in a more active role of university presidents in setting priorities, while the new governmental programme *Université du troisième millénaire* encouraged stronger synergies with regional and local stakeholders (Quinio 1998).

## The student union landscape

French student unions generally operate at the national level with local factions at individual universities. Like public teachers unions, the student union landscape is characterized by its leftist inclinations and attachment to the notion of educational equality. The largest union – the *Union nationale des étudiants de France* (UNEF) – sees itself as a labour union representing future workers in training (Interview FR 02). Thus, it generally advocates the preservation of a state-centred higher education system, which is supposed to guarantee a level playing field. The second-largest union, *Fédération des associations générales étudiantes* (FAGE) is less political and primarily concerned with increasing student representation on the *Conseil national de l'enseignement supérieur et de la recherché* (CNESER), a consultative body within the Ministry.[11] By contrast, the *Union nationale inter-universitaire* (renamed *Mouvement des Étudiants* in 2010) is more closely affiliated with the Gaullist *Union pour un mouvement populaire* (UMP) and views itself as a centre-right counter-force to the strike-friendly leftist unions.

Another notable feature of the union landscape is the proximity of higher education and secondary education unions due to the strong presence of higher education staff – which often hold the same public-servant status as secondary education teaching staff – within the FSU (formerly FEN) and UNSA. This frequently results in contagion effects, as secondary education strikes often spill over into higher education strikes, which are then joined by student unions.

## Reactions of relevant actors in French higher education

As hinted at above, the Bologna reform of study structures was not a highly contentious issue in French education politics, as most university academics and students were either receptive or ambivalent towards the reform. Most stakeholders welcomed the simplification that allowed for easier recognition of French higher education degrees as well as the new potential for study programme innovations (Malan 2004; Interview FR 04). However, as was the case with the attempted *baccalauréat* reforms in secondary education, students expressed concerns over the loss of national validity of diplomas as institutions gained autonomy to create their own study diplomas (Malan 2004; Witte 2006). A further concern was the feared decline in status of vocational diplomas (for example, *bac + 2*; *Brevets de technicien supérieur* – BTS and *Diplômes universitaires de Technologie* – DUT) and intermediary diplomas (*maîtrise, bac + 4*). In addition to perpetual worries over the aggravation of inequalities and budgetary austerity, students feared excessive competition due to increasing university diversification (Interview FR 02). In fact, a new union – SUD Education – was formed in parallel to the Bologna Process as a conglomeration of strike-friendly and adamantly leftist students and teachers who oppose any form of educational deregulation, privatization, and liberalization.

However, the scattered protests and strikes were mitigated by the gradual implementation of the reforms through contract-based agreements (*contractualisation*) between higher education institutions and the Ministry (MESR). Moreover, the Ministry provided assurance that the national character of diplomas would be protected by a ministerial accreditation and evaluation procedure.[12] Thus, the main lines of action of the Bologna Process only had a limited impact on French higher education policies, aside from the emergence of the far-left SUD.

Instead, the main by-products of Bologna and internationalization processes – the changes to the system of governance – not only provoked fierce reactions by major stakeholders, but have also transformed the higher education policy playing field and political process. With explicit reference to the Bologna Process and European standards, the French government first attempted to transform university governance with the so-called *loi de modernisation universitaire* (university modernization law; 2003; also *Loi Ferry*), which promoted autonomy in teaching and university administration (for example, through global budgets) (Witte 2006: 295–6). However, the proposal reignited the French student movement, which had been relatively tame since the mid-1980s. The drive to increase university autonomy was met with bitter resistance by the UNEF, SUD Education, and the *Fédération Syndicale Étudiante*, another far-left student union which emerged during the early 2000s. Here the unions argued that the modernization law was a neo-liberal plot that would lead to unfettered university competition and undermine the principle of equality. However, the movement died down due to a scission within the UNEF; the reformist faction abandoned the union to create the *Confédération étudiante* (CE), which was favourable to the LMD reform and subsequent governance reforms, but still maintained close ties with the Socialist Party and the CFDT (Institut Supérieur du Travail 2006).

### The academic uprising

Irrespective of the failed passage of the university modernization law, a series of other modifications stirred up resentments among the French research community, leading to strikes and protests which later intensified amid the 2007 LRU reform. The new *Agence Nationale de la Recherche* (ANR) (see above) was viewed by large segments of the research community as being based on a short-term and production-oriented vision of research and hence undermining the public servant status of French researchers. Fearing detrimental effects on the quality of their work and their academic autonomy, a group of researchers gave rise to the *Sauvons la recherche* (Save Research) movement, which called for a substantial boost in the research budget and fixed employment status for young researchers. The movement staged nationwide strikes and occupied the offices of AERES and ANR while at the same time initiating a Europe-wide campaign against research performance evaluation and, in particular, the introduction of bibliometric data (Interview FR 03; Sauvons la Recherche 2009a; 2009b; 2010)

Initially, the 2007 LRU law also sparked negative reactions among students. In addition to *Sauvons la Recherche*, two new organizations emerged – the *Collectif contre l'autonomie des universités* and *Sauvons l'université* – which organized countrywide protests. The participants expressed fears that the law would lead to large quality-related disparities in higher education and thus a "slippery slope" towards the privatization of universities (Le Monde 2008).

## A transforming student advocacy landscape

It is safe to say that the array of new education legislation led to the largest academic uprising since 1968. However, it is important to distinguish that the broader protest movement (*mouvement universitaire*) was not so much driven by student activism but rather by the research community. On the passing of the LRU law, researchers feared being subject to a new form of "academic feudalism" due to the simultaneous reintegration of research into universities and the massive expansion of authority for university presidents. For example, university presidents were granted extensive powers over personnel affairs, which were perceived by many researching lecturers (*enseignants-chercheurs*) as undermining the democratic nature of university decision-making.

However, the responses to the LRU law were much more differentiated than during past reform efforts, and actually are likely to have facilitated its passing. As anticipated, the leftist SUD Education was the most visible opponent to the LRU governance reform, labelling it a degradation of an already unacceptable status quo (Interview FR 02). The organization – along with the "collective against university autonomy" – feared the penetration of enterprises and their "short-term" objectives into the university system and, like the research community, saw the civil servant status of academic personnel endangered. Moreover, leftist union forces viewed the *pôles de recherche* as a means of "giving more to the rich", as "good universities" would benefit from partnerships with already privileged *grandes écoles*, while weaker-performing institutions would be abandoned by the state (Interview FR 02).

Crucial, however, was the reaction by the two largest student unions, FAGE and UNEF, who pursued a different political rationale than in the past. FAGE refused entirely to become involved in the strike movement and instead opted for a consultative strategy through the CNESER. Like SUD Education, UNEF feared the emergence of a two-tier system and chronic underfunding, despite agreeing with numerous aspects of the reform (for example, university autonomy, performance controls). However, the leftist factions suffered a major setback when the UNEF withdrew from the protests once the state abandoned its plans for restrictive access to master's programmes.[13]

Importantly, the "leftist clout" of the student unions was counterbalanced by the increasing presence of centre and centre-right student organizations. This pertains in particular to the organization *Promotion et défense des étudiants* (PDE), which has deliberately broken with a major tradition in French education politics – the high politicization of decision-making, which in turn can be traced back to its centrist character (Archer 1979; Duclaud-Williams 1985). Instead PDE pursues a nonpolitical logic and seeks to influence governmental policy in advance, instead of resorting to ex post strikes (Interview FR 02). Altogether, the organization has favoured reform and progress over the status quo and has attempted to promote student interests by collaborating directly with the Ministry. Contrary to the leftist forces, PDE explicitly favours closer ties between universities and enterprises, which are seen as injecting valuable input into universities, as well as a further differentiation of the higher education landscape due to regional socio-economic specificities (Interview FR 03).

A similar logic applies to the *Union Nationale Universitaire* (UNI), which aligns itself with the centre-right UMP and advocates competition- and performance-oriented higher education in line with European standards. This organization sought to mobilize students against participating in strikes against the LRU law. More recently, in fact, it actually abandoned its student union status and renamed itself the *Mouvement des Étudiants* (MET). In doing so, it has embraced a new political tactic like that of PDE, which – as described above – seeks to collaborate more closely with the Ministry during the policy formulation process. Thus, it sees itself as a countermovement to the "hostage-taking" leftist forces

(MET 2010), which have relied on coordinated nationwide strikes to bring down government proposals. Various leftist groups, in turn, have accused MET of being created and financed by former Minister Pécresse with the specific purpose of rallying support for its policies (Interviews FR 02; FR 03).

Another noteworthy development, which is indeed indicative of the central government's efforts to reshape the organizational landscape, is the creation of the *Conférence des chefs d'établissements de l'enseignement supérieur* by the Ministry, not by the academics themselves. Consisting of several previous organizations representing different university types, the body has been constructed to collectively represent the interests of university managers *vis-à-vis* the Ministry.[14] The organization is not only symbolic of the state-enforced cooperation between universities and other higher education providers, but also reflects the rational-tactical attempts of the Ministry to increase the clout of its likely political allies, that is, actors whose autonomy has been strengthened by the reforms.

### Reactions of university management and business

Altogether, the recent higher education reforms have given rise to a new system of polycentric governance with numerous new channels of access for multiple stakeholders (Aust and Crespy 2009). Not surprisingly, the reactions of those actors whose influence has been strengthened are overwhelmingly positive. This pertains, above all, to most university presidents. After years of perceived sclerosis (*immobilisme*), the LRU law has reportedly added new dynamics to university governance, in particular regarding programme design, and allowed institutions to more effectively manage the flow of funds (Ouabdesselam 2011). According to one university president, the LRU reform has been viewed by most university managers as a "rejuvenating cure", which has enabled French universities to catch up with world-class foreign institutions (Boudou 2011). In fact, numerous university presidents have expressed their astonishment that student unions have remained relatively subdued during the implementation of the reforms.

However, it is also emphasized that numerous universities have yet to fully benefit from the newly endowed autonomy. For the first time, there have been cases of bankruptcy among French universities, while others have been embroiled in false diploma scandals (Interview FR 03). Moreover, observers have cited difficulties in managing autonomy and building up research capacities. The most prominent critique by university managers, however, is that they have been endowed with new managerial tools to promote entrepreneurialism, but still lack sufficient government funds to do so (CPU 2009). The French business community generally views the higher education reforms positively. The gradual marketization of French higher education has resulted in new university management structures and institutional structures (for example, PRES), which offer various new platforms for partnerships. The main business association *Mouvement des entreprises de France* (MEDEF) quickly signed a pact with numerous universities which provides a new framework for partnerships between higher education, large enterprises, and other interested professionals. Moreover, the new autonomy of French higher education institutions to procure additional funding to fill gaps has made French university presidents more willing to engage with MEDEF, which in turn has provided enterprises improved access to public research (Fikri 2011).

### The academic community back in uproar

The relative calm during the implementation of the LRU was once again disrupted by the mobilization of the university research community (*enseignants-chercheurs*). The so-called "decree to modify the status of teaching researchers"[15] transferred further discretion to university presidents over individual research activities. Previously, the principle of equal time for teaching and research applied, along with uniform rules for academic promotions. However, the law significantly strengthens the authority of university management over research evaluation. It foresees a recurring evaluation of individual researchers on a quadrennial basis and effectively authorizes university presidents to punish poorly evaluated researchers with more teaching hours. This in turn was perceived by university researchers as an attack on their academic freedom and the principle of collegiality.

The initially restrained resistance of individual organizations (for example, *Sauvons la recherche*) spilled over into nationwide protests after a speech to leading French researchers by President Sarkozy in 2009.[16] The President directly criticized the poor performance of French higher education institutions and researchers in international rankings,[17] which was interpreted by the research community as an attack on their professional expertise. This, in turn, prompted not only numerous left-leaning student unions and academic associations, but also the university managers association (*Conférence des chefs d'établissements de l'enseignement supérieur*), to join the protest movement. The protests escalated to the extent that teaching activities were suspended at 28 universities for several months.

**Summary**

Returning to our theoretical framework, *voice* was clearly the most common reaction to the recent higher education reforms, albeit with different intensities and significant variations between stakeholders. The Bologna-inspired study structures were widely accepted, while reforms relating to governance and quality assurance were much more controversial. The varied reactions have had numerous consequences for the political arena. The organizational landscape has become increasingly diversified. Fearing the loss of their public employment status and academic freedom, large segments of the research community mobilized within new organizations, such as *Sauvons la Recherche* and the *Collectif contre l'autonomie des universités*. As for the student community, the initial emergence of leftist organizations, such as SUD Education and the *Fédération Syndicale Étudiante*, was balanced out by the increasing presence of centre- and right-leaning forces such as PDE and MET, who rejected the strike tactics and pursued more consultative strategies.

Altogether, it is safe to say that centre-right forces have more effectively mastered new opportunity structures, as the reforms have opened new channels of access for those who refrain from strikes and pursue a more corporatist approach and collaborate in advance with the state. This finding is in line with other studies that show that France is becoming more corporatist (Siaroff 1999; Schmidt 2003). However, it remains to be seen whether the new opportunity structures are contingent on party-related factors and if those groups who have expressed *loyalty* to the reforms will pursue the same strategies *vis-à-vis* the current socialist government. Along these lines, it is noteworthy that the new government has no current plans to reverse the LRU reform and new study structures, but instead has only proposed rather vague plans to "democratize" university governance and simplify research funding (Parti Socialiste 2012). This speaks for the relatively high acceptance of the reforms. Finally, despite more *exit* opportunities due to the internationalization of the higher education market, *exit* is generally not viewed as an option, even for the most vehement reform critics.[18] As one Bologna and LRU adversary put it: "Why would one want to leave France, only to find the Anglo-Saxon system elsewhere?" (Interview FR 01).

## Conclusion

The analysis has shed light on the different developments in secondary and higher education. Internationalization and efforts to boost the competitiveness of French higher education have generated a new playing field with more polycentric opportunity structures, combined with a new state governing approach. This has given rise to new strategies (for example, higher education–business collaborations) and forms of cooperation (for example, PRES). These include, in particular, the less conflict-oriented and more corporatist political approach of student representatives, but also the more assertive, reactionary approach of the research community. To this extent, one might be inclined to speak of a "Humboldtization" of French higher education policy.

The students' points of view were heterogeneous and represented in unions of different political affiliation. Given that they saw the main problems of the higher education system not in its funding, but rather in its perceived lacking quality, accountability, and market-orientation, most non-leftist groups supported the reform. This is in line with rational reasoning because the utility of standardized and internationally comparative degrees is high from their perspective. In contrast, the "academic uprising" was rational from the researchers' view because they perceived the reforms as detrimental to the quality of their work. Unlike in secondary education though, the *voice* tactic of the research community did not hinder significant policy change. This was due to the recent diversification of actors and the increasing presence of loyal actors. Thus, there was no united front to hinder reforms and prevent the transformation of the *politics of education*.

As for secondary education, a different logic of action applied. Powerful teachers unions exploited their privileged access to the policy-making apparatus to prevent significant policy change and, even more importantly, a transformation of secondary education *politics*. The *voice* was employed in concerted fashion by teachers unions to prevent any tactic measures which would have strengthened local school autonomy. For the teaching corps, it was not so much a matter of hindering policy change but rather hindering *changes in politics*, as decentralization would have radically altered the favourable opportunity structures and channels of access for the "republic of teachers". Thus, even loyal political forces joined the "*voice* front" to prevent the dismantling of public state-centred education. In view of the recent change in government in France, it will be interesting to see whether the present dominance of secondary education by teachers unions can further persist amid severe budgetary pressures, and whether the new higher education policy field has taken on a new irreversible dynamic despite the more market-sceptical new socialist government.

## Notes

1  For example, Pech (2012) points out that French teachers spend less time in class than their OECD counterparts, while French pupils attend more hours of class in total.

2  This performance disparity and France's alleged inability to cope with school underperformance and underprivileged students was then highlighted in the widely publicized study *Que vaut l'enseignement en France?* (What is education worth in France?) (Forestier et al. 2007).

3  Moreover, the reform provides for the possibility to select specialized courses (*filières*) later than previously and the introduction of transitional courses of instruction *(stages-passerelles)* during vacation for pupils wishing to switch specialized courses. Two 90-minute lesson units (*enseignements d'exploration*) are also being introduced in the first upper secondary grade to more effectively prepare students for graduation.

4  *Loi Fillon d'orientation scolaire.*

5  However, subjects such as history and geography were to become optional in the last school year, which was harshly criticized by intellectuals (France24 2009).

6  Specifically, the current reforms of the *lycée* provide two hours of personalized special lessons in small groups and individualized systematic support and development tracking for all pupils. In addition, integrated class lessons (*enseignements communs*) (MEN 2010b; 2010c) are to be expanded as well as voluntary additional lessons during vacation to support students wishing to avoid repeating a class. Moreover, students are now provided the possibility to select specialized courses (*filières*) later than previously.

7  See Kaiser (2007) for an overview of the previous and current diploma structures.

8  *Comité national d'évaluation – CNE, Comité national d'évaluation de la recherche – CNER, Mission scientifique, technique et pédagogique – MSTP.*

9  The agency was established with *Loi de Programme du 18 avril pour la recherche* of 2004.

10  Certain *grand établissements* are not under the authority of the Education Ministry.

11  This body consists of university lecturers and administrative personnel and must be incorporated into all-important higher-education–related decisions by the Ministry. It only has a consultative status, though (Chevaillier 2007).

12  The MESR also made it clear that the establishment of a European higher education area would not endanger existing diplomas.

13  Here once again, the UNEF argued in line with the *égalité* principle that admissions must be free and open to all *baccalauréat* holders.

14  It consists of members of two previous organizations, the *Conférence des présidents d'université* (CPU) and the *Conférence des directeurs des écoles françaises d'ingénieurs* (CEDEFI), and representatives of French education providers abroad.

15  *Décret modifiant le statut des enseignants-chercheurs.*

16  *Discours à l'occasion du lancement de la réflexion pour une stratégie nationale de recherche,* January 2009.

17 Particularly unacceptable, in his view, was the fact that French researchers publish between 30 and 50 per cent fewer articles than their British colleagues despite a comparatively high level of funding and that French universities allegedly do not create any jobs through technology transfer (Sarkozy 2009).

18 Altogether the expatriation rates of French researchers are lower than European counterparts, although there are currently some indications of a minor increase (Les Echos 2007). The government has also recently initiated targeted measures to attract French researchers abroad back to France (*retour postdoctorants*). Therefore, it is difficult to pinpoint the "exit" numbers and whether any increase or decrease is due to the most recent reforms.

## References

Aghion, Philippe and Élie Cohen (2004) *Education et Croissance*, Paris: La documentation française.

Archer, Margaret (1979) *Social Origins of Educational Systems*, London: Sage.

Aust, Jérôme and Cécile Crespy (2009) "Napoléon renversé? Institutionnalisation des Pôles de recherche et d'enseignement supérieur et réforme du système académique français", *Revue française de science politique*, 59(5), 915–38.

Baudelot, Christian and Roger Establet (2009) *L'Elitisme Républicain. L'école française à l'épreuve des comparaisons internationale*. Paris: Seuil.

Baumgartner, Frank R. and Jack L. Walker (1989) "Education Policymaking and Interest Group Structure in France and the United States", *Comparative Politics*, 21(3), 273–88.

Boudou, Alain (2011) Interview in *Capital*, Universités: Enfin une réforme qui marche, 29 September, http://www.capital.fr/carriere-management/dossiers/universites-enfin-une-reforme-qui-marche-630375/%28offset%29/1, retrieved 20 August 2013.

Bronner, Luc (2004) "Le SNES appelle seul à la grève dans le second dégrée", *Le Monde*, 7 December 2004.

Bruneel, Lise (2008) "Organisation et politique de l'enseignement finlandais", *L'école démocratique*, http://www.skolo.org/spip.php?article478&lang=fr, retrieved 30 August 2013.

Chayet, Delphine and Marielle Court (2005) "La démonstration de force des enseignants", *Le Figaro*, 21 January 2005.

Chevaillier, Thierry (2001) "French Academics: Between the professions and the civil service", *Higher Education* 41(1), 49–75.

Chevaillier, Thierry (2007) "The Changing Role of the State in French Higher Education", in Don Westerheijden and Stefanie Schwarz, eds., *Accreditation and Evaluation in the European Higher Education Area*, Dordrecht: Springer.

Cody, Edward (2009) "French teachers resist neo-liberal reform", *Washington Post Foreign Service*, 11 July 2009.

Cole, Alistair (2001) "The New Governance of French Education", *Public Administration*, 79(3), 707–24.

Cole, Alistair and Peter John (2001) "Governing Education in England and France", *Public Policy and Administration* 16(4), 106–25.

Corbett, Anne (1996) "Secular, free and compulsory: Republican values in French education", in Anne Corbett and Bob Moon, eds., *Education in France: continuity, change in the Mitterrand years 1981–1995*, London: Routledge, 3–21.

CPU (2009) Réforme des statuts et moyens afférents: la CPU réaffirme ses positions, http://www.fabula.org/actualites/reforme-des-statuts-et-moyens-afferents-la-cpu-reaffirme-ses-positions_28767.php, retrieved 20 August 2013.

Dalsheimer, Nadine and Denis Despréaux (2008) "Les classements internationaux des établissements d'enseignement supérieur", *Éducation et Formations* 78.

Darcos, Xavier (2009) Tout le monde souhaite la réforme du lycée, Interview in *Le Figaro*, 19 December, http://www.lefigaro.fr/le-talk/2008/12/19/01021-20081219ARTFIG00545-darcos-tout-le-monde-souhaite-la-reforme-du-lycee-.php, retrieved 14 November 2011.

Dobbins, Michael (2012) "How market-oriented is French higher education?", *French Politics*, 10(2), 134–59.

Dobbins, Michael and Kerstin Martens (2012) "Towards an education approach à *la finlandaise?* French education policy after PISA", *Journal of Education Policy*, 27(1), 23–43.

Dobbins, Michael and Christoph Knill (2009) "Higher Education Policies in Central and Eastern Europe: Convergence towards a Common Model?", *Governance*, 22(3), 397–430.

Duclaud-Williams, Roger (1985) "Local Politics in Centralized Systems: the case of French education", *European Journal of Political Research*, 13(2), 167–86.

Duru-Bellat, Marie, Nathalie Mons and Bruno Suchaut (2004) "Inégalités sociales entre élèves et organisation des systèmes éducatifs: quelques enseignements de l'enquête PISA", *Les Notes de L'IREDU*, 04/02.

Duru-Bellat, Marie and Brigitte Marin (2010) "La mixité scolaire, une thématique (encore) d'actualité?", *Revue française de pédagogie*, 171, 5–8.

Fikri, Mehdi (2011) Le Medef s'invite dans les facs, in Humanité, 6 January, http://www.humanite.fr/06_01_2011-le-medef-s%E2%80%99invite-dans-les-facs-461483, retrieved 20 August 2013.

Forestier, Christian, Claude Thélot and Jean-Claude Ernin (2007) *Que vaut l'enseignement en France?*, Paris: Stock.

Fowler, Frances C. (1992) "Teacher Unionism as Mission and Battle: Success and Crisis in French Teacher Unions", *American Educational Research Association*, San Francisco, California.

Frajerman, Laurent (2008) "Le syndicalisme enseignant français et la grève: normes et normalisation d'une pratique (1948–1959)", *Paedagogica Historica*, 44(5), 543–54.

France24 (2009) "French intellectuals slam new controversial education bill", http://www.france24.com/en/20091206-french-intellectuals-slam-controversial-new-education-bill, retrieved 20 August 2013.

Geay, Bertrand (2005) *Le syndicalisme enseignant*, Paris: Editions La Découverte.

Gombert, Philippe (2008) "Les associations de parents d'élèves en France: approche socio-historique et mutations idéologiques", *Revue française de pédagogie – Recherches en éducation* 162, January–March 2008, 59–66.

Grenet, Julien (2008) *PISA – Une enquête bancale? La Vie des Idées*, http://www.laviedesidees.fr/PISA-une-enquete-bancale.html, retrieved 20 August 2013.

Gurr, Ted R. (1970) *Why Men Rebel*, New Jersey: Princeton University Press.

Hirschman, Albert O. (1970) *Exit, Voice, and Loyalty. Responses to Decline in Firms, Organizations, and States*, Cambridge: Cambridge University Press.

Institut supérieur du travail (2006) Les organisations étudiantes et lycéennes en France, http://istravail.com/article292.html, retrieved 20 August 2013.

Institut Thomas More (2012) Éducation Analyse comparée de la dépense publique en France et en Allemagne. Note de Benchmarking No. 8., http://www.institut-thomas-more.org/upload/media/notebenchmarckingitm-8.pdf, retrieved 20 August 2013.

Jacob, Antoine (2008) Le lycée finlandais, un modèle qui inspire Xavier Darcos, *LeFigaro,* http://www.lefigaro.fr/actualites/2008/02/06/01001-20080206ARTFIG00304-le-lycee-finlandais-un-modele-qui-inspire-xavier-darcos-.php, retrieved 20 August 2013.

Kaiser, Frans (2007) "Higher Education in France: Country Report", *International Higher Education Monitor,* Twente: CHEPS.

Le Monde (2008) La loi sur l'autonomie des universités mise en œuvre progressivement, 25 July, http://www.sauvonsluniversite.com/spip.php?article597, retrieved 20 August 2013.

Les Echos (2007) La France épargnée par la fuite des cerveaux, 29 October, http://www.lesechos.fr/29/10/2007/LesEchos/20035-64-ECH_la-france-epargnee-par-la-fuite-des-cerveaux.htm, retrieved 2 December 2013.

Loi n° 82-213 du 2 mars 1982 relative aux droits et libertés des communes, des départements et des régions, http://www.legifrance.gouv.fr/affichTexte.do?cidTexte=LEGITEXT000006068736&dateTexte=20090318, retrieved 20 August 2013.

Loi n° 83-8 du 7 janvier 1983 relative à la répartition de compétences entre les communes, les départements, les régions et l'Etat, http://legifrance.gouv.fr/affichTexte.do?cidTexte=JORFTEXT000000320197, retrieved 20 August 2013.

Malan, Thierry (2004) "Implementing the Bologna Process in France", *European Journal of Education,* 39(3), 289–97.

MEN (2010a) *La maîtrise des dépenses publiques à Éducation Nationale,* http://www.education.gouv.fr/cid52031/la-maitrise-des-depenses-publiques-a-l-education-nationale.html, retrieved 20 August 2013.

MEN (2010b) *Réforme du lycée: publication des premiers textes réglementaires au journal officiel du 28 janvier 2010,* http://www.education.gouv.fr/cid50434/reforme-du-lycee-publication-de-textes-reglementaires.html, retrieved 3 September 2013.

MEN (2010c) *Vers une nouveau lycée en 2010,* http://www.education.gouv.fr/cid49667/vers-un-nouveau-lycee-en-2010.html, retrieved 20 August 2013.

MET (2010) L'UNI et le MET disent «stop à la grève», http://www.mouvementde-setudiants.fr/spip.php?article196, retrieved 20 August 2013.

Meuret, Denis (1994) "L'efficacité de la politique des zones d'éducation prioritaires dans les collèges", *Revue française de pédagogie,* 109, 41–64.

Meuret, Denis (2003) "Pourquoi des jeunes Français ont-ils à 15 ans des compétences inférieures à celles de jeunes d'autres pays?", *Revue Française de Pédagogie,* 142, 89–104.

Meuret, Denis and Sophie Morlaix (2006) "L'influence de l'origine sociale sur les performances scolaires: par oú passe-t-elle?", *Revue française de sociologie,* 47(1), 49–79.

Moisan, Catherine and Jacky Simon (1997) *Les déterminants de la réussite scolaire en zone d'éducation prioritaire,* Paris: Ministére de l'éducation nationale.

Mons, Nathalie and Xavier Pons (2009) "La réception de PISA en France", *Knowledge and Policy in Education and Health Sectors Working Paper 12.*

Mouriaux, René (1996) *Le syndicalisme enseignant en France,* Paris: PUF.

Musselin, Christine (2001) *La longue marche des universités françaises,* Paris: PUF.

Musselin, Christine and Catherine Paradeise (2009) "France: From Incremental Transitions to Institutional Change", in Catherine Paradeise, Emanuela Reale, Ivar Bleiklie and Ewan Ferlie, eds., *University Governance: Western European Perspectives*, Dordrecht: Springer.

OECD (2001) *Knowledge and Skills for Life. First Results from the OECD Programme for International Student Assessment (PISA) 2000*, Paris: OECD.

OECD (2002) *Bildung auf einen Blick – OECD-Indikatoren*, Paris: OECD.

OECD (2007) *PISA 2006. Science competencies for tomorrow's world, Volume 1*, Paris: OECD.

Ouabdessalm, Farid (2011) Interview in *Capital*, Universités: Enfin une réforme qui marche, 29 September, http://www.capital.fr/carriere-management/dossiers/universites-enfin-une-reforme-qui-marche-630375/%28offset%29/1, retrieved 20 August 2013.

Parti Socialiste (2012) *Les 60 engagements de François Hollande – Engagement 39*, http://www.parti-socialiste.fr/articles/engagement-39, retrieved 20 August 2013.

Pech, Marie-Estelle (2009) Les réseaux de parents d'élèves se multiplient, *Le Figaro*, 19 October, http://www.lefigaro.fr/web/2009/10/17/01022-20091017ARTFIG00727-les-reseaux-de-parents-d-eleves-se-multiplient-.php, retrieved 3 September 2012.

Pech, Marie-Estelle (2012) Les profs français travaillent moins que les autres, *Le Figaro*, 29 February, http://elections.lefigaro.fr/presidentielle-2012/2012/02/29/01039-20120229ARTFIG00651-les-profs-francais-travaillent-moins-que-les-autres.php, retrieved 20 August 2013.

Pech, Marie-Estelle and Aude Sérès (2008) "La réforme Darcos renvoyée à des jours meilleurs", *Le Figaro*, 13 December.

Pons, Xavier (2011) *L'évaluation des politiques éducatives*, Paris: PUF.

Quinio, Paul (1998) "Pour financer le plan Université du troisième millénaire. Allègre compte sur les régions", *Libération*, 3 December, http://www.liberation.fr/societe/0101264216-pour-financer-le-plan-universite-du-troisieme-millenaire-allegre-compte-sur-les-regions, retrieved 20 August 2013.

Radio France Internationale (2010) Education nationale: une logique purement économique, Le Débat du Jour, http://www.rfi.fr/emission/20100906-education-nationale-une-logique-purement-economique, retrieved 20 August 2013.

Rémond, Martine (2006) "Eclairages des évaluations internationales PIRLS et PISA sur les élèves Français", *Revue française de pédagogie*, 157, 71–84.

Robert, Paul (2008) *La Finlande: un modèle éducatif pour la France – les secrets d'une réussite*, Paris: ESF.

Sarkozy, Nicolas (2007) *Lettre de mission de M. Nicolas Sarkozy, Président de la République, adressée à M. Xavier Darcos*, http://www.sauvonsluniversite.com/spip.php?article115, retrieved 21 August 2013.

Sarkozy, Nicolas (2009) Discours à l'occasion du lancement de la réflexion pour une stratégie nationale de recherche, 22 January, http://www.dailymotion.com/video/xc7xqr_reflexion-strategie-nationale-de-re_news, retrieved 20 August 2013.

Sauvons la Recherche (2009a) Dire publiquement nos vérités sur l'AERES, http://sauvonslarecherche.fr/spip.php?article2771, retrieved 20 August 2013.

Sauvons la Recherche (2009b) L'AERES occupée, http://sauvonslarecherche.fr/spip.php?article2660, retrieved 20 August 2013.

Sauvons la Recherche (2010) Happy Birthday Lisbologna!, http://sauvon slarecherche.fr/spip.php?article3107, retrieved 20 August 2013.

Schmidt, Vivien (2003) "French Capitalism: Transformed, Yet Still a Third Variety of Capitalism", *Economy and Society*, 32(4), 526–54.

Sérès, Aude (2008) "Enseignants: le front syndical se fissure", *Le Figaro*, May 28.

Siaroff, Alan (1999) "Corporatism in 24 Industrial Democracies", *European Journal of Political Research*, 36(2), 175–205.

Sud Education (2006) Contre la décentralisation la lutte continue, http://www. sudeducation.org/Contre-la-decentralisation-la.html, retrieved 20 August 2013.

Thélot, Claude (2005) L'évaluation dans le système éducatif. Conférence introductrice du 18ème colloque international de l'ADMEE,24-26 octobre 2005, Reims, http://www.pedagopsy.eu/claude_thelot.htm, retrieved 20 August 2013.

UNSA (2010) Communiqués: Les fausses assertions du président de la République, http://web.unsa-education.org/modules.php?name=News&file=pdf& sid=1794, retrieved 2 December 2013.

UNSA (2011a) Communiqués: Luc Chatel doit sortir du déni, http://web.unsa–education.org/modules.php?name=News&file=article&sid=1777, retrieved 2 December 2013.

UNSA (2011b) Communiqués: Recrutement des enseignants: l'éducation doit rester nationale!, http://web.unsa–education.org/modules.php?name=News&f ile=article&sid=1752, retrieved 2 December 2013.

van Zanten, Agnès (2002) "Educational Change and New Cleavages Between Head Teachers, Teachers and Parents", *Journal of Education Policy*, 17(3), 289–304.

Walker, Iain and Heather J. Smith (2002) "Fifty Years of Relative Deprivation Research", in Iain Walker and Heather J. Smith, eds., *Relative Deprivation. Specification, Development, and Integration*, Cambridge: Cambridge University Press, 1–12.

Witte, Johanna K. (2006) *Change of Degrees and Degrees of Change*, Enschede: CHEPS.

# 6
## On Silent Wings – PISA, Bologna, and the Debate about Internationalization in England

*Philipp Knodel*

### Introduction

As a result of international developments, such as intensified global competition, increased influence of international organizations, or the creation of a European Higher Education Area, reforms can be observed in many European countries. Unlike Germany (see chapter 4 by Niemann in this volume) or Switzerland (see chapter 8 by Bieber in this volume), England has not reorganized its education system. In both the field of secondary and higher education there were only a few changes following international and European developments. The Organisation for Economic Co-operation and Development's (OECD) Programme for International Student Assessment (PISA) Study has been noticed by policy-makers, but it has only played a minor role in the discourse about the future for schools in England (Knodel and Walkenhorst 2010; Grek 2009). In higher education there were some slight adjustments in the context of the Bologna Process and other European initiatives, but general interest has not been very high.

However, England is an interesting case to study the consequences of internationalization for domestic politics because it shows that non-national levels of policy-making have not been on the agenda of government and interest groups for quite a while. These reactions can be interpreted as a form of *exit*: even though actors are well informed and know what was going on outside the British Isles, they have intentionally remained silent for a long time. This chapter also shows, however, that the situation is about to change and relevant actors in the English education sector have started to engage in debates about PISA and Bologna. In the following section, I briefly introduce England's institutional setting. By discussing the major reforms in secondary and higher education, I outline the characteristics of the opportunity structures in the field of education. The second part takes a closer look at politically relevant actors and shows their strategies of dealing with the OECD's PISA Study in secondary education and the Bologna Process in higher education. Finally, I summarize the findings and discuss them in relation to the typology of *voice, exit, loyalty,* and our theoretical framework.

## Policy-making in England

British institutional structures are peculiar compared to other European states. For a long time the political structures and institutions were described by the Westminster model: a single-party government, one-party opposition, elections ruled by plurality, unitary state that dominates the administrative hierarchy, and ministers responsible to parliament (James 2009). In theory, this model is clearly structured and there is little space for disorder that may lead to suboptimal policies or gridlock because clear majorities in the House of Commons for the governing party guarantee stable conditions and political continuity. In addition, legitimacy of government decisions is high because there is no higher authority than the parliament and, in theory, all decisions could be controlled by the parliament. This institutional setting is complemented by a politically neutral civil service (Smith 1999: 10).

Generally, there is only one chamber that is worth being influenced by interest groups, namely the House of Commons. The importance of the second chamber, the House of Lords, has continuously decreased. Nevertheless, accessing the members of the British parliament is more difficult than in other countries, for example, the United States. Thus, attempts by groups to influence policies take place mainly outside the formal institutions. Interest groups "try to 'push' them in their preferred direction from outside of Whitehall and Westminster, not 'pull' them in it from inside" (Heffernan 2011: 192). Over the years this has created a system of governance in English education that can be characterized by deregulation, institutional autonomy, and decentralization.

However, the central state, that is, the government and education departments, do not have direct control over the direction of education policy. Both in secondary and higher education there is a relatively high level of control by the state. As Bache (2003) argues, for secondary education the fragmentation within the policy field has increased the government's capacity to enforce its objectives over the interests of other powerful institutions. In a similar vein, in higher education "it is the state, the interaction of its political and bureaucratic arms, which has the power" (Tapper 2007: 228). Given the multilevel governance structure in English education policy, representatives of education organizations, for example, interest groups or trade unions, have multiple channels to influence policies.

## Secondary education

This section examines the consequences of international initiatives in education. More specifically, I take a closer look at the reactions of politically relevant actors in England to the PISA Study and the Bologna Process. First, however, the most important policy changes in English secondary and higher education are described.

### Changes in education policy

Education policy changed substantially after the election in 1979. The rhetoric of Conservative politicians focused on the freedom of choice and the need to improve the quality of education by fostering competition. Earlier concepts of education were reinvented as a type of "Victorian laissez-faire individualism" (Ball 2008: 75). The Education Reform Act 1988 is a milestone in English education policy and has reorganized secondary education. A national curriculum was introduced, and the financial responsibility was transferred to the schools. In addition, a regime was introduced that evaluated school performance. The consequences of these reforms were fundamental: market mechanisms should dominate the provision of education. For example, parents were able to compare and select schools according to their performance, new types of schools were created, and the publication of the results increased the pressure on schools with poor evaluation scores. These reforms can also be characterized as a process of centralization since national standards were controlled by the state. At the same time, however, schools and parents have become more powerful at the expense of the local authorities. After the Education Reform Act 1988, English education policy has been remarkably stable. The overall direction has remained the same, even after the change of government in 1997 (Power and Whitty 1999). New Labour adopted the Conservatives' rhetoric and emphasized the need of education for economic growth and the modern knowledge society. This economic understanding of education has dominated political speeches and put it at the heart of debates about globalization and its consequences (Ball 2008: 14–18).

The reforms in the 1980s and the continuity in education policy has led to an education system that is remarkably close to the general ideas and policy recommendations of the OECD. Usually, the OECD does not formulate explicit guidelines since education policy is still in the hands of governments. However, by means of soft governance, the OECD has had substantial influence in the past (Martens et al. 2010; Breakspear 2012). Put more generally, the OECD's and the English idea of education is closely related to concepts of New Public Management (see Papado-poulos 1995; Henry et al. 2001). Even though there are many variants of this concept, it can be boiled down to a number of characteristics: controlling efficiency and performance of schools, organizing and coordinating education institutions on the basis of contracts, distinguishing between providers and recipients, competition, as well as decentralized funding and personal responsibility of individuals (Clarke et al. 2000: 6).

## Actors' reactions

The story of PISA and actors' reactions in England is special compared to other countries (Knodel et al. 2010; Knodel et al. 2013). In general, there have not been any policy changes in England as a consequence of PISA. The government followed a "pick-and-choose" strategy: trying to ignore bad results and taking good results as proof of good governance. Other actors in English education policy, such as teacher unions and other interest groups, have remained mostly silent regarding international initiatives. There are various reasons for these reactions: First, the English education system underwent a fundamental reform at the beginning of the 20th century, and in the 1980s there was no need for further reforms. Second, England already has a complex system to measure performance in education. In other countries, PISA was the first systematic assessment of pupils' performance, while this was already everyday business in English schools.

Figure 6.1 shows all newspaper articles that discuss the PISA Study. The selected newspapers are *The Guardian* and *The Times* since they can be considered as two of the most influential quality newspapers in the British media. At a first glance there is a clear trend towards a growing interest in PISA. While in the first round of PISA only 16 articles were published, the number of articles has increased in 2006 after the third round. With the publication of the fourth round in 2010, the interest in PISA has increased again. However, compared to other countries, the overall number of articles is very low (Niemann 2010; Bieber 2010). It

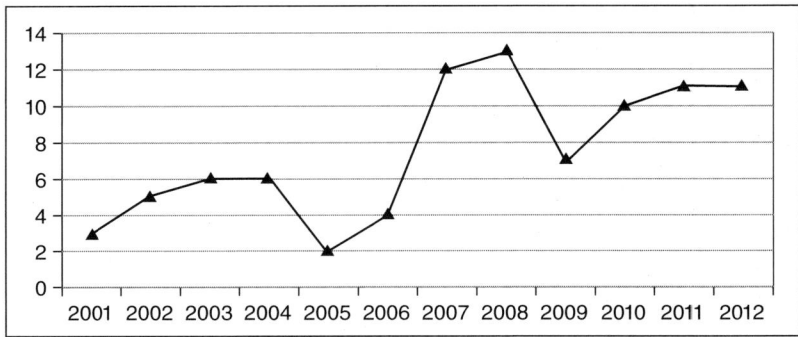

*Figure 6.1*   PISA articles in English newspapers.
*Source:* Factiva.

can be reasonably argued that the discourse about international comparative assessments in education has intensified. As the media analysis and interview data show, the PISA Study has changed the debate about education policy. In order to understand the actors' reactions to this international initiative, the following sections take a closer look at each PISA round.

In the first round of PISA in 2000, English students received surprisingly good results: in all categories they could be found in the top ten; they were even in fourth place for science. Politicians celebrated these good results extensively; Education Secretary Estelle Morris heralded, "it is a moment to be very proud. We now have a system which is working towards world class." She also mentioned the reasons for the English success, namely "the extra money we have put into our education system over the last four years has been very well spent" (in Times Educational Supplement 2001a). In a similar vein, the head of the Prime Minister's Delivery Unit, Michael Barber, praised the results and the robustness of the OECD's study. He argued that PISA 2000 was the "most sophisticated and reliable set of international comparisons ever undertaken" and a tribute to the teachers and head teachers (in Times Educational Supplement 2001b).

Things changed in the second round of PISA. Instead of confirming the good results, England dropped in the ranking. The results, however, were not published because the response rates from schools were too low. While Scotland and Northern Ireland were included in the official publications, it was argued by government officials that English results were not comparable. This decision has provoked criticism both within and outside. Even the OECD, which usually follows a more reluctant strategy, criticized the government for not having been active enough. At the end of the day, however, the decision to leave the English results out of the ranking was a win–win situation. In doing so, the government could ignore the bad PISA results by referring to the statistical problems and thus avoid too much media and opposition attention. The OECD could keep their statistical standards high and save the assessment's good reputation (The Economist 2004). However, after the exclusion of English results from the official OECD publication, the debate became controversial. Analysis of the data proved that the response rates were only marginally lower than in the first PISA round. It would thus be possible to control for response bias. The results of English students were thus comparable to those of PISA 2000 and to other countries (Micklewright et al. 2010).

In 2006, the response rate was sufficient for the English scores to be compared to other national-level data. In contrast to the first PISA round, the average reading scores dropped in 2006. While England's science scores were still above the OECD average, the results in mathematics fell below it. If one takes a look at all three PISA rounds, the latest survey confirms an overall decline in England's PISA performance (see OECD 2006). This is remarkable because the first PISA cycle took place when Prime Minister Tony Blair put "education, education, education" on the top of the government agenda. Furthermore, despite the rather poor performance in this international comparison, the discourse has only slightly increased (Interview ENG 12, ENG 02; see also Grek 2008). Just before the publication of the next round's results, the government published the white paper "The Importance of Teaching". As it was clearly stated by Prime Minister David Cameron and Deputy Prime Minister Nick Clegg in the foreword of the paper, the basis for it was the PISA Study: "The only way we can catch up, and have the world-class schools our children deserve, is by learning the lessons of other countries' success" (in Department for Education 2010: 3).

The main argument of the white paper was to improve education standards by strengthening the education of teachers. Following the models of Finland and South Korea, the paper outlines strategies to improve the teaching profession in general. Only one month later, in December 2010, the OECD published the results of the fourth study. While other countries were able to improve their results in the PISA Study, English pupils scored the same results. The head of the OECD's PISA group, Andreas Schleicher, characterized the situation of the English performance in the international comparison as "stagnant at best" (The Guardian 2010).

In general, PISA initiated a political discourse that has led to a growing recognition of other countries' education policy. The English political dialogue has recently begun to change "because of the concern to be world class" (Interview ENG 06). Political actors in England have started looking at other countries that have scored higher in terms of participation and performance, for instance, Finland (Interview ENG 12). Put more drastically, "in the war to create the world's best schools, the fight's to the Finnish" (The Times Education 2009). In recent years, political actors in Britain have become aware of the fact that they need to compare themselves to other countries (Interview ENG 05).

These changes have been a "gradual progressive realization" (Interview ENG 06). What has changed in recent years is the attitude of political actors towards the work of the OECD: nowadays, the studies and publications of the OECD are taken more seriously (Interview ENG 08). The capability of the OECD to influence education policy-making in England is limited due to a traditional English skepticism regarding international activities. Yet PISA has become a "brand" in England well marketed by the OECD (Interview ENG 12; see also Grek 2009). Although the slow-growing pressure has not actually translated into concrete initiatives, political actors are beginning to outline concepts to improve England's performance in the PISA Study (Interview ENG 11; ENG 12). Still, English policy-makers still use PISA rather selectively. Whenever it helps, they refer to the OECD's data or the good performance of English pupils, such as in the first round of the study. Usually, however, international comparisons do not play an important role in political arguments and debates about how to improve the education system. As was argued before, one reason for this is that already since the late 20th century England has implemented a complex system of assessing pupils' performance. There are also critical sceptical voices about PISA and the way policy-makers use the study. Beth Davies, president of the National Union of Teachers, strongly criticized the assessment and said that she is "thoroughly sick of hearing about PISA" because the results are used to "drive forward a false agenda of school and local authority reform" (in BBC 2013).

Michael Gove, Secretary of State for Education, was especially engaged in bringing PISA back into the public debates. In his speeches or written statements he frequently praised the need for international comparisons in education and the work of the OECD. For example, in a speech to the Education World Forum in January 2012, Gove emphasized the importance of comparative education assessments for governments: "no nation that is serious about ensuring its children enjoy an education that equips them to compete fairly with students from other countries can afford to ignore the PISA and McKinsey studies" (in Department for Education 2012).

These findings certainly should not be overestimated. First and foremost, this is political rhetoric and thus part of the game. Yet, the fact that PISA has slowly become part of discourses about educational quality and the future of the English education system shows that international initiatives are now taken more seriously. As argued at the beginning of this book, there are three possible interpretations of actors' reactions on international initiatives: intentionally ignoring an initiative (*exit*); criticizing and opposing it (*voice*); and supporting and complimenting it (*loyalty*). English reactions on PISA include all three. While at the beginning policy-makers responded with *loyalty* and praised the study as proof of good governance, it quickly changed to *exit* and *voice*. With the latest PISA Study, however, reactions of state actors such as the Secretary of State for Education can be characterized as forms of *loyalty* expressed by acts of positive speech. At the same time other actors and organizations have started to publicly express *voice* with regards to the international assessment and the way that policy-makers use it.

## Higher education

Similar to the discussion of the PISA Study, I first give a brief overview of changes in English education policy. The second part takes a closer look at actors' reactions to the Bologna Process.

### Changes in education policy

As many of today's policies in England, the transformation of higher education has its origins in the Thatcher era. With the elections of 1979 and the government change from the Labour Party to the Conservatives, the implementation of New Public Management at English universities began. Large parts of the education sector were weakened by a "discourse of derision" (Ball 1990) that attacked public education. The conservative government referred to the aftermath of the financial crisis in 1970 to dramatically cut down financial resources. The rapid massification of higher education posed more problems for the sector than it could handle at a time. Between 1989 and 1995, student numbers in higher education increased by almost 70 per cent (Eurydice 2000: 492). At the same time, funding per student was halved (Greenaway and Haynes 2003: 153).

With the Further and Higher Education Act 1992, many polytechnics were transformed into universities. Polytechnics had served as a second tier in the United Kingdom (UK) postsecondary education. These institutions' governance structures were already close to the ideas of New Public Management that dominated the era. They were strongly regulated by the state while controlled by regional external actors (Lange and Schimank 2009: 527).

Another major change that came with the Further and Higher Education Act 1992 was the introduction of the so-called Research Assessment Exercise (RAE): a "carrot and stick" instrument through which the government evaluates universities' performance on a regular basis. All universities were graded upon their research activities on a scale from one to four (since 1996, from one to five). These changes had consequences for the strategies of universities. One consequence was a significant increase in competition between universities that caused a "downward spiral": a department's success in raising external funding affected the external evaluation and thus the RAE scale (Henkel 2000: 131). At the same time, however, private foundations or other potential funding institutions started referring to evaluation results. As a result, strong universities have become stronger, while universities with the lowest performance received "no money at all" (Henkel 2000: 115).

The massification of higher education has been accompanied by the question of how to finance expansion. A review commissioned by the government suggested solutions for the pressing question of under-funded universities. Lord Dearing, the author of the report, came up with a simple but controversial proposal: those who benefit from tertiary education should contribute to its costs, rather than the taxpayer. The report recommended further growth and widening participation towards disadvantaged groups, more emphasis on teaching quality and staff training monitored by a national agency, increased higher education spending, modernized university governance, and the introduction of tuition fees (National Committee of Enquiry into Higher Education 1997). Dearing's ideas of higher education were consistent with those of New Public Management or "new managerialism" (Robertson 2010: 195). Even though the report had been commissioned under the Conservatives, it was published in 1997 when Tony Blair had already assumed office.

Consequently, in 1998 tuition fees became applicable for domestic students. At the same time, with the introduction of tuition fees the government cut funding for higher education (Ryan and Carroll 2005: 91). This pushed universities to rethink their strategies, for example, regarding attracting foreign students and competing internationally with other institutions. Increasing frictions in Parliament and within the Labour Party itself culminated in 2004 when the Blair government pushed the Higher Education Act, which allowed universities to charge variable tuition fees, through Parliament.

Unlike in other countries, the Bologna Process or other higher education initiatives coming from the European level have not triggered substantial reforms (Witte 2006; Knodel and Walkenhorst 2010; Knodel et al. 2013). Nevertheless, both in secondary and higher education, developments on the international and European levels have changed the conditions for policy-making. Thus, the following sections focus on the reactions of politically relevant actors and their strategies in the context of internationalization. Following the typology of Hirschman, the question is if domestic actors respond with *voice, exit,* or *loyalty* to the increasing prominence of international and European developments.

### Reactions to the Bologna Process: from exit to voice

There are a variety of actors in English higher education policy-making, and the field is highly decentralized. Despite this high degree of decentralization and the independence of universities, the state still has power to regulate (Tapper 2007). Thus, the underlying logic of higher education policy-making can be described as institutional autonomy and indirect regulation. In order to understand the reactions of actors on internationalization, I focus in particular on the government and actors of the higher education sector.

When the British Minister of Education, Tessa Blackstone, signed the declaration of Sorbonne in 1998, she did not consult any other important actors within the higher education sector, nor with Scottish, North Irish, or Welsh policy-makers or higher education stakeholders. As she has later clarified, she was convinced that the agreement would not have any consequences for the UK higher education sector (Witte 2006: 329). One year later, Baroness Blackstone signed the official Bologna declaration together with education ministers from 29 different countries. The guidelines were still very vague at this point. This time, however, there had been consultations with stakeholders such as the Committee of Vice-Chancellors and Principals (CVCP). Yet, both within the sector and the broader public, the Bologna Process was not on the agenda in the early years.

The government and the ministers responsible for higher education have long remained silent regarding the Bologna Process and its implications for the UK. Moreover, it can even be argued that, at first, they ignored the developments in other European countries. In 2003, the government published the white paper "The Future of Higher Education" (DfES 2003). The focus of the paper was on major issues for UK higher education, most importantly raising participation and funding of universities. This paper reflects the inward-looking perspective of British policy-makers at that time: many of the issues raised in the paper were very close to what has been discussed at the European level in the context of the Bologna Process, for example, quality assurance, employability, and creating a higher education area in order to be more competitive on the international market. It seems as if the authors of the white paper talk about the Bologna Process and its goals without naming it: "higher education is becoming a global business. Our competitors are looking to sell higher education overseas, into the markets we have traditionally seen as ours" (DfES 2003: 11). This strategy of the government to avoid implicating Bologna can be interpreted as a form of *exit*: even though the education department was well aware of the Bologna Process and its objectives, they intentionally did not mention it.

In July 2004, the House of Lords debated the European Higher Education Area for the first time. Baronness Ashton of Upholland, parliamentary Under Secretary of State for Education represented the government's position in this debate. Several Lords expressed concerns about the growth of European cooperation in higher education. In particular, they questioned if the UK government will "resist any pressures under which they may come from the European Commission towards a harmonisation that could interfere with the flexibilities of the UK system, such as our one-year Masters degree and the quality control provisions" (in House of Lords 2004: 2). They strongly criticized the absence of a clear position and statement by the government. The response by the Under Secretary of State on the question about future UK policy on European integration of education was in line with the vague position of the government years before: "my Lords, we see processes such as Bologna (. . .) as a good example of how best to develop the right kind of links in both a European economy and a global economy" (in House of Lords 2004). Interestingly, it was the higher education sector that criticized the strategy of the government and called for a clear position towards the Bologna Process. In a statement, the President of Universities UK argued, "the UK government, and most universities it must be said, have largely stood aside from the Bologna Process" (in House of Lords 2004: 2). So while the government's strategy was to ignore the Bologna Process, the biggest organization of the higher education sector, Universities UK, has started to raise its *voice*. As will be shown later, it was also Universities UK (UUK) that set up an institutionalized forum for information exchange in the context of the Bologna Process.

An important part of the Bologna Process is the so-called ministerial conference. These events take place every two years and are organized by the member countries. Since London was selected to host the conference in 2007, the House of Commons ordered a select committee to oversee the debate. The final report can be summarized in three major points (House of Commons 2007). First, it has been extensively argued that the UK has a unique position among the members of the Bologna Process because it already has a two-cycle degree structure, quality assurance, and a higher education system with an excellent global reputation. The report, however, also acknowledged that other European countries have started improving their higher education systems and could turn into competitors that should be taken seriously. Second, the question about Bologna's comparability or standardization runs throughout the report. The then Minister for Higher Education, Bill Rammell, diplomatically stated that the goal of the Bologna Process is not about standardization, it "is about enabling a greater mobility of students and academics across that wider European area, and it is about facilitating interaction and movement between global higher education institutions [. . .]" (in House of Commons 2007: 17). Finally, there was a consensus among the higher education sector, agencies, and representatives of the government that the role of the European Commission raises important concerns. As the President of Universities UK Drummond Bone put it, "there is a continual danger [. . .] that the bureaucratization [. . .] does actually take over" (in House of Commons 2007: 6). These concerns were shared by Bill Rammell, who stressed that the government "pushed back strongly" on attempts of the European Commission to "overstep its competence in that area" (in House of Commons 2007: 36). Yet the strongest claim in the report of the Select Committee was that the UK government should take an active role in the Bologna Process and shape its future development towards British interests.

The intention of the report was to facilitate discussion and to prepare the upcoming Bologna conference in London. Interestingly, however, all witnesses invited by the Select Committee were representatives of organizations from within the British higher education sector. This created a sceptical and rather negative notion of the Bologna Process. As a British higher education expert put it, the Select Committee "got the answers it wanted by having the interviewees they wanted" (Interview ENG 13). In an official response to the Select Committee report after the

2007 ministerial conference in London, the government summarized the major outcomes of the Bologna conference: (1) the establishment of Register of Quality Assurance Agencies, (2) the development of strategies to advance the social dimension of Bologna, and (3) the promotion of the Bologna Process (House of Commons 2007b: 1). The Department for Education and Skills (DfES) was also keen to stress its activities in the context of the ministerial conference, such as the publication of the booklet "Bologna Process – Excellence through Engagement" as well as agreements to cooperate more closely with the British Council to promote Bologna in the UK (DfES 2007).

In June 2011, the Department for Business, Innovation and Skills (BIS) published the white paper "Students at the Heart of the System" (BIS 2011). Again, this report covered topics that were close to what had been discussed in the context of the Bologna Process over the previous years: workload, student mobility, social dimension, and quality assurance. Furthermore, the authors of the report avoided any reference to the Bologna Process or the European Union. It was again an inquiry of the House of Lords in 2011 that brought the Bologna Process back on the agenda. The aim of the inquiry "Modernisation of Higher Education in Europe: The EU Contribution" (House of Lords 2012) was to turn the attention to internationalization in higher education, both at the European and international levels. After having collected written and oral evidence from a range of individual and collective actors, the report was published in March 2012. It covered various topics, including student mobility, funding of higher education, and EU initiatives in higher education in general. With regards to the Bologna Process and the engagement of state authorities, the Select Committee criticized the government. They argued that the government is still too passive when it comes to the English master's and the Bologna guidelines. Following the evidence of several witnesses, the House of Lords Select Committee called on the government "to be more proactive in ensuring that the one-year Masters degree, which is already recognized in theory, is accommodated within the European Higher Education Area in practice" (House of Lords 2012: 15). The fact that the Department for Business, Innovation and Skills lacks any reference to the developments at the European level was also strongly criticized. The government and the universities should promote the Bologna Process more actively and "exploit the actual and potential benefits of the Bologna Process to their students and staff, including the utility of the European Credit Transfer and Accumulation System and the Diploma Supplement" (House of Lords 2012: 45).

To sum up, the story of the Bologna Process in England and the role of the government seem to be ambivalent. On the one hand, the UK had been among those countries that initiated the process and signed both the Sorbonne Declaration in 1998 and the Bologna Declaration in 1999. The government and departments responsible for higher education participated in the events and sent delegations to ministerial conferences in Prague, Berlin, and Bergen. They submitted all the required information and reports, such as the stocktaking reports that are due every two years. On the other hand, the Bologna Process has not been on the agenda in early years and the government has not taken a clear position towards it. This hesitation of the British government towards the Bologna Process can thus be seen as a strategic decision to be on board the Bologna train without prioritizing it. As argued above, given that the UK government signed the declaration in 1999 and has always been well informed, this behaviour and strategy can be interpreted as a form of *exit*: intentionally ignoring the Bologna Process and the European-level policy-making. The next section takes a closer look at interest groups in English higher education.

### The higher education sector and Europe: slowly awakening

The higher education sector in England consists of various organizations. The biggest organization of the higher education sector is Universities UK. Established in 1930 as Committee of Vice-Chancellors and Principals of the Universities of the United Kingdom (CVCP), UUK represents all British universities. As a consequence of devolution in the late 1990s, the group fragmented into various so-called mission groups (Reichert and Teixeira 2009: 24–5): the Russell Group represents large research universities, the 1994 group was set up to represent smaller research universities, and million+ is a think tank that works on behalf of former polytechnics and new universities. Another important player is the National Union of Students (NUS). Divided into the sub-organizations NUS-Scotland, NUS-Wales, and NUS-Northern Ireland, the NUS represents the interests of over 600 student unions.

An important landmark in the context of the Bologna Process was the creation of the High Level Policy Forum (HLPF). Established in 2003 by the head of the Higher Education Funding Council (HEFCE), it should be the main forum to exchange views on international initiatives in higher education. Closely related to these developments was the launch of the Europe Unit in late 2003 (see Witte 2006: 344–54 for a more detailed discussion). HEFCE and Universities UK agreed on funding the Europe Unit. The goal was to create an organization that should make "the sector aware of the Bologna Processes and being a repository of knowledge of Europe" (Interview ENG 14). In 2006, the Europe Unit was complemented by a section that should focus on the international level; both were merged in 2010. The creation of these forums, in particular the HLPF and the International Unit, shows that the higher education sector responded to the Bologna Process by establishing new forms of cooperation.

The conducted interviews have shown that there is limited awareness of the Bologna Process in the higher education sector. The following section takes a closer look at the agendas and activities of a selection of interest groups (UUK, Russell Group, 1994 group, National Union of Students). It is based on an analysis of news archives where higher education sector organizations comment on various issues. For example, ongoing debates of higher education policy, policy proposals by the government, or other developments that are of interest for their organization. The underlying assumption is simple: whatever is mentioned in the News and Policy Statements sections is expected to be of great importance for the organization. By coding and analysing this data we can learn more about their priorities and strategies. This assessment of news archives is complemented by interview data. Table 6.1 summarizes all news and policy statements between 2008 and 2011.

I distinguish between three categories. The first category (*domestic*) includes all news and statements that deal with developments on the national level. This covers a variety of topics, ranging from debates about tuition fees to the accreditation of new universities. In the second category (*European*) all articles were coded that contain a reference to the European level of higher education. We intentionally defined this category rather broadly. This means that, by definition, it covers topics such as the Bologna Process, activities of the European Commission in the context of higher education, EU programmes, but also references to

*Table 6.1*   Share of News and Press Statements in per cent, 2008–11.

|  | Domestic | International | European | Articles total |
|---|---|---|---|---|
| Universities UK | 97.1 | 2.3 | 0.7 | 306 |
| Russell Group | 79.6 | 18.5 | 1.9 | 211 |
| 1994 Group | 94.5 | 5.5 | 0 | 146 |
| National Union of Students | 91.3 | 8.1 | 0.6 | 715 |

*Source:* http://www.universitiesuk.ac.uk; http://www.russellgroup.ac.uk; http://www.1994group.co.uk; http://www.nus.org.uk, retrieved 5 December 2013.

umbrella organizations at the European level. Finally, a third category (*international*) is coded that refers to the international level of higher education policy. It includes all articles that made reference to issues such as visa regulations for international students, branch campuses, international organizations, or the publication of global rankings and the performance of British universities.

As Table 6.1 clearly shows, the focus of all organizations has been on the national level. Universities UK, 1994 group, and the National Union of Students have intensively commented on domestic issues. The share of articles that refer to the national level is over 90 per cent. Only the Russell Group's share of news and press statements in the category *domestic* is lower than 80 per cent. If we look at the share of articles that refer to the international dimension of higher education policy-making the numbers show a similar pattern; there has been some interest in international higher education policy. All organizations have publicly discussed international trends and developments. Many of the coded articles were contributions to the debate about UK's immigration policy and its implications for the reputation of British higher education. Almost 20 per cent of all Russell Group articles deal with the international dimension of policy-making. What is more interesting, however, is the category *European*. In general, the share of articles that deal with European issues is very little. The selected organizations have rarely published news and press statements on developments on the European level. More specifically, in the years between 2008 and 2011 only ten of all 1378 articles discuss higher education in a European context, for example the Bologna Process and its implications for the UK or the Erasmus programme. The results of the analysis show that the Bologna Process has not been a top priority for the selected organizations. Apparently, discourse and interaction has only taken place in collective forums such as the HLPF. Yet, there is evidence that in recent years sector organizations and interest groups have turned their attention towards the European level. The Russell Group, for example, has increased the attention towards the international level of policy-making. As an expert of the group put it, "it becomes more important to get policy-makers to understand the impacts that higher education make to the country and the global large economy, not just in the local economy" (Interview ENG 15). International competition has increased the pressure on the UK higher education sector. It "became important to think about: do we have world class universities? In a way, that maybe would have been taken for granted once upon a time. But other countries have massively invested and concentrated resources" (Interview ENG 15).

While there has been some visible interest in the international dimension, the Bologna Process and developments on the European level have been followed only recently (Interviews ENG 13; ENG 14; ENG 15; ENG 17; ENG 18). This is, of course, not too surprising since the pressure for institutional adaptations in the context of the Bologna Process has not been as high as in other countries. The Bologna Process, however, has established a European dimension of higher education that is much more competitive for British universities than it was a decade ago. In the words of an expert in the higher education sector: "in some respects the biggest difference the Bologna Process has made to the UK in general has been about opening up the rest of Europe to compete rather than us having to change a great deal" (Interview ENG 14). Given that the Bologna Process is still a moving target and not fully implemented in all countries, its consequences for global higher education are not yet entirely clear. Even though some higher education sector organizations have not yet begun to realize the potential of the Bologna Process, policy experts are already aware of them: "[. . .] if the goal of the Bologna Process was to increase the possibility for an academic market and if it is creating what is essentially seen as a European academic credential it could mean that the European Higher Education Area is able to outmanoeuvre places like Australia and Canada and possibly the U.S." (Interview ENG 16). With regards to the analytical framework, the reactions of higher education organizations can be interpreted as *exit*. Even though they have been well aware of these developments, these organizations have overlooked international- and European-level activities in higher education for a long time. As long as the interests of their members are not directly affected or penalized, there simply was no need to take these issues on board. Yet as was shown above, this strategy appears to have slightly changed recently – *exit* has turned into *voice*.

## Conclusion

The discussion of PISA and the Bologna Process in England has shown that actors' reactions vary compared to other countries. Both in secondary and higher education these international initiatives have not played an important role. They have been overlooked for quite a while. On the one hand, this is not surprising because the need for institutional adaptations and policy change was low. With regards to PISA, England already had a testing regime to assess and compare pupils' performance. Similarly, the two-cycle degree structure that can be considered as the core of the Bologna Process has always been part of the UK higher education system. On the other hand, the English case shows how selectively government actors and interest groups cope with international initiatives. Reactions on the PISA Study are different in each cycle of the assessment – they range from praising and heralding the importance of PISA to criticizing and ignoring it. Referring to our theoretical framework, this strategy of the government is quite rational. Because testing pupils' performance has become a standard in the English education system, the risk of triggering a critical public debate has been low. The benefits, however, are clearly visible: the government could use good results to emphasize their reform endeavours and the quality of English education institutions. At the level of interest groups, reactions have been, if at all present, rather negative, and we can observe a potpourri of *voice, exit,* and *loyalty* in each cycle of the PISA Study. This could be explained by the low importance and visibility of the PISA in England. Put differently, because the overall interest in PISA was low, there were no benefit in putting the international assessment on the agendas of interest groups.

Even though the British government has signed the Bologna declaration, it has remained silent for a while. It was the higher education sector that has called on the government to engage in the process. Consequently, reactions have turned from *exit* to *voice*, that is, the government has started to come up with a clearer position towards the Bologna Process. They realized that the costs of ignoring the developments at the European level could be higher than expected. As this chapter has also shown, the Bologna Process has not played an important role for the day-to-day business of organizations in the higher education sector. Yet recently, some organizations have started to put international-level issues on their agenda. This can be interpreted as turning internationalization strategies from *exit* to *voice*. Again, they started realizing that the Bologna Process might be more important than they have expected and the costs of missing the Bologna train could be high.

## References

Bache, Ian (2003) "Governing through Governance: Education Policy Control underNew Labour", *Political Studies*, 51(2), 300–314.

Ball, Stephen J. (1990) *Politics and Policy Making in Education. Explorations in Policy Sociology*, London: Routledge.

Ball, Stephen J. (2008) *The Education Debate*, Bristol: The Policy Press.

BBC (2013) *Schools can measure themselves against Pisa tests*, http://www.bbc.co.uk/news/education-22002525, retrieved 2 October 2013.

Bieber, Tonia (2010) "Playing the Multilevel Game in Education – the PISA Study and the Bologna Process Triggering Swiss Harmonization", in Martens, Kerstin,

Alexander-Kenneth Nagel, Michael Windzio and Ansgar Weymann, eds., *Transformation of Education Policy*, Basingstoke: Palgrave Macmillan, 105–31.

Breakspear, Simon (2012) "The Policy Impact of PISA. An Exploration of the Normative Effects of International Benchmarking in School System Performance", *OECD Education Working Papers*, 71.

Clarke, John, Sharon Gewirtz and Eugene McLaughlin (2000) *New Managerialism, New Welfare*, Thousand Oaks: SAGE Publications.

Department for Business, Innovation and Skills (2011) *Students at the Heart of the System*, London: The Stationary Office.

Department for Education and Skills (2003) *The Future of Higher Education*, London: The Stationary Office.

Department for Education and Skills (2007) Bologna Process. *Excellence through Engagement*, http://www.see-educoop.net/education_in/pdf/11%20Excellence_FINALv2.pdf, retrieved 2 October 2013.

Department for Education (2010) *The Importance of Teaching*, London: The Stationary Office.

Department for Education (2012) *Speech: Michael Gove to the Education World Forum*, https://www.gov.uk/government/speeches/michael-gove-to-the-education-world-forum, retrieved 2 October 2013.

The Economist (2004) *Bad marks all round – Education*, 11 December, London: The Economist Newspaper Limited.

Eurydice (2000) *Two Decades of Reform in Higher Education in Europe: 1980 Onwards*, Eurydice: Brussels.

Greenaway, David and Michelle Haynes (2003) "Funding Higher Education in the UK: The Role of Fees and Loans", *The Economic Journal*, 113 (February), 150–66.

Grek, Sotiria (2008) "PISA in the British Media: leaning tower or robust testing tool?", *CES Briefing*, No. 45, Edinburgh: Centre for Educational Sociology.

Grek, Sotiria (2009) "Governing by Numbers: The PISA 'Effect' in Europe", *Journal of Education Policy*, 24(1), 23–37.

The Guardian (2006*) The Vice-chancellors new velvet glove: Interview Wendy Piatt*, November 14, London: Guardian News and Media.

The Guardian (2010) *UK schools slip down world rankings. OECD study shows that despite comparatively high levels of per-pupil spending, the UK is behind Poland and Norway*, 7 December, London: Guardian News and Media.

Heffernan, Richard (2011) "Pressure group politics" in Richard Heffernan, Philip Cowley and Colin Hay, eds., *Developments in British Politics 9*, Basingstoke: Palgrave Macmillan.

Henkel, Mary (2000) *Academic Identities and Policy Change in Higher Education*, London: Jessica Kingsley.

Henry, Miriam, Bob Lingard, Fazal Rizvi and Sandra Taylor (2001) *The OECD, Globalization and Education Policy*, Amsterdam and London: Emerald.

House of Commons, Education and Skills Committee (2007) *The Bologna Process. Fourth Report of Session 2006–07*, http://www.publications.parliament.uk/pa/cm200607/cmselect/cmeduski/205/205.pdf, retrieved 2 October 2013.

House of Lords (2004) *Daily Hansard. 14 Jul 2004: Column 1239 – Column 1242*, http://www.publications.parliament.uk/pa/ld200304/ldhansrd/vo040714/text/40714-01.htm, retrieved 2 October 2013.

House of Lords (2012) "The Modernisation of Higher Education in Europe", *House of Lords Paper*, 27th Report of Session 2010–12.

James, Oliver (2009) "Central State", in Matthew Flinders, Andrew Gamble, Michael Kenny and Colin Hay, eds., *The Oxford Handbook of British Politics*, Oxford: Oxford University Press, 342–65.

Knodel, Philipp and Heiko Walkenhorst (2010) "What's England Got to Do with It? British Underestimation of International Initiatives in Education Policy", in Kerstin Martens, Alexander-Kenneth Nagel, Michael Windzio and Ansgar Weymann, eds., *Transformation of Education Policy*, Basingstoke: Palgrave Macmillan.

Knodel, Philipp, Kerstin Martens, Daniel de Olano and Marie Popp (2010) *Das PISA-Echo. Internationale Reaktionen auf die Bildungsstudie*, Frankfurt, New York: Campus.

Knodel, Philipp, Kerstin Martens and Dennis Niemann (2013) "PISA as an International Roadmap for Policy Change: Exploring Germany and England in a Comparative Perspective", *Globalisation, Societies and Education*, 11(3), 421–41.

Lange, Stefan and Uwe Schimank (2009) "Germany: A Latecomer to New Public Management", in Catherine Paradiese, Emanuela Reale, Ivar Bleiklie and Ewan Ferlie, eds., *University Governance – Western European Comparative Perspectives*, Dordrecht: Springer, 51–75.

Martens, Kerstin, Alexander-Kenneth Nagel, Michael Windzio and Ansgar Weymann, eds. (2010) *Transformation of Education Policy*, Basingstoke: Palgrave Macmillan.

Micklewright, John, Sylke V. Schnepf and Chris Skinner (2010) "Non-Response Biases in Surveys of School Children: The Case of the English PISA Samples", *IZA Discussion Paper*, No. 4789.

National Committee of Inquiry into Higher Education (1997) *Higher Education in the Learning Society (the Dearing Report)*, London: HMSO.

Niemann, Dennis (2010) "Deutschland – Im Zentrum des PISA-Sturms", in Philipp Knodel, Kerstin Martens, Daniel de Olano and Marie Popp, eds., *Das PISA-Echo. Internationale Reaktionen auf die Bildungsstudie*, Frankfurt, New York: Campus, 59–90.

OECD (2006) Education at a Glance 2006. Briefing Note for the United Kingdom, http://www.oecd.org/unitedkingdom/37392956.pdf, retrieved 2 October 2013.

Papadopoulos, George (1995) "Looking Ahead: An Educational Policy Agenda for the 21st Century", *European Journal of Education*, 30(4), 493–506.

Power, Sally and George Whitty (1999) "New Labour's education policy: first, second or third way?", *Journal of Education Policy*, 14(5), 535–46.

Reichert, Sybille and Pedro Teixeira (2009) "Institutional Diversity in English Higher Education" in Sybille Reichert, ed., *Institutional Diversity in European Higher Education. Tensions and Challenges for Policy Makers and Institutional Leaders*, Brussels: European University Association, 21–44.

Robertson, Susan L. (2010) "Corporatisation, Competitiveness, Commercialisation: New Logics in the Globalising of UK Higher Education", *Globalisation, Societies and Education*, 8(2), 191–203.

Ryan, Janette and Jude Carroll (2005) *Teaching International Students. Improving Learning for All*, London: Routledge.

Smith, Martin J. (1999) "Centre of Power: the institutions of government", in Ian Holliday, Andrew Gamble and Geraint Parry, eds., *Fundamentals in British Politics*, London: Macmillan, 96–118.

Tapper, Ted (2007) *The Governance of British Higher Education*, Dordrecht: Springer.

Times Educational Supplement (2001a) *Shocking news - we are doing OK*, 7 December, London: TSL Education Ltd.

Times Educational Supplement (2001b) *Pupils will never have had it so good*, 7 December, London: TSL Education Ltd.

The Times Education (2009) *Thoughts for the week: Why Finland is best for education*, 8 August, London: Times Newspapers Ltd.

Witte, Johanna K. (2006) *Change of Degrees and Degrees of Change. Comparing Adaptations of European Higher Education Systems in the Context of the Bologna Process*, Enschede: CHEPS (Center for Higher Education Policy Studies).

# 7
# New Culture, Old System – Reactions to Internationalization in Spanish Education Policy

*Marie Popp*

## Introduction

Spain's economy was hit hard by the international financial crisis. Hence, youth unemployment is extremely high in Spain, at over 50 per cent among 15- to 29-year-olds in May 2013. International experts recommended making structural adjustments to the educational sector (OECD 2012). Taking action, Spain began to cooperate with other countries, such as Germany, in order to establish a high-quality system of vocational training. The growing attention towards vocational training in Spain is only one example of this phenomenon. In general, Spanish governments tend to present specific reform ideas "as the best way to improve students' abilities and skills" (Bonal and Tarabini 2012: 337). After all, education policy has become an issue of major relevance in Spain independently, despite *and* due to the Programme for International Student Assessment (PISA) Study and the Bologna Process.

In Spain, both PISA and Bologna played an important role in introducing changes to higher education and secondary education. In order to integrate Spain into the European Higher Education Area (EHEA), the higher education system was restructured. As part of this, the overall study structure was changed in line with the Bologna guidelines. In the various rounds of the PISA Study, Spanish pupils performed below average (MECD 2013). These results raised questions about the quality of secondary education and triggered public debates on how to improve the Spanish school system. So far, few studies address changes in Spanish education policy in the context of PISA and Bologna (for example, Bonal and Tarabini 2012; Popp 2010; Salaburu et al. 2011). Thus, we know very little about how the most important actors were affected by these international initiatives.

This chapter describes reactions of key actors by focusing on their subjective interpretation of the overall situation and the instruments at hand referring to Hirschman's (1970) typology as adapted for this volume (see Introduction to this volume). Results are based on expert interviews in combination with reviews of political documents and newspaper articles.[1] Since the transition to democracy in 1975, education has been a policy field of permanent transformation but characterized by a division of interest groups favouring either private or public schooling. It is assumed that processes of internationalization in education policy may result *in new constellations of the state* and, therefore, increase the possibilities of interest groups to seek alternative venues where policy-making could be influenced.

In the first part of this chapter, I describe the general opportunities key actors have to exert influence on Spanish education policy-making. I then focus on the consequences of reforms in Spanish secondary education. First, changes in response to PISA are described briefly. Later, reactions of key actors towards these changes and their impact on Spanish secondary education are explained. The following section deals then with the consequences of transformations in Spanish higher education and starts with some insights regarding Bologna reforms in Spain. This may serve as background information in order to understand the reactions of key actors in response to the internationalization of the Spanish higher education system. In the last part, I summarize the main findings.

## Education policy-making in Spain

In Spain, the process of education policy-making is quite complex. Regional differences were once a source of longstanding tensions in Spain. The Constitution of 1978 addressed these conflicts by providing regional autonomy and more responsibilities that had once corresponded to the central government but over the years had transferred a large amount of decision-making power to the authority of the Autonomous Communities. Consequently, the decentralization of state power also resulted in the decentralization of the education system (Pereyra 2002). Nowadays, responsibilities for educational administration are shared between three levels: national, sub-national and municipal.

In education policy, the Spanish government has a predominant position in the definition and implementation of the political agenda. In secondary education, the Education Ministry (*Ministerio de Educación*) formulates requirements of educational institutions, core curriculum and education standards. Governments of Autonomous Communities have the power to define national norms corresponding to regional conditions and specific interests. Additionally, regional governments formulate norms for the regional educational system. The municipal level is responsible for infrastructure and the provision of educational services (Martínez Usarralde 2010).

In general, school policy in Spain is marked by historical dualism between public and private education (Bonal 2000). As a consequence, the landscape of key actors in Spanish secondary education policy is divided into two blocks of interests: conservative and progressive. While conservatives prioritize the application of market ideology in education and fight for religious education or free schooling, progressive actors are in favour of public education (Bonal 2000: 205). The division in education is symbolized by the two major parties. The conservative party (PP) tends to support conservative positions and is strongly connected to the Catholic community. In contrast, educational principles and programmes of the socialist party (PSOE) are linked to the progressive perspective on education in Spain. It is one of the reasons why changes in government are generally followed by changes in education policy (Bernecker 2008).

In higher education, administrative responsibilities are distributed among the federal Ministry of Education, governments of the 17 Autonomous Communities and 71 universities. Institutional autonomy of universities is guaranteed by the Spanish Constitution of 1978, which has been re-emphasized by more recent reforms in the context of the Bologna Process (Hernández Sandoica 2009). At the national level, the Education Ministry is the key department. Major changes in higher education also affect the interests of other departments, such as the Ministry of International Relations and Cooperation. Regional governments have the main responsibility for universities' financial and organizational matters.

In both sectors, the participation of interest groups is mainly directed to the government. In secondary education, interest groups have formal access to the decision-making process through its participation in the State School Council (CEE). This is the highest consultative and participatory body of the education community. In higher education, prior to Bologna, activities of interest groups were mainly targeted to the single university and the corresponding boards and committees.

## Spanish secondary education under discussion

From PISA 2000 to PISA 2012, Spanish pupils performed poorly compared to pupils from other European countries (MECD 2013). As a consequence, growing public concern about the quality of education turned PISA into a political instrument (Bonal and Tarabini 2012). In this section, I analyse reactions of key actors on PISA. Prior to this, the most important changes in Spanish secondary education are described.

### Raising quality in Spanish schools

Spanish secondary education policy has been a field of permanent transformation. In the last decade, there have been major debates about the innovation of education and the improvement of educational quality in the sector of secondary education. In this context, PISA has had a major impact on public opinion in Spain and has turned into an international reference for the quality of education (Marchesi 2006; Massot Verdú et al. 2006).

For governments, PISA serves as a source of legitimacy for reform. In Spain, both sides – the conservative and the socialist party – selectively used the PISA Study to legitimize each party's reform ideas. Since the results of the first PISA Study were published in 2001, three education reforms have been presented by three different governments. First, the education reform *Ley Orgánica de Calidad de la Educación* (LOCE) of the conservative government. Second, the education reform *Ley Orgánica de Educación* (LOE) of the socialist government. Third, the education reform *Ley Orgánica para la Mejora de la Calidad Educativa* (LOMCE) currently proposed by the new conservative government.

Although all of these education reforms aim to enhance educational quality, they differ profoundly in direction and instruments: While the conservative party seeks to strengthen the principle of merit, the socialist party supports the principle of equality. To give an example, the PP promotes tracking in the last two years of secondary education in order to meet the needs of each student, whereas the PSOE is an advocate of comprehensive schooling in order to guarantee qualitative education for all students (Popp 2010).

Politicians of both parties made references to education systems of other countries, such as Finland, where pupils' performance in PISA was above average. Despite these references, it is difficult to identify those policy changes that in fact resulted from the PISA Study. PISA itself is merely about demonstrating data that may reveal countries' successes and deficiencies in international comparison. Ideas about how to improve the effectiveness of an education system are the result of inter-pretation. As in the case of Germany (see chapter 4 by Niemann in this volume), the most important transformation in secondary education policy was the paradigm shift from content to competence. At the politi-cal level, this shift resulted in the formulation of education standards. In schools, the orientation towards competences introduced a new cul-ture of teaching and learning, which was strengthened by other reform aspects, such as school autonomy.

## Actors' reactions in secondary education

PISA results raised questions about the quality of secondary education in Spain. Consequently, actors involved in this field were obliged to respond to the international study and its effects with regard to reform-ing the Spanish education system. Reactions of support and *voice* can be assessed. Reactions are strongly linked to the established constellations in the field but have to be differentiated with respect to the specific reform under discussion.

In secondary education, the group that is most affected by policy changes are pupils. Yet they are less influential than other organizations in this policy field. At the federal level, pupils' interests are represented by four student organizations, which include students from university *and* pupils from school.[2] In the State School Council, teachers' interests are defended by only eight representatives coming from these organiza-tions. The National Confederation of Students Associations (CANAE), for example, has three representatives in the State School Council and therefore is an important agent of the youths' interests. With respect to PISA, the organization reacted positively on the international study and its impact on Spanish school policy. CANAE linked the PISA Study to the modernization of teaching methods. In this context, the interna-tional assessment was helpful to bring in a new perspective on teaching and learning to the Spanish schools and the actors involved. Neverthe-less, the organization criticized "that the PISA debate was dominated by the rankings" (Interview ES 08) and that most actors highlighted sub-jective interpretations while ignoring academic literature. Due to lim-ited resources, the organization supported ideas to modernize teaching practice through proposals in the State School Council, and by training teachers, parents and students. For this reason, CANAE cooperated with other student organizations, parent associations and teacher unions (Interview ES 08).

Another group with interests in school policy are parent organiza-tions. At the national level, the interests of parents are represented by two organizations. These organizations show the dualism of the Spanish education system: The Catholic Parents Confederation (CONCAPA) represents the interests of religious private schools with public substitutions, and the Parental Associations Confederation (CEAPA) defends parents' interests in compulsory public education. Both organizations are members of the State School Council, but they "never agree in their ideological positions nor in their understanding of parents' rights in the educational system" (Bonal 2000: 210).

Within the conservative alliance, CONCAPA is one of the most powerful actors. It represents about three million parents and is strongly linked to the Catholic Church in Spain. The organization's influence on the priorities of the conservative party in education policy is very high (Feito 2011). That is why CONCAPA supported and shaped the reform LOCE in 2002 to the same extent as it supports and shapes the current reform project of Ignacio Wert, education minister of Rajoy's conservative administration. Consistently, the organization protested against the reform of the socialist party during the time when Zapatero was the Spanish prime minister. CONCAPA became a motor of the anti-LOE movement that tried to stop the reform by organizing mass demonstrations and collection of signatures. The movement was very successful in blocking the introduction of this reform and forced the government to make additional changes.

In the case of CEAPA, reactions were directly opposed to those of CONCAPA. The organization protested against the reform LOCE of the conservative government and supported the reform LOE in order to secure quality education for all. With respect to PISA, the organization sees the study as a good measure to compare the Spanish education system with those of other countries. Changes such as competence-based learning, individualization and school autonomy match with the interests of the organizations. CEAPA supported the international assessment by informing parents, teachers and directors at the local level and collaborating with other organizations. However, similar to the student organization, CANAE, the parent association, CEAPA, criticized that "PISA has turned into a political weapon" (Interview ES 03).

Introducing changes to secondary education always affects the groups of schoolteachers. In Spain, many schoolteachers are organized in unions. However, the landscape of teacher unions in Spain is quite complex (Bonal 2000: 208). Working conditions for teachers differ from private to public schools and from the regions of Catalunya to Andalucia. This is one of the reasons why schoolteachers are represented by a large number of organizations that try to defend the members' interests and influence the regulations of each Autonomous Community. At the federal level, seven different associations represent teachers of public and private schools.[3] In the State School Council, teachers are defended by 20 representatives coming from these organizations.

In general, teacher unions in Spain tend to make use of symbolic activities in order to shape education policy-making. Mobilization of members for the collections of signatures, mass demonstrations or strikes are common instruments to attract public attention and to influence policy-making. Reactions to PISA were ambivalent among teachers unions. On the one hand, some organizations, in particular FE-CC.OO, criticized that PISA is often reduced to the international ranking. On the other hand, many teacher unions selectively used PISA results in order to legitimize the organizations' proposals. Recently, PISA has been used as an argument to protest against financial cuts in the educational sector. Teacher unions claimed that high salaries are strongly linked to students' achievement (El País 2011).

With regards to changes in education policy that are connected to OECD recommendations or best practices from other countries, reactions of teacher unions are less obvious. For example, FETE-UGT supported the reform of the socialist party PSOE but criticized the party's conclusion that school autonomy would improve student achievement in international evaluations. In a similar way, the creation of a new master's programme for the preparation of teachers "provoked strong and polemic reactions" (Egido Gálvez 2011: 41). To this end, resistance towards competence-based learning in secondary education (as PISA highlights and tests) and internationalization in higher education (as the Bologna Process promotes) culminated in this point. All in all, PISA has become an important aspect of school policy in Spain. Teacher unions are obliged to respond to the OECD's PISA Study and spread their interpretation of the Spanish results.

PISA was a topic of public attention in Spain. Accordingly, societal actors got involved in the debate on educational quality. The overall mission of these organizations is to "improve society through education" (Interview ES 02). Related to PISA, some organizations adopted the role of experts or mediators. As experts, they shared their knowledge on successful education systems and projects from other countries. As mediators, they offered a forum for discussions about how to improve student achievement and raise the quality of education. To give an example, the foundation Santillana organized conferences and roundtables on PISA and its consequences for Spanish secondary education. Andreas Schleicher of the OECD was invited to Madrid to give lectures on the Spanish PISA results. Since foundations and think tanks do not have formal access to the political sector, they have to rely on informal channels to exert their influence. Combining the power of PISA in media with financial resources and expertise was a successful strategy to increase the visibility of an organization's goals and activities.

Within the Ministry of Education, the National Institute for Evaluation in Education INEE (*Instituto Nacional de Evaluación Educativa*) tried to act in a similar way on the dynamics which accompanied every PISA Study. The organization's objective was to enhance evidence-based policy-making in the field of education. The INEE is responsible for the collaboration with international organizations and the implementation of international studies of student achievement at the school level. Unlike the agency *Agencia Nacional de Evaluación de la Calidad y Acreditación* (ANECA) in higher education, INEE was created before PISA. However, the prominence of the organization has increased substantially with the turn towards educational performance data and evaluation.

From the INEE's perspective, "PISA has become an international reference and has changed the culture of evaluation in Spain" (Interview ES 04). These changes resulted in a shift from content to competence and therefore affected teachers, school principals and pupils. In contrast to the politicians, who tended to politicize PISA results for each party's own purpose (Bonal and Tarabini 2012; Popp 2010), the administrative level tended to depoliticize the PISA debate by providing additional background information that could explain the PISA results in more detail. It was the organization's interest to adapt findings from the international study to the national context and to inform key actors on the conclusions for the Spanish education system. By doing so, INEE cooperates with universities, schools and regional institutes of evaluation.

To conclude, PISA was used as a political instrument by various actors to legitimize different proposals of reform. Reactions on PISA and corresponding changes to education policy were shaped by ideological constraints: Depending on the political party in government, actors reacted with *voice* or *loyalty* to the respective reform under discussion. This can be explained by the strong division of progressive and conservative ideologies guiding school policy reforms. As a result, an organization's opportunities to exert influence on education policy-making were dependent on whether the conservative party or the socialist party was in power. Put differently, PISA was able to raise public attention towards education quality, but was not able to overcome the internal logic of the system.

## Spanish higher education in transition

As in many other countries, the Bologna Process was the main reason for major changes in Spanish higher education policy. In this section, I first highlight some aspects of higher education reform and then focus on reactions of different key actors in the field.

### Adopting Spain to the European model

The integration of Spain into the EHEA started in 1999 when Mariano Rajoy, the former education minister of the conservative party, signed the declaration of Bologna. Since then, much has changed in Spanish higher education policy. First, political power has shifted several times. In 2004, the right-wing government of José María Aznar was replaced by the left-wing government of José Luis Rodríguez Zapatero. In 2012, the conservative party won the elections and Rajoy became prime minister. Second, the Spanish higher education system has been transformed profoundly. Contents, structures and responsibilities have been changed in order to meet the Bologna guidelines (European Commission 2012).

Reforms in line with the Bologna Process affected the overall study structure. In Spain, it takes four years to get a bachelor's degree (*Grado*), but only one year to get a master's degree (*Máster*).[4] This structure is compatible with the Bologna guidelines, but only six out of 47 countries which voluntary joined the Bologna Process opted for this solution. Most countries implemented a study system of three plus two years for the combination of bachelor's and master's degrees (European Commission 2012).

Another important aspect of the reforms was the introduction of a system of quality assurance and accreditation. As many other countries, Spain did not have significant experiences in quality assuring or accreditation. Before Bologna, study programmes were designed by state authorities. Enabled by the reform acts of 2001 and 2007, universities have gained more autonomy in terms of curriculum and funding. As a result, ANECA was created in 2002. In addition to ANECA, other state agencies were created in order to meet the challenges which resulted from the trends of internationalization. In 2011, the National Council of University Students (CEUNE) was founded to offer a formal channel of students' participation. Similar to the State School Council CEE, this body is connected to the national Ministry of Education and has only an advisory role.

In general, the process of implementation was chaotic. Pello Salaburu and his colleagues (2011: 73) claim that "the way was longer and harder in Spain than in other countries". Due to changes in political leadership and moving responsibilities, the process of adoption in Spain was interrupted several times. During 1999 and 2012, six different ministers were in charge of adapting the Spanish higher education system to the European model. As a consequence, the implementation of reforms was slowed down, modified or even stopped. In comparison to the situation in secondary education, differences between conservative and socialist positions were not that extreme in the context of Bologna.

### Actors' reactions in higher education

The Bologna Process was a starting point for a set of reforms that aimed at modernizing and internationalizing the Spanish higher education system. In general, most actors supported the basic idea to create an EHEA. Nevertheless, a lot of other actors sharply criticized the way in which the Spanish government tried to introduce major changes to the national higher education system in order to meet the Bologna guidelines.

In the field of higher education policy, students are the group of actors that is most affected by changes. From 1999 until 2008, the Bologna Process was nothing more than an abstract political vision to most students in Spain. The situation changed dramatically when reform ideas were implemented. In 2008, new study structures which were necessary to adapt the Spanish higher education system to the Bologna guidelines became obligatory for all universities in Spain. In reaction to this reform, thousands of students filled the streets all over the country to show their protest against ongoing reforms. From this day on, the internationalization of the Spanish higher education system ceased to be a political concept that was discussed in expert forums and began to have visible effects for all actors involved in the field of higher education policy.

Student organizations played an important role during this time. In Spain, the landscape of student associations is diverse. In contrast to France (see chapter 5 by Dobbins in this volume), most student associations do not operate at the national level. Rather, they aim to influence the decision-making process at the university level or at least at the level of each Autonomous Community. There are only a few associations that are represented at the federal level. For example, the students union (SE) is one of the largest and most powerful student associations in Spain due to the large number of members. Ideologically, the students union is leftist. The organization strongly opposed the internationalization of Spanish higher education and became a motor of the anti-Bologna movement. In order to raise *voice* against the Bologna reforms, the organization mobilized students and university teachers through coordinated public campaigns and members' mobilization at almost every university in the country (Interview ES 05).

In response to this, the more moderate student organizations formed an alliance of support.[5] In order to defend the advantages of internationalization, these actors began to coordinate their positions and actions. The dissemination of information about Bologna and its positive and negative consequences for Spanish higher education in general and for Spanish students in particular, was their main concern. They mobilized their members at universities across the country and organized a number of information events. In addition, there were joint campaigns to spread a positive image of Bologna in Spain. This active form of *loyalty* – "Yes to Europa. Yes to Bologna" (Interview ES 05) – made these student associations important partners for the Education Ministry. In the beginning, the alliance predominantly used informal power, such as campaigns, discussions and trainings, to exert influence at the university level. After the creation of CEUNE, the Bologna-supporting organizations had formal access to the political level, which allowed them to have a favourable position (Interview ES 07). In contrast to this, the SE refused to participate in CEUNE because the organization rejected the whole project of internationalization. With reference to Hirschman's typology, this specific reaction may be interpreted as a form of *exit*.

In sum, reactions of student organizations were not consistent. On the one hand, the student union played an active and important role within the Spanish anti-Bologna movement. On the other hand, other student associations formed an alliance of support to enhance the acceptance of Bologna reforms among students.

It is worth taking a closer look at education providers. As argued before, professors and lecturers of some universities supported the student protests. They especially criticized the way in which the European reform model was adapted to the Spanish system. At the same time, many university teachers supported the idea of harmonization in higher education. However, unlike the reactions of students, activities of professors, lecturers and researchers were marked by a low level of coordination.

In contrast to this, the *Conferencia de Rectores Universidades Españolas* (CRUE) is an organization with a high level of internal coordination. CRUE represents almost all public and private universities in Spain, and therefore, has been one of the most important actors in Spanish higher education policy since its creation in 1994. CRUE defines itself as a connector between government and universities.[6] The organization generally supports the idea of modernization and harmonization of higher education, which fits well with the members' view that the process of internationalization was accompanied by regionalization. This means that the autonomy of universities is strengthened by the transfer of responsibilities from the level of political administration to the university.

Although CRUE stressed the importance of Bologna-related reforms and supported the governments' activities, they criticized the process of implementation. Universities had to deal with changing regulations and a high level of administrative work as a consequence of accreditation and quality assurance. For example, in 2005 universities were obliged by law to design new master's programmes of two-year duration. Some years later, the government restructured its study structures by shortening the master's programmes to one year. As a consequence, universities had to redesign their master's programmes once more. As connector, CRUE observes the progress and assesses the impact of Bologna-related reforms. The annual studies are an important measure for each government's improvements or regressions. Another related group of actors, economic actors, was not directly involved in Spanish higher education policy-making. Nevertheless, some of these actors are among the strongest supporters of the idea to integrate Spain into the EHEA. Santander, for instance, one of the world's leading banks based in Spain, plays an active role in promoting the idea of internationalization of the higher education sector.[7] For them, working in a globalized world is not a vision but a reality. Therefore, the bank supports student mobilization programmes by offering scholarships.

Making Spanish universities competitive at the international level is a goal that cannot be achieved by state actors alone. For this reason, the Education Ministry and its technical bodies had to find strategic partners supporting Bologna-related reforms. For instance, ANECA's strategy was to develop programmes of support to administrators and university teachers. A more cooperative approach was necessary because the agency's activities were sharply criticized in the beginning. Today ANECA cooperates with a wide range of organizations representing universities, teachers and students. In the future, the agency aims to be seen "as an advisor" (Interview ES 06) and contributor to a culture of quality in Spanish higher education. In sum, many actors support the vision of Bologna but sharply criticize the way it was implemented. The government was initially slow to adapt the national higher education system to the European model, and in some points, opted for isolated solutions (for example, study structure). Various actors' reactions indicate that ongoing reforms offer new venues for participation in higher education, but transformation in this policy field has just begun.

## Conclusion

In the Spanish case, PISA and Bologna appear to have caused great sensation. Whereas PISA sparked a debate about the quality of school education and about the means by which the system is to be improved, Bologna gave the impetus for a comprehensive redesign of the Spanish university system.

The analysis of actors' reactions shows that PISA and Bologna, in combination with corresponding education reforms, triggered reactions of a variety of actors involved in the system. Many actors supported the main messages of both international initiatives, that is, improving the quality of education and introducing an international perspective in national education systems. In comparison to other countries, the Spanish case stands out because the changes in education were accompanied by an atmosphere of approval (*loyalty*). Nevertheless, actors had different points of view (*voice*) related to the effects of reforms and the measures that should be adopted in order to raise the quality of Spanish schools or internationalize the higher education system.

In secondary education, various actors have exploited the PISA Study (Bonal and Tarabini 2012). PISA has not reduced the ideological division of interest groups within the field of education policy – it has rather exaggerated the differences between them. Nevertheless, education policy in Spain has changed in the aftermath of PISA, especially with regard to the quality of education, competences, evaluation, teaching methods and individual support in the classroom.

The scope of analysis is limited because only actors from the national level were taken into account. Future research should therefore concentrate on comparative studies at the regional level. Over the past years, evaluating the effectiveness of education systems with the help of PISA has turned into a political instrument where the comparison within Spain is even more important than the comparison with other countries. The Autonomous Communities compete for the best education programmes, allowing them to reach the highest points in the next PISA Study. In times of economic crisis and massive financial cuts in education, increasing the effectiveness of education requires all the more creativity on the part of involved actors.

In higher education, the reforms and discussions brought about by the Bologna Process included not only the organization and content of the Spanish courses, but also the orientation and influence of stakeholders, especially where new venues of participation were created. Some players have been able to take advantage of the modernization of Spanish higher education, namely by responding with an interest in developing more *loyalty* partnerships with other actors and thereby increasing their own visibility in the field. In addition, new tasks developed within these partnerships brought about the creation of new institutions and negotiation fields with it.

This analytical result is only tentative. The fact that Spain has only more recently begun the implementation process of the Bologna guidelines suggests that policy changes in this field are still in full swing. Further studies are necessary to evaluate the reactions of different actors and their impact on the political process in Spanish higher education. Particularly worth investigating are the questions: Which inherent dynamics can be observed in the newly created institutions, such as CEUNE, and the role of economic actors, such as Santander, and how will these dynamics develop in the long term in relation to the design of higher education policy in Spain.

## Notes

1 Interviews with representatives of relevant organizations were conducted by the author in March 2012. Press analysis was conducted with *Factiva*, covering the newspapers *El País* and *El Mundo*.
2 *Confederación Estatal de Asociaciones de Estudiantes* (CANAE), *Sindicato de Estudiantes* (SE), *Federación de Asociaciones de Estudiantes* (FAEST) and *Unión Democrática de Estudiantes* (UDE).
3 *Asociación Nacional del Profesorado Estatal-Sindicato Independiente* (ANPE), *Central Sindical Independiente y de Funcionarios* (CSI.F), *Federación de Enseñanza de Comisiones Obreras* (FE-CC.OO), *Federación de Trabajadores de la Enseñanza-Unión General de Trabajadores* (FETE-UGT), *Confederación de Sindicatos de Trabajadoras y Trabajadores de la Enseñanza-Intersindical* (STES-I), *Federación de Sindicatos Independientes de Enseñanza* (FSIE) and *Unión Sindical Obrera-Federación de Enseñanza* (USO).
4 Some programmes derivate from this standardized structure: For example, in pharmacy or dentistry, it takes five years to complete the first cycle and six years in the case of medicine or architecture.

5 FAEST (*Federación de Asociaciones de Estudiantes*), CANAE (*Confederación Estatal de Asociaciones de Estudiantes*) and CREUP (*Coordinadora de Representantes de Estudiantes de Universidades Públicas*).
6 www.crue.org, retrieved 9 December 2013.
7 The bank's global division is responsible for the project Universia, a global network of universities. News about Bologna is often posted on the project's website: "Bologna improves the quality of higher education", www.universia. es, retrieved 5 December 2013.

## References

Bernecker, Walther L. (2008) "Politik zwischen Konsens und Konfrontation: Spanien im 21. Jahrhundert", in Walther L. Bernecker, ed., *Spanien heute. Politik, Wirtschaft, Kultur*, Frankfurt: Vervuert, 85–106.
Bonal, Xavier (2000) "Interest Groups and the State in Contemporary Spanish Education Policy", *Journal of Education Policy*, 15(2), 201–16.
Bonal, Xavier and Aina Tarabini (2012) "The Role of PISA in Shaping Hegemonic Educational Discourses, Policies and Practices: the Case of Spain", *Research in Comparative and International Education*, 8(3), 335–41.
El País (2011) "A más salario, mejor nota", 10 February 2011.
Egido Gálvez, Imaculada (2011) "Cambios y dilemmas en la formación del profesorado (1961–2011). Ciencuenta años de historia de España en perspectiva europea", *Tendencias Pedagogicas*, 18, 33–50.
European Commission (2012) *The European Higher Education Area in 2012: Bologna Process Implementation Report*, http://eacea.ec.europa.eu/education/eurydice/documents/thematic_reports/138EN.pdf, retrieved 10 December 2013.
Feito Alonso, Rafael (2011) *Los Retos de la Participación Escolar. Elección, Control y Gestión de los Centros Educativos*, Madrid: Morata.
Hernández Sandoica, Elena (2009) "La Crisis de la Universidad", in Walther L. Bernecker, Diego Iñiguez Hernández and Günther Maihold, eds., *Crisis? Qué Crisis? España en Busca de su Camino*, Madrid: Vervuert, 237–72.
Hirschman, Albert O. (1970) *Exit, Voice and Loyalty. Responses to Decline in Forms, Organizations, and States*, Cambridge: Cambridge University Press.
Marchesi, Álvaro (2006) "El Informe PISA y la política Eucativa en España. Revista de Educación", *Extraordinario: PISA. Programa para la Evaluación Internacional de Alumnos*, 315–55.
Martínez Usarralde, Maria Jesús (2010) "Spanien", in Hans Döbert, Wolfgang Hörner, Botho von Kopp and Lutz R. Reuter, eds., *Die Bildungssysteme Europas*, Baltmannsweiler: Schneider, 735–48.
Massot Verdú, Margarida, Gerard Esteban Ferrer and Ferran Ferrer Julia (2006) "El Estudio PISA y la Comunidad Educativa. Percepciones y Opiniones sobre el Proyecto PISA 2000 en Espana Revista de Educación", *Extraordinario: PISA. Programa para la Evaluación Internacional de Alumnos*, 381–98.
MECD – Ministerio de Educación, Cultura y Deporte (2013) *PISA 2012. Programa para la Evaluación Internacional de los Alumnos. Informe Español. Volumen I: Resultados y Contexto*. Madrid: MECD.
OECD (2012) *Education at a Glance. OECD Indicators 2012. Country Note: Spain*, http://www.oecd.org/edu/EAG2012%20-%20Country%20note%20-%20Spain.pdf, retrieved 10 December 2013.

Pereya, Miguel A. (2002) "Changing Educational Governance in Spain: Decentralisation and Control in the Autonomous Communities", *European Educational Research Journal*, 1(4), 667–75.

Popp, Marie (2010) "Spanien – Konkurrierende Leitideen beim PISA-Absteiger", in Philipp Knodel, Kerstin Martens, Daniel de Olano and Marie Popp, eds., *Das PISA-Echo. Internationale Reaktionen auf die Bildungsstudie*, Frankfurt: Campus, 145–69.

Salaburu, Pello, Guy Haug and José-Ginés Mora (2011) *España y el Proceso de Bolonia. Un Encuentro Imprescindible*, Madrid: Academia Europea de Ciencias y Artes.

# 8
## Cooperation or Conflict? Education Politics in Switzerland after the PISA Study and the Bologna Process

*Tonia Bieber*

### Introduction

In the past 15 years, education policy-making in Switzerland has experienced important changes. In the field of Swiss secondary education, international school rankings turned out to be major drivers of policy change. The Programme for International Student Assessment (PISA) of the Organisation for Economic Co-operation and Development (OECD) has been the most prominent example of such comparative evaluations of student skills. In the Swiss higher education sector, European and transnational influences led to diverse governance changes as well as structure-related reform activities. Above all, the European Bologna Process emerged as a novel approach in harmonizing the diverse cantonal study structures in Switzerland.

Being a small non-EU member state with an inimitable decentralized educational tradition, federalist Switzerland is a special case when it comes to internationalization. Over the last decade, the soft governance of international organizations has resulted in far-reaching structural and governance-related change in the Swiss education landscape. This relationship has been the investigation of several academic studies (Benninghoff and Leresche 2009; Griessen and Braun 2010; Trampusch and Mach 2011; Bieber 2012). The country succeeded in introducing new forms of steering to better coordinate its education systems: the political power relationships of federal and cantonal players in Switzerland have experienced trends towards harmonization. In addition, new policies were passed to foster equity and access as well as modernize the relationship between education providers and state authorities.

Being not throughout excellent but, in some areas, also of medium quality, Swiss results in the PISA Study have contributed to the aggravation of existing pressure to harmonize structures of secondary education. In addition, references to the comparative result of this OECD study served as an argument to legitimate political reform activities, which include the various aims of Swiss conservatives, social democrats, liberals, and leftists against the resistance of the right-wing populists (Bieber 2012). In higher education, university rankings, the Bologna Process, and the rising importance of education as a source of economic wealth in information societies triggered new modes of governance and renewal of previous study structures (Bieber and Martens 2011; Bieber 2012; Criblez 2008b). As a consequence, output orientation and evidence-based policy-making have come to the forefront, which also has been the case in Germany (see Niemann, chapter 4 in this volume).

By contrast, it has rarely been assessed how these new policies have actually changed the level of politics. In this contribution, therefore, I aim to assess in which ways the new policies in the Swiss education field have influenced its political processes and the underlying political opportunity structures. How do the main stakeholders concerned perceive and evaluate the change in politics as a result of the internationalization of the political decision-making processes in education at the secondary- and higher-education level? Do they accept the new policy frameworks in terms of *loyalty,* express *voice,* or even seek *exit* opportunities?

This chapter demonstrates that the consequences are mainly perceived positively in Switzerland by the involved actor groups in education (*loyalty*).[1] Like in Germany but in sharp contrast to France (see Niemann and Dobbins, chapters 4 and 5 in this volume), few political actors see recent reforms critically and protest (*voice*) or even opt for the *exit* strategy; they mainly refer to technical implementation problems. In addition, I show that the Swiss actors' constellation in reaction to reforms facilitated by PISA and Bologna did not fundamentally change.

Overall, this chapter intends to provide insights into the impact of policies induced by internationalization on education politics in Switzerland. In this context, the *new constellation of statehood* in education policy and its consequences in secondary and higher education can be conceived as the independent variable. The reactions of the affected political actors to internationalization are regarded as the dependent variable and are categorized in line with the typology of *loyalty, voice,* and *exit* (Hirschman 1970). According to the theoretical framework (see introductory chapter by Knodel et al. in this volume), reactions are expected to hinge on actors' patterns of interpretation, organizational capacity, and specific interests. The domestic political opportunity structures and the rational calculations of actors offer explanatory power in assessing their choices and reactions to policy changes.

The chapter is structured as follows. First, the overall Swiss education polity, political opportunity structures, and actor groups' resources for political participation are presented. Second, for the field of secondary education, the reactions of actors to the *new constellation of the state* and the consequences of this internationalization are investigated. Against the background of far-reaching transformations in educational statehood due to international initiatives such as PISA, I demonstrate that the political reactions turned out to be rather temperate and mostly *loyal* to the reforms. Third, I present the reactions to the recent reform activities in the higher education arena. As an answer to changes in Swiss higher education based on the Bologna Process, reactions of *loyalty* were predominant. Fourth, I highlight the main findings and the consequences of this internationalization for Swiss education politics.

## Political opportunity structures and relevant actors in the education field

The historic policy-making and negotiation processes in Switzerland's education system reflect the country's federal fragmentation, consociationalist politics, and direct-democratic principles. In addition, the Swiss political culture of autonomy, multilingualism, and multiculturalism play a great role. The cantons principally have legal competencies in the education field. With a total of 26 education systems, the cantons have always had extensive autonomy in school matters, which in the 19th century resulted in diverse governance challenges regarding domestic mobility and recognition of degrees. According to consociationalism, associations of concerned actors are included in the policy-making process on a prelegislative basis (*Vernehmlassung*), which enables them to participate and, thus, guarantees a high degree of consensual decision-making.

These traditional Swiss principles involve many instances for the use of the veto right, which complicates collaboration with other countries and international organizations. However, increasing demands for international cooperation as a precondition for competitiveness required stronger domestic coordination of the cantonal systems to enable

Switzerland to act as a global player in the education field in a coherent and strategic manner. In the last decade, Switzerland succeeded in better coordinating its education systems: the political power relationships of federal and cantonal players have experienced tendencies of harmonization.

The Swiss constellation of educational actors mainly consists of five groups: state institutions, education providers and demanders, employer representatives, and civil society.

In the spirit of cooperative federalism, three different state actor groups, namely Federation, communities, and cantons share power over education and culture, primarily based on the Federal Constitution of 2006 (Art. 61a). Swiss sectors of secondary and higher education are presided over by different political authorities and funded in different ways. While secondary education is still under cantonal authority, the responsibilities for higher education are shared between the cantons and the Federation.[2] Consequently, both sectors exhibit strong variances in their legislative and funding responsibilities, with cantonal responsibility for obligatory schooling, cantonal universities and universities of teacher education, and federal responsibility for universities of applied sciences, the two federal institutes of technology, and *Höhere Fachschulen* (Benninghoff and Leresche 2009: 207). However, from 2012 on, the higher education area, which embraces universities, universities of applied sciences, and universities of teacher education, has been steered jointly by the Federation and the cantons (Art. 63a BV).

The cantonal education departments have primary responsibility for education and culture and coordinate at the intercantonal level via the Swiss Conference of Cantonal Ministers of Education (EDK). This organization represents the cantons and is the traditional guardian of diversity within the Swiss education system (Osterwalder and Weber 2004: 14). The foundations for its work are legally binding intercantonal agreements, so-called concordats. The intercantonal Swiss Council of universities of applied sciences is the strategic political organ for intercantonal cooperation concerning universities of applied sciences and is the steering organ for universities of teacher education. It represents the seven Swiss regions with universities of applied sciences through cantonal education directors and assumes coordinative tasks jointly with the Federation.

Significantly, until 2013 a single education ministry has been lacking in Switzerland. At the federal level, responsibility for higher education institutions has been divided between two federal education authorities with different responsibilities: the State Secretariat for Education and Research (SBFI) and the Federal Office for Professional Education and Technology (BBT). Located within the Federal Department of Home Affairs, the SBFI was the authority for national and international tasks in general and university education, research, and space; it was also responsible for the *Eidgenössische Technische Hochschule Zürich* and the *École Polytechnique Fédérale de Lausanne*. In contrast, the BBT has been part of the Federal Department of Economic Affairs and supervises vocational education and training, universities of applied sciences, and innovation. Following decades of debate, the demand for uniting the two federal education offices has been realized. Since 2013, the SBFI in the Federal Department of Home Affairs has been dissolved and integrated into the Federal Department of Economic Affairs.

Swiss education providers consist of diverse coordinating organs at the national level and promote cooperation between the different political levels. In the field of secondary education, providers of education consist of the teacher organization *Syndicat des Enseignants Romands* and the umbrella organization of Swiss teachers. Higher education providers consist of representatives of university administrations as well as teaching and research staff, who are represented through unions and professors' associations. Political umbrella organizations in higher education comprise the Swiss University Conference[3] and the EDK's intercantonal council for universities of applied sciences.[4] Academic umbrella organizations include three executive bodies, namely the Swiss Rectors' Conference of Universities, of Universities of Applied Sciences, and of Universities of Teacher Education. These three rectors' conferences represent Swiss higher education institutions. The Rectors' Conference of Universities represents all universities externally and is responsible for the coordination of the executive management of the universities. The Rectors' Conference of Universities of Applied Sciences is an association of seven public and one private university of applied sciences and represents the schools' interests in matters relevant to the Federation, cantons, other institutions in charge of education and research policy, and the general public. The Rectors' Conference of Universities of Teacher Education represents the universities of teacher education.

The actor group of education consumers consists mainly of student representatives, namely the National Union of Students in Switzerland *(Verband schweizerischer Studierendenschaften)* and pupils' representatives. Employers' representatives and trade unions belong to the actor group of Swiss social partners. Swiss trade unions are *economiesuisse*, *Travail. Suisse*, and the *Schweizerische Gewerkschaftsbund*, while employers' representatives include the Swiss Employers' Confederation and the umbrella organization *economiesuisse*. Traditionally, in Switzerland trade unions do not have a big say in politics, let alone in the education field. In contrast, employers' representatives have a strong influence, which has even increased in the last decade.

## Secondary education: the consequences of reforms

The publication of the PISA results on December 7, 2001, posed new challenges to Switzerland. As the country had not participated in the Progress in International Reading Literacy Study (PIRLS) of the International Association for the Evaluation of Educational Achievement (IEA), PISA presented its only source of comparable and reliable data on student performances in secondary education (SKBF 2010; Baechler 2010). The study revealed unexpected shortcomings of the Swiss system, confirming that the quality and equity of Swiss outcomes were often only average. Along with other countries, such as Germany (Niemann 2010: 84) and Denmark, before PISA Switzerland had shared the belief that it had the best education system in the world due to comparatively high public spending on education and its excellent OECD country reviews. PISA's findings therefore resulted in a *Bildungsschock*. The concern grew even bigger as the OECD framed the educational outcomes as an economic issue, where deficits in students' performances would endanger their entrance into working life and consequently hamper economic growth of the national economy. The great variance in students' test scores from different cantons (OECD 2009) increased the existing problem pressure of the lack of harmonization between cantonal education structures.

### Changes in policy-making of secondary education

Swiss PISA findings triggered fierce public and scientific debates on the future of the education system and catapulted the issue to the top of the political agenda. The central question was how to improve the system's structure in order to be capable of playing in the league of PISA 'winners', drawing on a set of potential success factors highlighted by the OECD in a series of international thematic reports in the PISA context (OECD 2004a; 2004b; 2009). Political reform trajectories in Switzerland since the late 1990s show that the *new constellation of the state* in secondary education policy was strongly influenced by the OECD's PISA Study. However, the international PISA events did not reinvent the wheel: the approximate direction of Swiss reforms was already pre-traced by previous discussions and attempts for more harmonization at the domestic level prior to the PISA era. Rather, PISA added the critical mass for reforms to occur and also redirected their course towards a more neo-liberal ideology. Despite the political opportunity structures of federalism and direct democracy, responsible for the weak state in education, PISA even had the force to neutralize the historical contradiction between centripetal and centrifugal forces in Swiss education politics to a certain extent as all actors started to orient on the external policy model, which resulted in harmonization processes.

In Switzerland, the principal reforms concerning secondary education were included in the constitutional revision of 2006, the intercantonal agreement for harmonization of obligatory schooling (HarmoS) of 2007, the language strategy, and the action plan PISA 2000. As a result, political change was tremendous. Comprehensive structural and content-related reforms were introduced within the framework of HarmoS. Reflecting the economic OECD ideology, these policies focused on promoting social integration and equity of chances. Likewise, the OECD's principles of accountability and efficiency (Morgan 2009) found an entrance into Swiss policies. The conception of education as a factor for personality development and civil right according to Dahrendorf (1965) moved towards the idea of education as tradable service within a market (Kehm 2003). This implied a paradigm change from input-orientation towards a logic of steering that aims at efficiency and controlling the output of education systems (Eckert 2009: 272; SKBF 2010: 55; Bieber 2010b). For Switzerland, the introduction of national education standards led to a stronger consideration of student competences and implied an entrance into a previously alien culture of testing, with regards to PISA.

These new policies impacted the arrangements of domestic actors in education politics. First, they implied new governance modes of evidence-based politics and provided new actors, such as the quality assurance organization and the Swiss university conference (SUK), with a say in education policy-making. As this development also entailed a novel output-based view of measurable performance and scientification, a key role was provided for scientific consultants to integrate evaluation procedures and systems for performance measurement of students. Second, the new policies changed the relation of the federal government and cantons towards more centralization (Criblez 2008b: 279). Third, the cantonal ministers of education started to foster cooperation within the EDK. As a result, the power of this coordinative institution has augmented since the 1970s particularly in furthering harmonization, which involved a slowly growing assimilation of the cantonal systems (Criblez 2008a; Bieber 2012).

The Swiss reforms were also stimulated by a novel competition in the secondary education area: from the results of the best-scoring countries, the OECD derived proposals for countries on how best to improve their system in order to assert themselves in increasing global economic competition. In Switzerland, these suggestions were adopted as there already existed an ongoing struggle on the degree of centralization for secondary education policy-making. The OECD provided Switzerland with policy advice, which was impressively reflected by the contents of the HarmoS reform. For example, Swiss lessons included a focus on school autonomy and the individualization of learning processes. The PISA findings on the remarkable deficits of the Swiss education system increased the reform dynamics in Swiss politics, which started to orient itself towards the OECD's best practice policies to dissolve the long-standing backlog.

However, one cannot regard PISA as the only trigger to political reforms in Swiss education. Rather, the high degree of domestic problem pressure that existed was the starting point for reforms in Switzerland, making it favourable for PISA to take effect. The PISA results of the internationally renowned OECD fell on fertile ground because they served reform protagonists – especially the federal actors that strived for more centralization of education politics – as an international scientific argument for legitimizing a wide spectrum of political positions, which enabled broad reform coalitions and eased the implementation of past-due reforms.

**Reactions of relevant actors in secondary education**

The education reforms in Switzerland have evoked different reactions from the concerned groups of actors. In the following, I will assume an actor-centred perspective to present the reactions of the main actors. The stakeholder types range from public state actors over social partners to school administrations and pupils. All in all, the reactions were close to *loyalty*. The political resistance of Swiss policy actors to the *new constellation of the Swiss state* in secondary education policy, especially with the introduction of the famous PISA-facilitated reform HarmoS, was rather low. This was because the PISA Study provided a unique chance to solve problems of international and domestic character, namely the insufficient scoring in the international PISA test and the lack of harmonization in the Swiss cantonal systems.

*State actors*

In Swiss secondary education, the state actors include the federal government called Federal Council, the federal ministries of SBFI and BBT, as well as the cantons represented by the EDK. In the federal council, the governing political parties stress different aspects of the HarmoS reform (Bieber 2010b). The Christian Democratic People's Party (CVP) focuses on early school enrolment and furthering language skills of schoolchildren, while the Free Democratic Party (FDP) underlines the political measures of school enrolment at an early age, free choice of school, and evaluation of student performances. In order to enhance equal opportunities, the Social Democratic Party (SP) intends to diminish the dependency of schoolchildren's performance on their socio-economic background by improving support structures including free day schools for all students and education plans for daycare and early learning centres.

The EDK has proposed the agenda for the intercantonal HarmoS project and still sticks to its positive evaluation of both the goals and the implementation of this harmonization reform (Interview CH 02). However, it is ambivalent on the new orientation on pupils' competencies, which has been introduced along with the HarmoS reform. Orientation on competences of students is appreciated; however, the EDK states that this cannot replace the learning content in the curricula. In addition, not every instance of learning that takes place can be illustrated by a specific competence. In the opinion of the EDK, education is more than what large-scale assessments are able to measure, and it criticizes the disregard of this fact in the discussions around the PISA Study (Interview CH 02).

Some reforms induced by PISA have been temporarily blocked, which was possible due to the Swiss political opportunity structure that includes many veto players such as the people (through referendums), cantons, and the Federation. In this line, the Swiss-wide introduction of the HarmoS concordat was impeded for a time; however, it was implemented in the majority of cantons. Next to parental forums and citizens' committees, the conservative political parties, the Young Liberals of Switzerland (jfs) and the Federal Democratic Union of Switzerland (EDU) hindered its implementation in some cantons. However, the major impetus to block the reform came from the Swiss People's Party (SVP) and *Junge SVP* in the cantons of Nidwalden, Lucerne, Thurgau, Aargau, Grisons, Zug, and Uri (Künzli et al. 2011). The SVP doubted the credibility of the PISA results and opposed reforms that were promoted in the PISA context by the other parties, reforms such as early school enrolment and daycare facilities in educational institutions. It lamented the overload of education offers and the abolishment of the kindergarten due to the introduction of an obligatory basic school level (Hagenbüchle 2004). As a consequence, the SVP launched a campaign named '*HarmoS ist nicht harmlos'*,[5] advertising against the accession of cantons to the intercantonal concordat. A facultative referendum was requested in 14 of 26 cantons, predominantly by the SVP. In these 14 German-speaking cantons, half of the referenda were successful, hindering HarmoS. The other half failed mainly due to increasing pressures of the problems that promoted the harmonization of the cantonal school systems' structures and curricula, which resulted in the introduction of HarmoS.[6] Thus, the conservative forces were not successful in their attempt to prevent the common consent to the HarmoS reform.

In sum, the leverage potential of the PISA Study was to some degree hindered by conservative players who called for a referendum against HarmoS. Thus the Swiss-wide implementation of the HarmoS reforms were blocked, resulting in a "two-speed Switzerland": the group of cantons that joined HarmoS and those refusing to accede to the concordat.

### Education providers

In Switzerland, education providers consist of the teachers' organization *Syndicat des Enseignants Romands* and the umbrella organization of Swiss teachers (*Lehrerverband Schweiz*, LCH). The teachers' organization stressed its general support of HarmoS itself because this reform was approved by the will of the people. It stated that it would express criticism concerning the conditions of implementation when the EDK reports on the realization of HarmoS in 2015 (Interview CH 04). The actual conditions of the school system and the trend towards harmonization were criticized, especially the teaching of foreign languages in primary school, which would need more assistance in terms of staff and funding. Likewise, the cancelling of team teaching and teaching in big groups were regarded negatively (Interview CH 04). In contrast to employers' associations, the teachers' organization assumes a critical attitude concerning the rising influence of inter-institutional competition in the education arena. Rather, it proposes to improve collaboration among the different education providers.

### Employers' representatives

Employers' representatives in Switzerland include the Swiss Employers' Confederation (SAV) and the umbrella organization *economiesuisse* of the Swiss economy. They welcomed the reforms of HarmoS induced by the PISA Study but underlined the necessity to push them further (Interview CH 01). Most of all, they stated that HarmoS and the *Lehrplan 21* only include the introduction of two foreign languages at the primary education level, but all other parameters have remained the same. In addition, the foreign languages after the primary level diverge between cantons, impeding mobility. *Economiesuisse,* in particular, demanded to facilitate mobility by making the school systems more comparable, especially in the field of compulsory education. This would also promote a system of competition among the different cantonal school systems (Interview CH 01). Contrary to the consensual culture in education politics, *economiesuisse* also expressed criticism in terms of the cooperative structures within the Swiss education system. Particularly, this concerned the collaboration with the major player, the EDK, which is regarded as a non-democratically legitimized institution. Moreover, the influence of *economiesuisse* addresses mainly the Federation, not the cantons (Interview CH 01).

## Summary

In Switzerland, the weak state power in the field of secondary education provides stakeholders with a variety of possibilities to access the political system. The standard procedure through which Swiss actors exert their influence is lobbying and normally involves reactions of *loyalty*; *voice* – or even *exit* – are used only as secondary means of expressing their respective political position. In order to raise their *voices*, the individual Swiss stakeholders depend on obtainable resources and utilize them to lobby for their opinion by providing empirical facts and arguments. In this section I have shown that political reactions in secondary education policy-making facilitated by internationalization processes and strong domestic problem pressure do not substantially diverge between the single relevant actors affected by education reforms. The majority of groups evaluate the change in politics positively, so that *loyalty* to PISA-induced reform processes in secondary education is the most frequent reaction to policy change – even among those actors that often block these policies in other countries (see Dobbins, chapter 6 in this volume). There may be three reasons for this fact. First, the specific nature of Swiss education politics, such as its highly consensual policy-making apparatus, makes *loyalty* and cooperative activities the most effective problem-solving strategy. Second, the great acceptance is due to backlog in the period before and the actors' perception that their specific situation was improved by the recent education reforms. Third, policy changes were regarded to be effective in reducing the existing problem pressure and drawbacks of the system. In contrast, the use of *voice*, such as protests and strikes, to hinder reforms has been rare, which is mostly because of the historical background of Swiss education and the traditional idea of education politics that is marked by a highly consensual system of cooperation between the state and concerned civil society interest groups. Finally, the tactic of *exit* was rarely chosen as a strategic option by corporate actors.

## Higher education: the consequences of reforms

While the period from the 1980s until the mid-1990s had experienced a backlog of reforms in Swiss university education, internationalization marked a range of higher education reforms in the last decade. Europeanization, the Lisbon strategy, international rankings of universities, globalization, and other international developments have facilitated far-reaching policy change in Switzerland. But most of all, it was the participation of the non-EU member country in the intergovernmental Bologna Process that fundamentally changed its higher education landscape (Bieber 2010a, Criblez 2008b: 281, Interview CH 07). As the country strongly needed reforms in the education field, actors used the window of opportunity to implement policy change in higher education.

### Changes in policy-making of higher education

Most of the Swiss transformations in the higher education landscape from the mid-1990s until today were brought about by the international undertaking of Bologna. A high number of far-reaching structural, rather than content-related, reforms were implemented by way of the constitutional revision, framework legislation for universities (UFG law) and universities of applied sciences (FHSG law), Bologna directives, and directives for quality assurance and accreditation. In addition, the law on the coordination and financing of universities (HFKG law) of 2012 introduced extensive policy amendments. Although some reform elements had already been discussed before Bologna, the majority of changes presented novelties to the Swiss system.

Changes in the sphere of polity resulted in transformations of politics by furthering vertical cooperation and coordination. The constitutional amendment provided the Federation and cantons with the joint responsibility for quality and permeability of higher education, which promoted vertical cooperation. However, the danger of a joint decision trap remained rather low because of the introduction of new institutional mechanisms: federal power vis-à-vis the cantons was increased, as the Federation was enabled to regulate if cantons failed to coordinate (Benninghoff and Leresche 2009: 208). In addition, the new constitutional provision of permeability required the development of a law that allowed for more coordination (HFKG law). According to this law, the three institutional pillars of Swiss higher education – universities, universities of applied sciences, and universities of teacher education – would be organized by one single higher education conference and by one single rectors' conference instead of three organizations. In other words, the tripartite structure of the higher education landscape would be reduced to one single organization and thus lead to an enormous simplification for both policy-makers and students. However, the dimension of politics also changed independently of constitutional amendments. There was an increase in power of the common organ SUK of the Federation and cantons, which was given more rights by the federal law on universities (UFG law). This increase in cooperative federalism, a genuine Swiss principle dating back to its foundation in 1848, blurred the clear vertical division of powers.[7]

At the policy level, Bologna resulted in a paradigm change from the Swiss focus on *Humboldtian* ideas towards a more economic worldview of education. Policies reflect a shift in the concepts from education as a means for humanistic personality formation and civil right (Dahrendorf 1965) towards education as a tool for promoting international employability and as a tradable good (Kehm 2003: 13). This trend is reflected by an increase of systems for performance measurement and rankings in higher education, the General Agreement on Trades in Services (GATS), the perception of students as clients, and enforced discussions on increasing study fees.

In terms of policy changes, bachelor's and master's studies as well as the doctoral cycle were introduced by the laws of UFG and FHSG and Bologna directives. Quality assurance and accreditation were addressed by corresponding directives. As a result of these legal acts, the conditions for establishing a European Higher Education Area have mostly been fulfilled. By the official Bologna deadline in 2010, Switzerland had reached a high degree of policy compliance with the international model. Compared to other Bologna countries, such as Austria, France, Germany, and Belgium, the liberal conservative country turned out to be a political "poster child" regarding both the speed and comprehensiveness of implementing the European Bologna reform (Universität Zürich 2009; Rauhvargers et al. 2009). Changes in Great Britain and the U.S. were rather negligible; Germany, on the other hand, underwent similarly strong changes as Switzerland (Martens et al. 2010). But while Germany transferred higher education competences from the Federation to the sub-national level, Switzerland experienced processes of centralization.

Astonishingly, these reforms have been possible despite the fact that Switzerland exhibits a reform-adverse political opportunity structure including referenda and two parliamentary chambers with highly diverse political positions. This paradoxical finding of a strong change in a federal state is due to the logic of multilevel games, according to which national actors promote Europeanization in order to overcome blockades in national reforms (see also Martens and Wolf 2006; Trampusch and Busemeyer 2010: 601). As the Bologna arena provided opportunities to reform the existing higher education system, the numerous veto players were circumvented in a unique way, which also posed questions about the democratic legitimacy of the decision-making procedures (Benninghoff and Leresche 2009). In this way, overdue reforms could be finally realized.

In sum, the Bologna Process has played a core role for the establishment of the latest reforms in the Swiss higher education arena, which resulted in a high degree of implementation of the European model. It had an immense influence on the Swiss *constellation of the state* in higher education policy-making by way of soft governance mechanisms, and the reform-blocking political opportunity structure was not as influential as expected.

### Reactions of relevant actors in Swiss higher education

Against the background of tremendous reforms in education, the reactions of Swiss political actors were rather moderate. In Switzerland, the assessment of the Bologna agenda was highly positive, and education politicians in general supported the broad goal of the European Higher Education Area (Bologna Declaration 1999). On the whole, general criticism of the idea behind the Bologna Process is quite rare. Rather, policy actors in the education field appear as reform proponents or underline the need for a better implementation of the single aims. However, the respective reaction depends on the class of the corporate stakeholder. Political and administrative actors tend to judge the phenomenon positively while student organizations and their representatives tend to have a more critical position or stress the need for ameliorating the implementation procedure, for example, by including more strongly the actors concerned by the policy changes, such as university members. The opinions of higher education institutes are split, with the humanities faculties refusing and the natural sciences approbating the reform process in Swiss higher education.

*Education consumers*

In the group of education consumers in Switzerland, the National Union of Students in Switzerland (VSS) takes a predominant position. The most important partners for cooperation of the student organization are the rectors' conferences, the EDK, and the federal state authorities. In addition, trade unions are crucial partners when it comes to the launch of initiatives, such as the stipends initiative. For the student organization, not only financial resources matter, but also ideational assistance, such as by the Swiss science academies.

In general, *loyalty* and moderate *voice* are the most common strategic reactions of the VSS. This is also due to the Swiss political opportunity structures, including consensus democracy. The basic strategy is cooperation with the political structures that are able to make decisions: the offices of education, state secretariats, and the utilization of the democratic means that they possess. In the last decade, there have been discussions about a more activist presence. The association also strongly collaborates institutionally with other organs such as the rectors' conferences, directors of education, and the Parliament, in order to exert political influence, especially during the prelegislative phase of the *Vernehmlassung* (Interview CH 05).

The reactions of *voice* by the Swiss student organization to the introduction of the Bologna reforms refer in the majority of cases to the implementation of policy changes, rarely to the reforms themselves. The VSS created a coalition with trade unions to change perceived problematic reform directions. The Bologna Process was often regarded critically because it has resulted in various problems. Before introducing respective national reforms, the organization would have welcomed being included in the political debates on how to cope with challenges, and not being subject to a top-down regulated European reform (Interview CH 05).

As protests were not successful, the student organization supported and participated in the education strike of 2009. Two main addressees of the students' *voice* reaction were present: the state and the higher education institutions themselves. The state authorities were requested to counteract the negative reform consequences by granting more flexibility and less detailed prescriptions, while university administrations were approached to allow for better accessibility to master's programmes and less strict study curricula.

The Swiss student organization joined the international education strikes and protests in 2009 in the "Global Week of Action" in Italy, Austria, France, Switzerland, Poland, and Germany, which included manifestations, demonstrations, and school blockades (Interview CH 05). Under the international slogan "Education is NOT for $A£€!", commercialization and privatization of public education was protested against. In addition, attention was drawn to the miserable conditions and the lack of free access to education. Students of the University of

Basel protested against too high study fees, the marketization of higher education, and the university council. They occupied the auditorium of the University of Basel, and different actions, such as concerts and poetry slams, drew Swiss-wide attention. The next day, university rector Antonio Loprieno joined discussions with students who posed their demands. Students pushed for less school-like teaching (*Verschulung*) and more transparency in the awarding of European Credit Transfer System (ECTS) credits and their unification. In addition, criticism concerned the insufficient improvement of international student mobility through the Bologna reform.

The main criticism of the student organization refers to the Bologna aim of the social dimension in higher education. In order to increase access to higher education, Switzerland runs a student grant system, which is the responsibility of the cantons. Concerning the living and studying conditions of students, Switzerland has established a nationwide statistical system for monitoring the situation, conducts extensive research on the subject, and provides access to public guidance and counselling (Bieber 2012). As the implementation of the Bologna Process entailed a *Verschulung* in Switzerland, the European reform brought additional difficulties concerning the Swiss stipend systems. Students were more strongly controlled, which complicated the chances of finding a part-time job (Interview CH 05). The student organization criticizes the lack of measures towards the goal of introducing domestic harmonization of and minimal standards for its student grant system. A huge challenge in Switzerland is that two students who attend the same university but live in two villages of a distance of some kilometers can be subject to totally different stipend systems depending on the canton where they live, the conditions of their parents, and the financial conditions (Interview CH 05). In order to increase the harmonization of grants, a federal grants system is intended to be established based on the educational constitution of 2006. In regards to the reduction of supportive funding through stipends, the assignment of more loans than stipends was often regarded as a step backwards. Reforms of the national grants and loans system (*Stipendien*) in higher education was successfully achieved by the student organization with the implementation of the 'grants initiative' in 2012, which they launched in 2010.

### State actors

In the group of state authorities, there was in principle no dissent about the positive evaluation of Bologna reforms, and the core goals of the Bologna Process are not questioned. The federal state actors are highly committed in consolidating the Bologna Process in terms of *loyalty*. There is no fundamental criticism of Bologna, only higher awareness of potential disadvantages of this new study system. Support for the Bologna aims has not changed and there is no movement to undo the reforms. Politicians expect rectors to address the negative collateral effects through collaboration with students and non-professorial academic staff and make improvements to the system (Interview CH 02).

In order to better identify the critical consequences of the Swiss higher education reforms, federal authorities provided a set of educational data. Since 2006, the 'education report', for example, includes statistics and data on the complete education system (BFS 2010). Moreover, the federal statistical office, BFS, regularly carries out student surveys to monitor the social situation of students (BFS 2005) and statistical surveys exist at the labour-force level (BFS 2007). Since 2008, Switzerland has participated in the Eurostudent project as a full partner. Based on this project, the BFS published a report that provides more background information and compares in detail the situation in Switzerland with other European countries (BFS 2007).

In addition, the Swiss Conference of Cantonal Education Ministers stated that the level of politics has been tremendously influenced by the Bologna-induced reforms in Switzerland (Interview CH 02). This concerns especially the cooperation of the different state levels in education. In this line, a representative commented that such projects of internationalization have strongly stimulated the cooperation between the Federation and cantons, meaning the vertical, federal cooperation that was made a constitutional duty in 2006; in addition, inter-cantonal cooperation was inserted into the constitution. This is in sharp contrast to the German situation that in the same year included the so-called interdiction of cooperation into its constitution. In general, the fostering of cooperation within the Swiss education landscape is regarded as a positive side effect of internationalization due to Bologna (Interview CH 02).

*Education providers*

In Switzerland, higher education providers such as representatives of university administrations and of teaching and research staff do not strongly differ regarding their reactions. In general, they regard the reforms facilitated by the Bologna Process to be effective. However, there are diverging opinions as to future developments. The SUK supported the goals of the Bologna Process because it provided an opportunity to revise university teaching (Benninghoff and Leresche 2009: 205). Likewise, the

Rectors' Conference of Universities of Applied Sciences (KFH) encourages the principle goals of the Swiss Bologna reforms (Interview CH 03). The means of influence of education providers mainly consists in the provision of information: the outward strategy based on information and communication is to engage in public relations and explain to the working world the structure and meaning of a bachelor's and a master's degree in relation to the former diploma degrees. They also invite universities of applied sciences to communicate in a more active way what kind of study courses they provide, both to their students and potential employers (Interview CH 03).

*Employers' representatives*

Swiss employers' representatives evaluated Bologna reforms positively and also lobbied for this position at different occasions. The Swiss business sector, especially the organization *economiesuisse,* supported the broad reform process with the aim of mobility promotion, international comparability, and reducing the length of study programmes, and of a qualitative and structural adjustment of higher education, decreasing the age of graduates entering the labour market (Benninghoff and Leresche 2009: 205, Interview CH 01). However, it criticizes that the reforms have not been as effective as desired and that the courses of study would never be comparable to each other. The association demanded that the aims be implemented more deeply and comprehensively and expressed criticism in terms of *voice* that this reform has not been as far-reaching as necessary. Particularly, it states that the competition of the single higher education institutions has not been promoted sufficiently by the Swiss Bologna reforms, which stands in sharp contrast to the position of the teachers' union, LCH, that aims to lower the influence of competitive processes in the education field. As a result, the expectations of employers have not been fully met by the Bologna Process (Interview CH 01).

### Summary

Overall, the general ideas of the reforms induced by the Bologna Process were more accepted than its actual realization in Switzerland. Most actors supported the reform goal of contributing to the establishment of a European Higher Education Area and promoting mobility and employability of students. Their motives were situated in meeting the strong domestic need for higher education reforms both in teaching and governance structures. However, criticism concerned the way in which reforms were finally implemented, especially the lack of inclusion of concerned actors, such as student representatives who saw their decision-making capacities dwindling.

Returning to the theoretical framework, the intensity of reactions of the policy actors concerned did not correspond with the intensity of the transformation of the *state's constellation* in the education sector. Compared to secondary education, the field of higher education showed similar reaction patterns. *Loyalty* was by far the most frequent response to the current reforms in higher education, such as employability of graduates, quality assurance of teaching, and a focus on learning outcomes. This was because of actors' willingness to overcome backlog and utilize reform projects for realizing their own political aims. However, actors substantially diverged in the intensity of their *loyalty* expressions. Quality assurance and accreditation were broadly supported as well as reforms concerning the new study structures. By contrast, *loyalty* towards the actual arrangement of the social dimension of the Bologna Process was less pronounced and more debated. *Loyalty* also included the wish of actors for more far-reaching reforms. For example, the student organization VSS proposed to back the mobility of students by improving access to student stipends and other financial resources. The choice of *voice* against the Bologna reforms was rare as policy actors did not want to be accused of blocking necessary reform processes. However, trade unions expressed protest because of the distinct economic orientation of reform proposals. In addition, they *voiced* that universities lacked financial resources and technical assistance for reform implementation. In contrast, *exit* is a political option which has not occurred in consociationalist Switzerland.

## Conclusion

Having experienced a multitude of comprehensive reforms in the last decade, the Swiss education landscape aimed at a consolidation of the passed reform projects. This chapter assessed the impact of these new internationally induced education policies in Switzerland on its education politics and provided a stocktaking of the country-specific reaction patterns to the change in secondary and higher education. Particularly, I analysed in which way the policies caused by the international initiatives of the PISA Study and the Bologna Process influenced Swiss political opportunity structures.

Drawing on the categories of corporate actors' reactions – *voice, exit,* and *loyalty* – Swiss education indeed presents a special case as the intensity of reactions did not correspond with the far-reaching transformations of the education sector. As assumed according to the theoretical framework, I have shown that reactions in both secondary and higher education could often be categorized as *loyalty*. In comparison with other countries, such as England (see Knodel, chapter 6 in this volume) or France (see Dobbins, chapter 5 in this volume), Switzerland showed more *loyalty* to the reforms, which may be due to the idiosyncratic political opportunity structures of consociationalist democratic elements of Swiss politics.

In general, the corporate actors' reactions strongly depend on both the political resources that are accessible to them, such as financial and ideational support, as well as the characteristic domestic structures of political opportunity. The high degree of decentralization and the consensus-oriented political system make Switzerland a weak state in education, which facilitates political participation. Actors spread their political positions by lobbying the normal points of entrance, such as the pre-legislative process of *Vernehmlassung* of the actors concerned. For example, trade unions and student organizations launched their own political campaigns, initiatives, and reports in order to provide the broader public with knowledge on their position.

The chapter has demonstrated that the consequences of education reform for Switzerland have been mainly perceived positively by the actor groups involved. Most of the Swiss actors have reacted with general approval and support (*loyalty*) of the achieved policy changes of the education system, even if the reforms are not fully implemented yet. This is mainly because they intended to use both international initiatives for legitimizing long-overdue reforms to renew teaching and to disentangle the complex policy-making structures, in addition to consensus-oriented policy-making. As in Germany (see Niemann, chapter 4 in this volume) and in sharp contrast to France (see Dobbins, chapter 6 in this volume), only a few political actors see recent reforms critically and show protest (*voice*) or even opt for the *exit* strategy. Criticisms mainly refer to technical implementation problems; most protests target certain elements of the reforms, such as the early schooling of students, not the whole reform as such, and few reform elements such as the introduction of cooperative school structures are controversial. Hence, the rationale behind these *voice* reactions is to improve the whole process. Rather than explicit *voice* against the reforms, this actually was a constructive way of expressing *loyalty*. Critics on technical implementation problems arose from groups such as teachers' and students' organizations that would substantially benefit from a smoother implementation, so these reactions are in line with the theoretical arguments on the rational choice of reactions.

Although their reactions differ significantly, the constellation of Swiss actors stays surprisingly constant. The chapter shows that the actors' constellation in reaction to reforms facilitated by PISA and Bologna did not experience a high degree of transformation. The state governance approach was not fundamentally changed neither in secondary education nor in higher education as the consensus-oriented political process was kept. In secondary education, the political decision-making procedures were not modified as a consequence of the OECD PISA Study's soft governance. Similarly, in higher education the Bologna Process has not had a considerable impact on the actors' constellations within the Swiss political arena. This fact contributes to a general reform-obstructive, conservative policy-making mode that sticks to traditional domestic structures of political opportunity and fits the theoretical assumptions (see introductory chapter by Knodel et al. in this volume).

## Notes

1  In Switzerland, semi-structured expert interviews were conducted in 2012 with the Swiss Conference of Cantonal Ministers of Education (EDK), the Rectors' Conference of the Swiss Universities of Applied Sciences (KFH), the Swiss trade union (*economiesuisse*), the Swiss teachers' association (LCH), and the Swiss student association (VSS).
2  In Switzerland, the sector of vocational education and training, which spans both secondary education-II and higher education, plays a much bigger role than in most other industrial nations and has always been subject to federal control.
3  At the behest of the Swiss university conference (SUK), the Accreditation and Quality Assurance Body (OAQ) fulfills a number of tasks relating to quality assurance and accreditation.
4  For its composition, see http://www.edk.ch/dyn/14623.php, retrieved 31 October 2013.
5  The campaign's title, translated '*HarmoS is not harmless*', alludes to traditional fears of centralization through a central body for educational control, the so-called '*Schulvogt*'.
6  However, the new constitutional articles of 2006 enable the federal government to make the HarmoS concordat binding if many successful referenda would hamper the national coordination of the education area.
7  This tendency was also stated by Obinger et al. (2005: 304) for the field of social policy.

## References

Baechler, Ariane (2010) *Die Bedeutung von PISA aus Bundessicht*, 7 December 2010, BBT.
Benninghoff, Martin and Jean-Philippe Leresche (2009) "The Internationalization of National Decision-Making Processes: The Case of the Bologna Declaration in

Switzerland", in Stéphane Nahrath and Frédéric Varone, eds., *Rediscovering Public Law and Public Administration in Comparative Policy Analysis: A Tribute to Peter Knoepfel*, Lausanne: Presses polytechniques et universitaires romandes, 197–215.

BFS (2005) *Das schweizerische Bildungssystem im europäischen Vergleich. Ausgewählte Indikatoren*, Neuchâtel: Bundesamt für Statistik.

BFS (2007) *Bildungsmosaik Schweiz. Bildungsindikatoren 2007*, Neuchâtel: Bundesamt für Statistik.

BFS (2010) *Das Bildungswesen in der Schweiz*, Neuchâtel: Bundesamt für Statistik.

Bieber, Tonia (2010a) "Europe à la Carte? Swiss Convergence towards European Policy Models in Higher Education and Vocational Education and Training", *Swiss Political Science Review*, 16(4), 773–800.

Bieber, Tonia (2010b) "Schweiz – PISA als Wegbereiter von Reformen", in Philipp Knodel, Kerstin Martens, Daniel de Olano and Marie Popp, eds., *Das PISA-Echo: Internationale Reaktionen auf die Bildungsstudie*, Frankfurt: Campus, 91–114.

Bieber, Tonia (2012) *Voluntary Convergence in Education and Training Policy. The Impact of Soft Governance through the PISA Study, the Bologna Process, and the Copenhagen Process on Switzerland*. Dissertation, Universität Bremen, Institut für Politikwissenschaft.

Bieber, Tonia and Kerstin Martens (2011) "The OECD PISA Study as a Soft Power in Education? Lessons from Switzerland and the U.S.", *European Journal of Education*, 46(1), 101–16.

Bologna Declaration (1999) *The European Higher Education Area*, Joint Declaration of the European Ministers of Education in Bologna, 19 June 1999.

Criblez, Lucien (2008a) *Bildungsraum Schweiz: Historische Entwicklung und aktuelle Herausforderungen*, Bern: Haupt.

Criblez, Lucien (2008b) "Die neue Bildungsverfassung und die Harmonisierung des Bildungswesens", in Lucien Criblez, ed., *Bildungsraum Schweiz: Historische Entwicklung und aktuelle Herausforderungen*, Bern: Haupt, 277–99.

Dahrendorf, Ralf (1965) *Bildung ist Bürgerrecht. Plädoyer für eine aktive Bildungspolitik*, Hamburg: Nannen.

Eckert, Manfred (2009) "Neue Steuerungsinstrumente in der beruflichen Benachteiligtenförderung", in Ute Lange, Sylvia Rahn, Wolfgang Seitter and Randolf Körzel, eds., *Steuerungsprobleme im Bildungswesen. Theorie und Empirie des lebenslangen Lernens*, Wiesbaden: VS, 267–82.

Griessen, Thomas and Dietmar Braun (2010) "Hochschulföderalismus zwischen Kooperationszwang und Blockadegefahr: Deutschland und die Schweiz im Vergleich", *Swiss Political Science Review*, 16(4), 715–46.

Hagenbüchle, Walter (2004) "Der Turm kommt nur langsam ins Lot – Verhaltene Freude über gute Noten in zweiter PISA-Studie", *Neue Zürcher Zeitung* of 8 December 2004.

Hirschman, Albert O. (1970) *Exit, Voice, and Loyalty. Responses to Decline in Forms, Organizations, and States*, Cambridge: Cambridge University Press.

Kehm, Barbara M. (2003) "Vom Regionalen zum Globalen. Auswirkungen auf Institutionen, System und Politik", in Barbara M. Kehm, ed., *Grenzüberschreitungen. Internationalisierung im Hochschulbereich, Themenheft die Hochschule, Special Issue 1*, 6–18.

Künzli, Rudolf, Moritz Rosemund and Anna-Verena Fries (2011) *Zeittafel: Harmonisierung des Schweizerischen Bildungswesens insbesondere in Bezug auf die Harmonisierung der Inhalte und Ziele seit 1848*, Zürich: Lehrplanforschung ch.

Martens, Kerstin, Alexander-Kenneth Nagel, Michael Windzio and Ansgar Weymann eds. (2010) *Transformation of Education Policy,* Basingstoke: Palgrave Macmillan.

Martens, Kerstin and Klaus D. Wolf (2006) "Paradoxien der neuen Staatsräson: Die Internationalisierung der Bildungspolitik in der EU und der OECD", *Zeitschrift für Internationale Beziehungen,* 13(2), 145–76.

Morgan, Clara (2009) *The OECD Programme for International Student Assessment: Unraveling a Knowledge Network,* Saarbrücken: VDM.

Niemann, Dennis (2010) "Turn of the Tide – New Horizons in German Education Policymaking through IO Influence", in Kerstin Martens, Alexander-Kenneth Nagel, Michael Windzio and Ansgar Weymann, eds., *Transformation of Education Policy,* Basingstoke: Palgrave Macmillan, 77–104.

Obinger, Herbert, Klaus Armingeon, Giuliano Bonoli and Fabio Bertozzi (2005) "Switzerland: The Marriage of Direct Democracy and Federalism", in Herbert Obinger, Stephan Leibfried and Francis G. Castles, eds., *Federalism and the Welfare State. New World and European Experiences,* Cambridge: Cambridge University Press, 263–304.

OECD (2004a) *Messages from PISA 2000. The Final Summary Report from the PISA 2000 Survey,* Paris: OECD.

OECD (2004b) *What Makes School Systems Perform? Seeing School Systems through the Prism of PISA,* Paris: OECD.

OECD (2009) *Education Today 2009: The OECD Perspective,* Paris: OECD.

Osterwalder, Fritz and Karl Weber (2004) "Die Internationalisierung der föderalistischen Bildungspolitik", *Schweizerische Zeitschrift für Bildungswissenschaften,* 26(1), 11–32.

Rauhvargers, Andrejs, Cynthia Deane and Wilfried Pauwels (2009) *Bologna Process Stocktaking Report 2009. Report from Working Groups Appointed by the Bologna Follow-up Group to the Ministerial Conference in Leuven/Louvain-la-Neuve, 28–29 April 2009.*

SKBF (2010) *Bildungsbericht Schweiz 2010,* Aarau: Schweizerische Koordinationsstelle für Bildungsforschung.

Trampusch, Christine and Marius R. Busemeyer (2010) "Einleitung: Berufsbildungs- und Hochschulpolitik in der Schweiz, Österreich und Deutschland", *Swiss Political Science Review,* 16(4), 597–615.

Trampusch, Christine and André Mach (2011) *Switzerland in Europe. Continuity and Change in the Swiss Political Economy,* London: Routledge.

Universität Zürich (2009) *Bericht über die 6. nationale Bologna-Tagung der CRUS. Studienbedingungen an den universitären Hochschulen im Bologna-System, 4 September 2008,* Zürich: Universität Zürich.

# 9
# A New Internationalization Trend? The PISA Study, the Bologna Process, and U.S. Education Policy

*Tonia Bieber, Michael Dobbins, Timm Fulge and Kerstin Martens*

## Introduction[1]

In this chapter, we analyse the United States' (U.S.) reactions to international initiatives in education policy. While the country has participated in the Programme for International Student Assessment (PISA) study since its beginning in 2000, the U.S. does not participate in the European Bologna initiative due to its geographical distance. However, the U.S. has assumed observer status in this process since 2005. Overall, the PISA Study and Bologna Process have not triggered any far-reaching reforms in the U.S. In fact, many political actors have only recently noticed these international initiatives. Key policy elements such as output orientation, evidence-based policy-making, an economic understanding of education, and quality assurance were already widespread in the American education system. Hence, the U.S. has shown limited tangible response to PISA, although it continuously has ranked below average. Only recently have policy-makers and stakeholders started to incorporate PISA findings into their decision-making processes. Conversely, Bologna has become a more prominently discussed topic in the higher education policy community mainly for reasons of compatibility with the new European systems. Along these lines, the scattered introduction of European-style, three-year bachelor's programmes at individual U.S. universities provide evidence of the increasing indirect influence of Bologna.

The concepts of *voice, exit,* and *loyalty* of Hirschman (1970) must be especially adapted for the case of the U.S. *Voice* is defined as criticism of the international initiatives. For example, organizations involved with education may comment critically on PISA and Bologna. They may stress American exceptionalism and the incomparability of the U.S. education system, which makes adaptations to policies of other countries or international organizations (IOs) impossible. For secondary education, this may result in the rejection of the PISA results in terms of usability and comparability. In higher education, we obviously do not expect many *voice* reactions as the U.S. is not directly affected by Bologna and already has a highly deregulated, market-oriented higher education system. In contrast to other country cases, the concept of *exit* refers in the U.S. case to ignorance of the international initiatives in terms of an *indirect exit* instead of non-participation. For secondary education, *exit* may refer to the initiatives being unknown or ignored in the U.S. context. It is also plausible that the U.S. or another country may withdraw from PISA. In the higher education sector, *exit* refers to stakeholder strategies that aim to weaken the Bologna system, for example, by proposing a counter-agenda. We describe *loyalty* as situations in which U.S. actors exhibit support for the international initiatives. In secondary education, this refers to policy-makers and think tanks who take the PISA results seriously and actively promote reforms using concepts from the corresponding Organisation for Economic Co-operation and Development (OECD) publications, often to justify their own policy ideas. For higher education, *loyalty* describes a situation in which actors join the "Bologna bandwagon" and initiate reform projects analogous to the European undertaking.

Our empirical study relies on academic literature, policy documents, and semi-structured expert interviews conducted in Washington, D.C, over the last years. Due to the highly decentralized nature of the American political opportunity structure and the high degree of institutional autonomy and privatization, official policy documents from federal or state authorities referring explicitly to Bologna reforms are rare (as an exception, see Spellings 2006). Thus, the documents studied are significant policy papers from prominent internationally focused educational associations and organizations such as the Institute of International Education, the Council of Graduate Schools, the Lumina Foundation, and so on. In addition, we concentrate primarily on national-level actors rather than on single U.S. states or universities. We first describe the education policy-making process in the U.S. We then explore actors' motives and political reactions to PISA and focus on the reactions of higher education organizations to Bologna. For both education sectors, we discuss reactions according to the actor type. We distinguish three categories: *state actors, interest groups,* and *education providers.* We focus on actors operating at the federal level. With regard to interest groups and education providers, however, these actors often represent aggregate local and state interests. Finally, we draw comparative conclusions for the two educational fields and evaluate to what extent both international initiatives have impacted the education sector of the U.S.

## Education policy-making process and reform initiatives in the U.S.

The U.S. education system can be characterized as highly decentralized and heterogeneous. Institutionally, the American federal government has very little influence over education as the U.S. Constitution principally gives jurisdiction in education policy to the state level. Before 1979, the American Federal Ministry of Education did not even exist. The Elementary and Secondary Education Act (ESEA, 1965) is considered the most important federal law in the education sector. It primarily regulates the federal expenditures for elementary and secondary schools.

Nonetheless, in the U.S., education policy has been an issue on the public and political agenda as early as 1957, when the Soviet Union launched the first satellite. From the American viewpoint, Sputnik demonstrated the Soviet Union's technological superiority or, at the very least, its strong technological competitiveness. The Sputnik shock led to the first comprehensive reform of the American education system, and diverse programmes were set up with the intention of improving the curriculum, particularly in the natural sciences (Ravitch 1983). Twenty-five years later when the 1983 report *A Nation at Risk: Imperatives for Educational Reforms* (National Commission on Excellence in Education 1983) revealed that the American education system was still in a desolate condition, it led to the revitalization of education policy issues at the federal level, where the necessity of developing standards and evaluation criteria was the pivotal point (Busemeyer 2007: 78). Ever since, several education reforms have been suggested and implemented which aimed at the establishment of standards, clarification of responsibilities, admittance of free school choice, and enhancement of teaching quality. Thus, the U.S. had experienced its *"Bildungsschock"* long before PISA.

The shortcomings of the American school system have ultimately become an undisputed fact followed by the consistent implementation of many reforms and new strategies. Similar to the guiding concepts of PISA, consecutive reforms following *A Nation at Risk* have propagated outcome-oriented types of educational teaching. Continuous reform efforts across and within U.S. states for improving secondary education have been on the political agenda ever since (Kosar 2005; McGuinn 2006). In particular, the *No Child Left Behind Act* (NCLB) of 2001 reauthorized a number of federal programmes that aimed to improve the performance of U.S. primary and secondary schools by increasing the standards of accountability for states, school districts, and schools, and by providing parents more flexibility in choosing schools for their children (McGuinn 2006). NCLB requires states wishing to receive federal school funding to develop assessments in basic skills to be administered to all students in certain grades. However, the act did not establish a national performance standard. On the contrary, each state can – in accordance with the principle of school autonomy – set its own standards. Unlike some other countries examined in this volume, current reforms are being undertaken without direct reference to PISA. Although the OECD makes a great effort to make PISA better known in the U.S. (OECD 2011), the *Race to the Top* (R2T) programme as part of the American Recovery and Reinvestment Act of 2009 or the reauthorized education act of March 2010 *A Blueprint for Reforms* do not mention the American PISA results, even though the major goals are parallel to what PISA propagates.[2] Thus, although many goals of PISA and the Obama government are similar, PISA is framed on domestic grounds rather than being oriented towards the OECD's paradigm.

Similarly, there are few signs that any substantive change in American higher education policy-making can be attributed to the Bologna Process. American higher education is predominantly driven by an economic rationale including supply-and-demand considerations, which recently have been strongly impacted by the economic and financial crisis. However, cross-country mobility has not been stressed as an important factor for the education or labour market in the U.S. as it has in Europe. Even as some governmental policy-makers are actively observing the sweeping changes across Europe through Bologna, there are significant obstacles for far-reaching changes to the American higher education system, not least due to its highly decentralized structure (Interview USA 06).

The American federal government indeed has a stake in the affordability of university education, which makes its involvement in policy implementation vital, but it is limited (U.S. Department of Education 2008). Federal influence is essentially limited to the federal student aid programme. There is nearly no formal dictation of higher education policies from Washington, and individual states also have little leverage over university operations – and if so only for the relatively few public universities. Hence, there are no institutional foundations for potentially devising a national strategy for internationalizing higher education or for dealing with Bologna. In contrast to Germany's nationwide internationalization strategy (BMBF 2008) for example, U.S. efforts to recruit international students are initiated by single host campuses' global outreach programmes and recruiting events, or by non-governmental organizations.[3] Along the same lines, Bologna-based credentials of student applicants are evaluated exclusively through case-by-case evaluation at individual higher education institutions, sometimes even at department or faculty level.

A further factor that may limit effective policy learning is a strong sentiment in both America and other countries that the U.S. has the world's best higher education system (Interview USA 05). This has been exhibited in notable university rankings, which boast that eight out of the top ten universities in the world are in the U.S. (Shanghai Jiao Tong University Institute of Higher Education 2011). However, when considering the hundreds of universities in America, these few elite institutions are by no means representative of the whole system. On the contrary, a "halo effect" from the top universities makes American higher education appear to be more cutting-edge as a whole – both in America and abroad (Interview USA 01). As expected, there are few signs of any substantive change to American higher education policy-making that can be attributed to the Bologna Process.

## Reactions to PISA in the U.S.

As mentioned, U.S. education policy has been in a state of continuous reform for the last five decades. Unlike in other countries investigated in this volume where secondary education policy has essentially been characterized by inertia, American secondary education has always been a policy priority. However, its overall quality has improved only very slowly, if at all. The U.S. has been aware of this problematic situation for a long time, and thus PISA is only one of many sources confirming the below-average performance of the U.S. It may, therefore, be no surprise that the OECD education study is not a major factor in ongoing U.S. efforts to reform the secondary education system. However, we argue that PISA does – perhaps with much more subtlety than in other countries – impact key actors formulating education policy.

More specifically, we find a stark discrepancy in the perception of PISA between the mass public and policy elites.

Compared to many PISA participants, there was limited perception of the study in the U.S. Although American results have consistently been below the OECD average in all PISA surveys, American policy-makers and the public seem to have paid very little attention to it (Dobbins and Martens 2010). Similarly, the media has paid little attention to the first three PISA cycles. As Martens and Niemann (2013) demonstrate, the U.S. national media response to PISA was the lowest of all OECD countries. A likely explanation of this inattention to PISA is that it did not increase pressure on the problem as it has done in other countries. There has already been a propensity to assess student performance in an output-oriented way through the use of standardized testing, perhaps further mitigating the potential impact of PISA as a new player (Dobbins and Martens 2010). Only the 2012 PISA Study received some media attention.[4]

As far as reactions of actors are concerned, we would like to advance a slightly different narrative. We argue that while the public disregards PISA and there is no policy output directly associated with it, the policy elite has been impacted by PISA in a variety of ways. Actors are not only aware of the study, but also have elaborate opinions about it and use it in forming their policy positions. The reason it has not played a role in the national discourse, according to virtually all interview partners, is that the notion of *American exceptionalism* (meaning in this context that comparisons of the U.S. education system with other countries are often deemed to be of limited value) is so overpowering that it prohibits a sensible discussion of an internationally comparative assessment such as PISA. For instance, according to one interviewee, a typical reaction to PISA is to invalidate the study by denying it represents "an apple-to-apple comparison" (Interview USA 07, see also Weingarten 2011).

In light of this explanation, it comes as no surprise that most interviewed actors have no formal position on PISA or use it publicly to argue their point. At the same time, we find virtually no *exit* (defined as ignorance) in our interview data. Instead, almost all actors had an elaborate position on the PISA Study, or at the very least, found it to be a salient piece of information in the wider context of secondary education policy. As a testament to this notion, reactions with regard to *loyalty* and *voice* are quiet varied. In terms of *loyalty*, two different reaction types can be distinguished. The first group emphasizes the importance of data-driven assessments of student performance and thus evaluates PISA positively, if only as a signalling device for how poorly the U.S. is performing comparatively. The second group shifts the focus to possible policy implications of PISA, such as better post-university teacher development and greater school autonomy. The crucial difference between these two groups is that for the first one, PISA seems to be a legitimacy tool rationally used to leverage their own ideological position (among policy elites only) and for the second one, PISA is used to directly derive reforms and best practices from other countries. There is also a substantial amount of *voice*. Here, we see quite elaborate critiques of the methodology of PISA. For example, one interest group argued that the concept of student performance tested for by PISA is insensitive to local and cultural idiosyncrasies and is also not goal-oriented with regard to local economic needs. Another group was dubious of the OECD's agenda and warned against the exploitation of PISA data by political actors. In addition, policy suggestions made by the OECD are said to be invalid because of the heterogeneity of tested countries and purported causal links that turn out to be correlational only.

## State actors

We define state actors as actors involved in the provision of secondary education policy at the federal level. These actors were exclusively members of the executive branch and therefore can be understood by extension as subsidiaries of the Obama administration. As is often the case in bureaucracies, organizational behaviour regarding the PISA Study is not exactly streamlined across different divisions. For instance, while one interview partner expressed unmitigated *loyalty* (Interview USA 04), another one articulated an extensive critique of the PISA methodology and consequently warned against deriving any meaningful policy prescriptions from it (Interview USA 05). What these actors have in common, however, is their assessment of reactions among their leading personnel. Alternatively labelling it as an "attention-focusing device" (Interview USA 05) or a "vehicle to create a sense of urgency" (Interview USA 04), the interviewees stated that PISA is very prominent in internal policy documents and speeches delivered to the education policy community. Quite interestingly, the study seems to have been partially successful in framing the debate about education policy in terms of international competitiveness:

> As global interdependence has risen, and as the United States feels the hot breath of competition from Europe and East-Asia, [international competition] is a dominant frame of reference in the education debate today. If the answer at one time had to do with issues of

equity, race, opportunity, democracy [...], the discourse has changed and measurably you could see the rise of the need to rise to the challenge of the international economy as this sort of dominant frame (Interview USA 05).

While PISA may not have been the primary cause of these developments, the interviewee expressed that the study may simultaneously be a consequence of growing competition between nations as well as a facilitator for further competition. This suggests a self-reinforcing impact of PISA. It was also acknowledged that the impact of PISA does not go beyond the policy elite to enter public discourse hindered by both American exceptionalism and the density of state-based assessments (Interview USA 05). Since states are the primary providers of secondary education, these assessments naturally carry more substantive meaning and provide a much broader information base than in countries without a culture of student performance assessment before PISA.

### Interest groups

Interest groups in secondary education include think tanks, lobby groups, and special interest representatives. Since organizations from both sides of the political spectrum were sampled, one could expect diverging reactions to PISA and its policy implications. We do not find this to be the case, however, as ideological outlook was not at all a predictor of positions towards the study. For example, the most pointed *voice* reactions came from a progressive think tank and an organization concerned with rural schooling, both of which critiqued that "PISA is testing all the wrong things" (Interview USA 06) but refrained from advocating the U.S. to drop out of the study. Aside from these groups, reactions to PISA by interest group actors can by and large be characterized as positive. In fact, some of the strongest *loyalty* expressions came from these actors, with interview partners saying they "love PISA" (Interview USA 07) and want to purposefully promote its influence in American secondary education policy (Interview USA 10). Described as *the* international benchmark (Interview USA 07), many interview partners not only found PISA to be salient as one more piece in the assessment puzzle, they also actively utilized the data to make reform suggestions, for example, regarding teacher recruitment (Interview USA 10) or school autonomy (Interview USA 03).

Moreover, a recurring theme in the interviews (again irrespective of ideology) was that participation in the study should be extended to individual states rather than just the nation as a whole (Interview USA 07,

USA 09, & USA 10). This has been actively lobbied for by some interest groups. Given the federal structure of secondary education policy, such a move could perhaps enhance the impact of the study. As gaps between the states and other countries become even more obvious, the study could potentially enter public discourse in a manner similar to that in other countries. Perhaps even more interestingly, the very same groups that most vehemently advocate state participation also advocate federal government involvement in secondary education policy. They hope that PISA would act as a legitimacy tool to justify far-reaching reform, similarly to those in countries such as Switzerland and Germany.

**Education providers**

Education providers are defined as organizations that represent actors involved in the delivery of education (not education policy) at the local level. They include teachers, school administrations, and boards of education. Again, we overwhelmingly find *loyalty,* with interview partners emphasizing the importance of data-driven assessments, expressing outright support for the PISA Study, and directly deriving policy implications. While warning against the political exploitation of its findings, education providers – compared to the other actor categories – were most willing to use PISA as a learning tool for foreign best practices. In the majority of cases, members of the interviewed organizations even undertook several research trips to well-performing countries such as Finland, Korea, and Singapore and had regular meetings with the OECD's Deputy Director for Education and Skills, Andreas Schleicher. It is perhaps unsurprising that education providers refer to policy details such as class size, teachers' pay, and school accountability with much more regularity than to the *politics* dimension of secondary education policy and are therefore more likely to discuss actual policy implications of PISA. More striking, however, is that they were also generally more outward-looking and more likely to frame secondary education policy in terms of international competitiveness and output orientation. Summarizing the position of his group on PISA, one interviewee stated:

> We organizationally believe that it is very important that we are doing more international benchmarking. And as you know, the Obama administration has instituted this notion of career readiness, being more globally competitive. I think PISA is an assessment tool that can inform us and [help us] to address the numerous issues that we may have competitively with other nations (Interview USA 02).

Similarly, another interviewee stated that PISA has been helpful "not only in terms of demonstrating what our children know and what our system is or is not able to provide them, but also how it stacks up our children for the global work force" (Interview USA 11). In addition, all interviewed groups advocated state participation in the next wave of PISA. In contrast to the interest groups, however, they do not want to involve the states to gain leverage for an education reform that would equip the federal government with more competencies. Rather, they simply want to "follow the evidence" (Interview USA 12) which, in their mind, points towards more authority at the state or local level.

**Summary**

In sum, while PISA did not elicit a response as dramatic as in other countries, we find that it has substantively impacted the thinking of the policy elite. The mainstream political discourse and, by extension, the mass public remain irresponsive to the poor comparative standing of the U.S. The reason for this discrepancy seems to be the overriding notion of American exceptionalism, denoting a reluctance to take comparative assessments seriously and an unwillingness to learn from other countries. As secondary education policy experts, all interview partners are very much aware of the PISA Study and without exception formulated an organizational opinion on PISA. While some disapprove of its methodology and doubt the validity of its indicators, most actors thoroughly approve it and, in some cases, are quite active in deriving policy implications and suggestions for reform. These reactions do not easily break down according to actor type. In other words, actors between categories do not necessarily have diverging positions on PISA, and actors within categories do not necessarily agree. The same is true for actors with clearly identifiable ideological roots. For instance, a conservative think tank may find itself more in agreement with a progressive lobby group than one of its ideological counterparts. However, we find that those actors involved in the delivery of education were most likely to substantively utilize the data and internalize the OECD's outlook on education policy.

## Higher education – cherry picking from the Bologna menu?

Even though it is directed at European countries, the Bologna Process has attracted attention worldwide. One of the main motivations behind Bologna was for Europe to again become a formidable global higher education competitor and even surpass the U.S. as the leading player in the knowledge economy. As a result, it is safe to say that Europe has become a "hot spot" for higher education innovations since the onset of Bologna. Therefore, it is worthwhile to explore the responses of the U.S. to the Bologna reform agenda, not least because European universities are increasingly competing with their U.S. counterparts for fee-paying international students. Has the U.S. learned from the European reform, or has the Bologna model remained a European solution to a European problem? What are the consequences of the Bologna reform for the European Higher Education Area's strongest competitor?

While Bologna's impact on European higher education systems has been widely studied, little knowledge is available regarding its potential effect on the U.S. system (Robertson and Keeling 2008: 221–40; Robertson 2010: 23–37). However, there is increasing evidence that "Bologna ideology" – such as programme transparency, structural compatibility, university autonomy, and multi-stakeholdership – has spread to nonparticipating countries (Vögtle 2010). Nevertheless, the U.S. has been slower to include Bologna concepts in its public discourse, let alone to undertake corresponding reform attempts (Dobbins and Martens 2010: 179–98; Dobbins et al. 2010: 77–94; Fulge and Bieber 2013). First and foremost, most American observers regard the Bologna reforms as a European answer to a European problem. However, there are initial signs that Bologna is beginning to directly and indirectly affect the American system at several levels – despite the abovementioned institutional and historical constraints.

In recent years, there is mounting evidence that American higher education policy-makers are increasingly drawing inspiration from foreign innovations. As hinted above, this is taking place with the aim of improving the global position of American higher education institutions while also effectively coping with the economic and financial crisis (Dobbins and Martens 2010: 179–98). Recently, Bologna has established itself as a reference for reform-minded policy-makers (Karakas 2013). Over the past five years a pick-and-choose strategy can be observed among individual American institutions that focused on specific Bologna-inspired instruments to improve transparency, accountability, and the recognition of degrees (Interview USA 01). For example, the European reform has triggered debates in the U.S. about the introduction of diploma supplements. Most notably, Bologna has inspired the so-called *Tuning Programme*, which can be interpreted as an attempt of American states to emulate the qualification frameworks that emerged in Europe during the Bologna Process. Furthermore, Bologna has been increasingly referred to in the design of programmes that simplify student lending, document credentials, increase student persistence, clarify learning aims, and increase financial support (Gaston 2010: 177). In addition, American policy-makers have drawn lessons from Bologna's more recent focus on associate's degrees, prompting some American state universities to incorporate community colleges into the university system, thus easing the transfer of credits and transition to a bachelor's degree (Gaston 2010).

There is also growing evidence of the impact of Bologna on educational supply and demand. The shift to a more market-oriented model in Europe (Dobbins 2012; Schimank and Lange 2009) has increased competitive pressures on the U.S. This has contributed to an ever more widespread perception that many other countries are now "educating citizens to more advanced levels" than the U.S. (Spellings 2006) and that students wishing to study abroad have numerous options outside the U.S. Thus, with Bologna, Europe has challenged U.S. dominance in education and forced U.S.-based higher education institutions to react (Interview USA 04). As one interviewee pointed out, "if you want to be called world-class, it is not sufficient to look at Ohio compared to Indiana, you also want to look at Ohio compared to Germany, or Japan, or someplace else" (Interview USA 08). Furthermore, since the implementation of Bologna reforms, the number of students in some European countries attending post-secondary education has surpassed the U.S. (Douglass 2008: 3). In addition, more and more top universities for specific research fields are located outside the U.S. The increased competition for foreign students is drawing away students, their tuition fees, and prestige from U.S. schools.

Interestingly, the economic recession and financial crisis may have inadvertently fostered transatlantic diffusion of the Bologna study structure. For example, many U.S. states are scrutinizing their expenditures more than they would have otherwise (Gaston 2010: 125). This has resulted in efforts to attract more fee-paying international students. According to the Open Doors Report of the Institute of International Education (IIE 2012), international students contributed over $22.7 billion to the U.S. economy and their enrolment rate increased 31 per cent over the last decade with 6 per cent specifically in 2012. However, the share of international students in American academic higher education is only 3.7 per cent in 2012 of all enrolled students with most students coming from China and India. Compared to Germany with 9.3 per cent and Australia with 20.9 per cent, the U.S. is lagging far behind (OECD 2012). In the global race for talent, competitors – particularly from Asia – are improving their branding techniques and spending more money on keeping their students in the country. In addition, the slowing increase in foreign students coming to the U.S. after the Bologna introduction represents a monetary loss for the American economy, aggravated by the reduction in the amount of scholarships available to foreign students.

One important measure to cope with the changing educational demand and the economic crisis is the introduction of three-year bachelor's programmes at American universities. Faced with declining public and private expenditure following the 2008 recession, prominent politicians such as former Secretary of Education Lamar Alexander actively pushed for three-year bachelor's degrees (ACE 2011). This new structure was seen as an important means of attracting fee-paying international students (Bieber and Martens 2012) and partially justified with the reference to three-year bachelor's degree as the new Bologna-inspired international standard.

### State actors

As the federal government is not a central player in American higher education, it is hardly a surprise that it has not *voiced* an official policy stance on Bologna. However, it is safe to say that it has fuelled the perception that other higher education systems overseas have become more effective, transparent, accessible, and better linked with labour markets. What is noticeable is a convergence of recently defined higher education policy goals by American governmental policy-makers and those of the Bologna Process and Europe's related efforts to become the world's most competitive knowledge economy. For example, the U.S. government has increasingly expressed support for the Bologna-friendly Lumina Foundation[5] in its efforts to increase the proportion of Americans with high-quality degrees by more than 50 per cent in the next decade. In terms of policy objectives, this broadly corresponds with the social dimension of Bologna that is strongly related with higher education completion rates and targeted efforts to support students during their studies (Bologna Press Briefing 2012).

Moreover, President Obama has recently proposed changes to the college/university accreditation system[6] which would enable higher education models and providers to receive federal student aid based on performance and results. Although no specific reference to Bologna was made, this ties into a growing European trend towards linking public funding to accreditation outcomes. Specifically, the President has proposed weakening existing accreditation institutions, which have held a monopoly over determining federal financial aid eligibility and access to Pell grants as well as student loans. This would either entail reforms to the existing accreditation system or the government-promoted establishment of a new system that allocates federal student aid to colleges/ universities and higher education programmes based on student performance and affordability. Thus, in an indirect sense, an increasingly widespread European strategy, that is, funding based on quality assurance outcomes, is being promoted to address America's problem of education affordability.

**Interest groups**

In line with the American tradition of anti-statism, it appears that private actors are the main conveyors of Bologna-based ideas in the U.S. Indeed, we can observe increasing efforts of private sector actors to bring one crucial component of the Bologna agenda into public policy – qualifications frameworks. The above-described tendency to transfer individual Bologna ideas *à la carte* is well reflected by the "Tuning USA" project. Jointly designed by European and American scholars (Wiarda 2009), Tuning USA is a pilot programme initiated by the Lumina Foundation for Education, the largest private foundation in the U.S. The project draws on both the Bologna model and like-minded activities in the U.S., Latin American and Caribbean countries, Central Asia, and Africa (Dobbins and Martens 2010: 179–98) and aims to comprehensively link learning outcomes to employability of graduates. This is an objective European universities have been required to meet in order to create a shared understanding among stakeholders of the subject-specific knowledge that students must demonstrate upon completing degrees. Similar to the Bologna qualifications frameworks, *tuning* aims to increase the practical relevancy of academic degrees for the labour market and to improve credit transfer among higher education institutions (Inside Indiana Business 2009; Bieber and Martens 2012: 9). On a voluntary basis, the involved universities have started to harmonize their qualification catalogues for degree programmes. The initial participating states – Minnesota, Indiana, Utah, Texas, and Kentucky – have developed accountability instruments in six disciplines, which included diploma supplements, qualifications frameworks, and the definition of student workload. In addition, they drafted learning outcomes and clarified the relationship of these outcomes with employment possibilities (Inside Indiana Business 2009).

While the impact of Tuning USA is limited because only a few higher education institutions in a few states take part, it is worth noting that the project explicitly draws on European expertise and offers a supplementary channel for transatlantic cooperation and communication (Fulge and Bieber 2013). Participating higher education institutions actively sought information on European procedures and applied it to their own setting (Interview USA 09). However, while it is still unclear if Tuning USA will ultimately extend to the entire U.S., the most populous state, California, has joined the endeavour. The fact that American history departments have already started to expand the project across the entire country also offers evidence of its increased popularity. If Tuning USA turns out to be successful, it may serve as a model for other states and higher education providers (Interview USA 05). This innovation would shift national guiding principles away from educational inputs towards outcomes and competencies. After all, the reputation of U.S. universities and colleges presently still counts more than concrete information on students' learning outcomes (Interview USA 07).

The first ever Tuning USA inaugural symposium was hosted in 2013 by the Midwestern Higher Education Compact in collaboration with the Institute for Evidence-Based Change. The event was the first opportunity in the U.S. for faculty, professionals, and stakeholders from around the country to exchange subjective perceptions on the progress of the project. Up to this point, the response has been highly positive, as reflected not only in the increasing number of participating states, but also the broad array of stakeholders involved in the process. There is a widespread perception that the benefits of the Bologna-inspired project will be immensely important, and it should be further pursued on an even broader scale (IEBC 2013).

There is also a growing array of actors who have begun to promote awareness of Bologna and its purportedly positive effects. One such American promoter of Bologna is the Institute for Higher Education Policy (IHEP) (for example, Adelman 2008; 2009; 2010). In policy documents, concrete ways that American higher education institutions can learn from its reform goals are proposed. Adelman (2009) goes as far as to claim that Bologna's core features are likely to become the dominant global higher education model and laments the blindness of top U.S. policy-makers towards Bologna. Along these lines, the IHEP study "The Bologna Process for U.S. Eyes: Relearning Higher Education in the Age of Convergence" (Adelman 2009) contends that European countries are producing degrees which are not only as good or better, but also more transparent, internationally compatible, and better define the qualifications of graduates. As for the U.S. though, the report laments the severe lack of transparency in degrees awarded to graduates. Besides its explicit support for the Tuning initiative, the Institute has also alluded to the social dimension of Bologna and advocated improved access to higher education for groups with low participation rates.

## Education providers

The introduction of new study structures in Europe, especially the three-year European-style bachelor's degrees, called for a new approach in recognizing foreign qualifications. In other words, Bologna posed novel problems of credit recognition for European students wishing to enter the U.S., since many U.S. graduate school requirements include undergraduate degrees based on four years of credit hours. Traditionally, when deciding on the admission of students, U.S. credentials assessors quantitatively evaluated education performance based on years of study, rather than through documented skills (Bell and Watkins 2006: 71). While some of the conventional one-track degrees of several European countries necessitated at least four years of study, the new Bologna bachelor's degrees are usually completed within three years. Therefore, European degrees no longer correspond in study length with U.S. undergraduate degrees, which require four years.

Given the decentralized character of American higher education and the pronounced diversity and autonomy of its universities (Slaughter and Cantwell 2011), it is no surprise that American responses to these degree recognition problems have been varied (Bell and Watkins 2006; Dobbins and Martens 2010). The country lacks a unitary policy for the admission of international students to graduate programmes. Admissions officers in different states and institutions have generally applied different approaches for the recognition of the three-year bachelor's degrees. While some providers have adopted an all-or-nothing approach by requiring four-year bachelor's degrees, others only recognize three-year bachelor's degrees from the Bologna zone and not from others (Bell and Watkins 2006: 71). However, the majority of institutions still have to develop an explicit recognition policy.

As indicated above, one additional and related development is the increasingly widespread introduction of three-year bachelor's programmes in the U.S. (Interview USA 08). For example, in the smallest state, Rhode Island, a new law requires all state higher education institutions to establish three-year bachelor's programmes starting in 2010 (Strauss 2009). Like in Europe, the motives for this policy modification were primarily economic, but were also additionally legitimated by the Bologna reforms and the attractiveness of shorter degrees for fee-paying international students (Interview USA 11). The introduction of Bologna-style undergraduate degrees thus makes U.S. degrees more compatible with European degrees and eases recognition matters with the European bachelor's. Some argue that this not only saves students time and financial resources, but also institutional resources, while increasing the efficiency of campus facilities. Opponents argue that this approach does not deal with underlying financial dynamics that affect college affordability and negatively impact students' life–work balance (Interview USA 08). Furthermore, the introduction of three-year bachelor's programmes would increase the workload for students immensely, and would require students to precisely know beforehand their intended field of study (Interview USA 11).

However, Bologna is making headway in changing how U.S. graduate schools evaluate their European applicants for admission. According to surveys conducted by the Council of Graduate Schools, many U.S. graduate schools have now adapted their evaluation procedures to accommodate European students with three-year degrees. Schools with high foreign student enrolment are also more likely to have implemented such procedures than schools with fewer students while other schools are also beginning to address this issue as three-year degrees originating from Europe become more common (CGS 2009).

This positive tenor towards processes of internationalization and transnational harmonization is shared by the American Association of Collegiate Registrars and Admissions Officers (AACRAO). This organization has drawn up numerous proposals for coping with Bologna and explicitly called on its members to acquire additional knowledge to identify European best practices regarding issues of credit recognition and admissions. Likewise, the National Association of Foreign Student Advisers (NAFSA) has compiled elaborate information on the origins, policy innovations, and potential benefits of Bologna for U.S. actors and institutions (NAFSA 2013). The American Institute of International Education Administration has also increased its information diffusion activities regarding Bologna with the aim of prompting American policy-makers to draw lessons from European experiences.[7] These activities have increasingly conveyed the perception that the U.S. – despite its highly market- and career-oriented higher education system – is now a laggard when it comes to degree transparency and accountability. As shown above, this played into the so-called tuning strategy.

### Summary

As indicated above, we have adapted our concepts of *loyalty, exit,* and *voice* to accommodate the special position of the United States regarding Bologna. Although still poorly understood and widely unknown, we were unable to find evidence of any political actors who actively rejected the European reform initiative in terms of the *voice* concept or who have devised an agenda to undermine Bologna's goals, such as the 3 + 2 study structure, the European Credit Transfer System (ECTS), quality assurance, and qualifications frameworks, in terms of an *exit* option. What we are seeing instead is a growing number of relevant stakeholders who are latching onto selected elements of Bologna to address challenges in the American higher education system. These elements comprise mainly the qualifications frameworks, the goal study content transparency, as well as diploma supplements and the definition of student workload. This development has reinforced the perception that other regions have not only caught up with but even surpass the U.S. in terms of transparency, affordability, and quality of higher education services. A broad array of U.S. actors aims to increase awareness of Bologna and individual Bologna initiatives as policy templates for the U.S. context. Altogether, *loyalty* can be identified as the prevalent strategy of the concerned U.S. stakeholders – at least among (primarily private sector) actors familiar with the process itself and its potential benefits. In other words, Bologna is no longer regarded by many American actors as a European solution to a European problem.

## Conclusion

U.S. reactions to the OECD's PISA Study can be viewed from two altogether different perspectives. On the one hand, there have not been any direct policy reforms induced by or derived from the continuously poor results of a significant share of American students. By the same token, PISA is not part of the public discourse even though secondary education has been high on both the public and the policy agenda for decades. On the other hand, our interview data clearly suggests that the study plays a considerable role in shaping beliefs among the policy elite. In these circles, reactions are surprisingly robust, with all interview partners expressing an elaborate opinion on PISA and most utilizing it for lobbying efforts or deriving policy implications (for example, with regard to teacher training). Moreover, many interview partners maintain close relations to the OECD and travel regularly to countries outperforming the U.S. in order to adopt best practices. Thus, the reactions of most actors can be characterized as *loyalty*, with a few actors expressing *voice* through elaborate critiques of the study and its political implications. These reactions, however, are only observable and consequential within the community of the policy elite and stand in stark contrast to the *ignorance* most actors seem to display publicly. This discrepancy can plausibly be explained by the overpowering notion of American exceptionalism impeding sensible public discussions of PISA results. In conclusion, in the case of U.S. secondary education, the PISA Study has not functioned as a legitimacy tool but rather as a device to shape the beliefs of the policy elite. Given the fact that in most other countries (see chapters 4 and 8 by Niemann and Bieber in this volume) it was the other way around, this is a testament to the OECD's ability to influence policy in a variety of ways.

In American higher education, the reactions of the three groups of stakeholders have been varied. While *private interest groups* are the leading receptors and promoters of goals drawing on the Bologna agenda, particularly concerning qualifications frameworks, the reactions of *state actors* has been more difficult to evaluate in terms of *exit, voice,* or *loyalty,* because essentially there has been no official stance by the federal government on the Bologna Process. However, many similarities can be identified between the Bologna agenda and President Obama's reform plans. Thus, one could argue that we are witnessing a subliminal convergence of overarching policy goals in the U.S. and Europe. Hence, this could be categorized as *loyalty. Education providers'* responses to the problems of the recognition of the three-year Bologna bachelor's degrees have been mixed, mainly due to the high degree of institutional autonomy and decentralization of the higher education landscape. Strategies for dealing with the new foreign degrees ranged from not accepting Bologna degrees, to recognizing the degrees on a case-by-case basis, to introducing three-year bachelor's programmes in the U.S. Although there are a variety of rationales in dealing with the Bologna Process in the heterogeneous educational landscape of the U.S., we predominantly find a pragmatic *loyalty,* which would further increase if the Tuning USA project continues to disseminate through the country. It seems that the prospect of remaining part of the globalized knowledge community in the future is a good incentive to do so – especially if competing higher education areas, such as Asia, gain in importance.

## Notes

1   Some of the interviews used in this study were conducted by Daniel de Olano. We thank him for this work.
2   http://www2.ed.gov/programs/racetothetop/executive-summary.pdf, retrieved 30 August 2013; http://www2.ed.gov/policy/elsec/leg/blueprint/ blueprint.pdf, retrieved 30 August 2013.

3 It is, of course, safe to say that in the past this approach has proven to be at least as successful in terms of internationalization as other countries' national-level strategies.
4 http://www.pisaday.org/, retrieved 17 December 2013.
5 http://www.luminafoundation.org/podcasts/2009-02-26.html, retrieved 30 August 2013.
6 See for example: http://chronicle.com/article/Obamas-Accreditation/137311/, retrieved 30 August 2013.
7 http://de.slideshare.net/AEISlides/bologna-process-presentation-final, retrieved 30 August 2013.

## References

ACE (2011) *House Subcommittee Holds Hearing on College Costs.* American Council on Education, http://www.acenet.edu/news-room/Pages/House-Hearing-on-College-Costs.aspx, retrieved 4 September 2013.

Adelman, Clifford (2008) *The Bologna Club: What U.S. Higher Education Can Learn from a Decade of European Reconstruction,* Washington D.C.: IHEP.

Adelman, Clifford (2009) *The Bologna Process for U.S. Eyes: Re-learning Higher Education in the Age of Convergence. Report for the Institute for Higher Education Policy with the Support of the Lumina Foundation,* Washington D.C.: IHEP.

Adelman, Clifford (2010) "The US Response to Bologna: Expanding Knowledge, First Steps of Convergence", *European Journal of Education,* 45(4), 612–23.

Bell, Jeannine E. and Robert A. Watkins (2006) "Strategies in Dealing with the Bologna Process", *International Educator,* 15(5), 70–5.

Bieber, Tonia and Kerstin Martens (2012) "Transatlantic Convergence in Higher Education? Comparing Current Trends of Policy Change in Germany and the U.S.", Paper presented at the IPSA World Congress, Madrid.

BMBF (2008) *Deutschlands Rolle in der globalen Wissensgesellschaft stärken. Strategie der Bundesregierung zur Internationalisierung von Wissenschaft und Forschung,* Berlin: BMBF.

Bologna Press Briefing (2012) The European Higher Education Area in 2012: Bologna Process Implementation Report, http://www.ehea.info/Uploads/(1)/Bologna%20Process%20Implementation%20Report.pdf, retrieved 3 December 2013.

Busemeyer, Marius R. (2007) "Bildungspolitik in den USA. Eine historisch-institutionalistische Perspektive auf das Verhältnis von öffentlichen und privaten Bildungsinstitutionen", *Zeitschrift für Sozialreform,* 53(1), 57–78.

CGS 2009. Institutional Strategies for Addressing Three-Year Degrees: Bologna and Beyond. Council of Graduate Schools, http://www.cgsnet.org/ckfinder/userfiles/files/am09_Bennett.pdf, retrieved 30 August 2013.

Dobbins, Michael (2012) "How Market-oriented Is French Higher Education?", *French Politics* 10(2), 134–59.

Dobbins, Michael and Kerstin Martens (2010) "A Contrasting Case – the U.S.A. and Its Weak Response to Internationalization Processes in Education Policy", in Kerstin Martens, Alexander-Kenneth Nagel, Michael Windzio and Ansgar Weymann, eds., *Transformation of Education Policy,* Basingstoke: Palgrave Macmillan, 179–98.

Dobbins, Michael, Christoph Knill and Eva Maria Vögtle (2010) "To What Extent Does Transnational Communication Drive Cross-national Policy Convergence? The Impact of the Bologna Process on Domestic Higher Education Policies", *Higher Education*, 61(1), 77–94.

Douglass, John A. (2008) *Universities, the US High Tech Advantage, and the Process of Globalization*, Berkeley: University of California.

Elementary and Secondary Education Act (1965) *Public Law 89-10 – April 11 1965*.

Fulge, Timm and Tonia Bieber (2013) "Atlantic Crossings of the Bologna Process – Analyzing the Diffusion of Higher Education Policies to the US and Germany", Paper prepared for the ISA Annual Convention, San Francisco, April 3–6.

Gaston, Paul L. (2010) *The Challenge of Bologna: What United States Higher Education Has to Learn from Europe, and Why It Matters That We Learn It*, Sterling: Stylus Publishing.

Hirschman, Albert O. (1970) *Exit, Voice, and Loyalty. Responses to Decline in Firms, Organizations, and States*, Cambridge: Cambridge University Press.

IEBC (2013) Tuning American Higher Education: The Process. Institute for Evidence-Based Change, http://tuningusa.org/Library/Newsletters-(1)/Tuning-Higher-Education-The-Process.aspx, retrieved 7 July 2013.

IIE (2012) Open Doors Report. Report on International Educational Exchange. Institute for International Education, www.iie.org/opendoors, retrieved 5 August 2013.

Inside Indiana Business (2009) Lumina Foundation Launches Tuning USA Project, http://www.insideindianabusiness.com/newsitem.asp?ID=34943, retrieved 3 September 2013.

Karakas, Scott L. (2012) "Bologna and Beyond: The Future of Higher Education in the United States?", *Synesis: A Journal of Science, Technology, Ethics, and Policy*, 3(1), 1–3.

Kosar, Kevin (2005) *Failing Grades. The Federal Politics of Education Standards*, Boulder and London: Lynne Rienner.

Martens, Kerstin and Dennis Niemann (2013) "When Do Numbers Count? The Differential Impact of the PISA Rating and Ranking on Education Policy in Germany and the US", *German Politics*, 22(3), 314–32.

McGuinn, Patrick J. (2006) *No Child Left Behind and the Transformation of Federal Education Policy, 1965–2005*, Lawrence: University Press of Kansas.

NAFSA (2013) The Bologna Process, http://www.nafsa.org/uploadedFiles/NAFSA_Home/Resource_Library_Assets/Bologna/bolognaprocess_ie_supp.pdf, retrieved 30 August 2013.

National Commission on Excellence in Education (1983) "A Nation at Risk: Imperatives for Educational Reforms", http://www2.ed.gov/pubs/NatAtRisk/index.html, retrieved 13 July 2013.

OECD (2011) *Lessons from PISA for the United States. Strong Performers and Successful Reformers in Education*, Paris: OECD.

OECD (2012) *Education at a Glance 2012*, Paris: OECD.

Ravitch, Diane (1983) *The Troubled Crusade: American Education, 1945–1980*, New York: BasicBooks.

Robertson, Susan L. (2010) "The EU, 'Regulatory State Regionalism' and New Modes of Higher Education Governance", *Globalisation, Societies and Education*, 8(1), 23–37.

Robertson, Susan L. and Ruth Keeling (2008) "Stirring the Lions: Strategy and Tactics in Global Higher Education", *Globalisation, Societies and Education*, 6(3), 221–40.

Schimank, Uwe and Stefan Lange (2009) "Germany: A Latecomer to New Public Management", in Catherine Paradiese, Emanuela Reale, Ivar Bleiklie and Ewan Ferlie, eds., *University Governance – Western European Comparative Perspectives*, Dordrecht: Springer, 51–75.

Shanghai Jiao Tong University Institute of Higher Education (2011) Academic Ranking of World Universities 2011, http://www.arwu.org/#, retrieved 3 September 2013.

Slaughter, Sheila and Brendan Cantwell (2012) "Transatlantic Moves to the Market: The United States and the European Union", *Higher Education*, 63(5), 583–606.

Spellings, Margaret (2006) *A Test of Leadership: Charting the Future of US Higher Education: A Report of the Commission Appointed by Secretary of Education*, Washington: U.S. Department of Education.

Strauss, Valerie (2009) "Colleges Consider 3-Year Degrees to Save Undergrads Time, Money", *Washington Post*, 23 May 2009.

U.S. Department of Education (2008) *Summary of the Higher Education Opportunity Act of 2008* (HEOA), http://www.tgslc.org/pdf/HEOA_summary.pdf, retrieved 3 August 2013.

Vögtle, Eva Maria (2010) "Beyond Bologna. The Bologna Process as a Global Template for Higher Education Reform Efforts", *TranState Working Papers* 129, Bremen University.

Weingarten, Randi (2011) *A Quality Agenda: How To Build Enduring Reform*. Speech delivered at the TEACH Conference in New York, 11 July 2011.

Wiarda, Jan Martin (2009) "Die Bologna-Kopie", *DIE ZEIT* 64 (16).

# 10
## Joining the World of Education? China's Reaction to Internationalization Pressures

*Alexander Akbik, Kerstin Martens and Chenjian Zhang*

## Introduction

Despite being politically closed, China has subjected itself to internationalization processes and pressures in education policy at both the secondary education level through Shanghai's participation in the Programme for International Student Assessment (PISA) as well as at the tertiary level, as China has the most students enrolled in higher educational institutions and the highest amount of students abroad. Although China as a whole does not participate in these international initiatives, ongoing structural reforms due to Bologna or PISA cannot be ignored. China, because of its political isolation, can also be seen as a test case: How does the country react to these internationalization pressures from abroad? To answer this question, we adapt Hirschman's (1970) typology – *exit*, *voice* and *loyalty* – on China (see Introduction by Knodel et al. to this volume). However, similar to the U.S. case presented in this volume, the question to apply the literature of political opportunity structures without engaging in conceptual stretching remains troublesome, particularly since this literature was developed for open, democratic Western states. In a nutshell, do political actors in China have opportunities to protest? What do we mean when we speak of *exit* or *voice* in the Chinese case?

In this chapter, we examine the reactions in China to the pressures of education internationalization. We focus in particular on the responses to PISA in secondary education and to the Bologna Process in higher education. We first examine the political opportunity structure that shapes how local actors can react to education policy in China. Moreover, we trace the general developments in education policies in China, the goals and measures. In the next section, we analyse China's reaction towards PISA. In the third section, we will depict the discourse surrounding the Bologna Process as part of ongoing internationalization and regionalization efforts in higher education.

In the field of *secondary education*, China first participated in the PISA Study in 2009, with Shanghai being the only region to be tested (OECD 2011: 105). Ranking first in all three areas of the test, China was able to positively evaluate its ongoing reform efforts of the secondary education system. However, since Shanghai was the only region that participated, the test results can hardly be considered representative for China as a whole (OECD 2011: 90; Zhang and Akbik 2012). Nevertheless, Shanghai's participation in PISA sparked strong national and international responses (Sellar and Lingard 2013). Arousing considerable reactions from diverse social groups, comments on the results lasted for several months. For our analysis we collected comments that were published from December 2010 through March 2011. In total, 42 documents, which were coded and analysed, are included in our analysis. Based on the arguments and reasoning for PISA results, we categorized the actors in two groups: first, the local education authorities, the Shanghai PISA team and journalists affiliated with government agencies, and second, independent educators as well as overseas researchers.

In the field of *higher education*, China is experiencing developments in internationalization, regionalization and harmonization; it is, for example, creating "world-class universities" that are able to compete in an international environment with the "Project 211" and "985" (Deem et al. 2008) and regionalize the education system (Cai 2008; Hawkins et al. 2008; Nguyen 2009; Zeng et al. 2012). These reforms aim at not only reversing the brain drain from China, but also attracting foreign students and raising the overall quality of the education system. Recently, China and the Association of Southeast Asian Nations (ASEAN) created the China-ASEAN Free Trade Area (CAFTA) in order to promote an Asian collective identity and create an Asian higher education area (Zeng et al. 2012). However when comparing the heated debate surrounding the PISA results to the discussion of the Bologna Process, its direct influence on China's higher education has remained limited. Therefore, the interpretation and discussion of Bologna remain at a rather abstract level. Despite using various online search engines and major Chinese newspapers, the number of relevant articles for our study remained considerably low. Instead, we searched for relevant articles in an online database provided by China National Knowledge Infrastructure (CNKI).[1] Based on this data, we were able to once more identify two major groups of actors, namely government officials of the education authority, on the one hand, and university educational researchers on the other.

## Political opportunity structures in China's education system

One should keep in mind that the People's Republic of China is *de facto* a one-party state, with highly centralized power in the hands of the Politburo Standing Committee (Martin 2010: 5). This political system sets barriers to social and political mobilization since political activity is confined to membership in a single political party and is characterized by mass media under state control, wherein individual citizenship rights and due process are not guaranteed (Osa and Corduneanu-Huci 2003). However, despite constitutional constraints, the political power in China is in reality rather diffuse, competitive and complex. With the death of Mao Zedong in 1976, Deng Xiaoping, his successor, introduced dramatic institutional change, such as a diffusion of power. These changes opened the political arena to new, involved actors to the educational field, such as government-sponsored research institutions, private education providers, parents and students (Mok 2005: 222; Zhang 2011: 78). In addition to the diffusion of state power at the national level, China undertook decentralization efforts by allocating "conditioned authority to local governments" (Cai 2008: 411). In this context, conditioned authority means that local authorities have more administrative and financial autonomy for dealing with local issues and responding to demands, enabling the state apparatus to act more efficiently at the local level, limit corruption and increase the resilience of the central government regime (Martin 2010: 15). China remains highly centralized and hierarchical, and local officials are appointed by the central state in order to avoid the danger of having these officials build a power base that can challenge the central government. The central government has the capacity to set up and implement new policies as well as appoint provincial and local leaders. In short, China has a top-down ruling structure.

Political stability is one of the core concerns of the central authority. Confronted with pressing social and economic inequalities, the Chinese government under the leadership of Hu Jintao declared the goal of a "harmonious society" on 11 October 2006 (Wang and Morgan 2012: 1). This statement was in response to uneven regional development and environmental damages caused by economic growth in China but was also meant as a response to quell recent social unrest. While protest movements are still at a nascent stage, with few citizens articulating their demands and successfully prevailing on the political stage, some predict that China's gradual opening to the world will increase the number of protests (Kuah and Guiheux 2009: 17).

While the accessibility of the political system in China is still mostly limited, the capacity of governments to implement new policies is hampered by coordination problems. The new actors that have emerged are predominantly actors at various state levels and within the government itself. For instance, within the Politburo Standing Committee, two camps compete for the direction of future developments in China: The progressive group heralds balanced economic growth and principles of a harmonious society, while the elitist group advocates rapid economic development (Martin 2010: 5). Most important to these developments is that the system itself has become more open, and political mobilization is nonetheless taking place within this restricted framework.

In the case of China, the dimensions of opportunity structures need to be complemented by the role of Confucianism. As noted by He and Feng (2008: 149), the Confucian political culture is one of the main obstacles of opening up the political system. Liu (2012: 3) observes that "education is at the center of Chinese people's lives". The form of examination-oriented education, in particular, has long been entrenched in Chinese society and culture (Dello-Iacovo 2009). Informed by the Confucian ideal of hierarchy to establish order and elite control as the best way to promote prosperity and harmony, for over 1000 years success in education was the main path for social mobility. One of the most prevailing characteristics of modern China is perhaps the "large population and a general recognition that the road to success lies in being admitted to one of its relatively few universities" (Hawkins et al. 2008: 215).

Furthermore, social and parental expectations contribute to the high pressure on students to excel in education, leading to the so-called *education fever*, wherein parents invest heavily in the tutoring of their children as well as facilitate, through legal and illegal means, their access to educational institutions. These investments can also be observed by taking into account the average household spending on education. Since 1990, customer surveys conducted by the China People's Bank have repeatedly identified children's education as the most important rationale for saving (Liu 2012: 4). Due to China's *One Child Policy*, parents have more money to invest in their only child, increasing the pressure and expectations on the child as the future caretaker of the family (Yu and Suen 2005), but also increasing pressures on policy-makers to provide facilities and structures to meet the demand for education.

## Reforms in China's education system[2]

Reforms in China's education system reflect the interplay between the global discourse on the knowledge economy and Confucian traditions (Liu 2012: 10): It displays decentralization under close guidance and control of the central government as well as massification and privatization of education services (Dello-Iacovo 2009; Mok 2005: 222). Essentially, the development of China's education system can be separated into two stages, the period between 1978 and 1998 as the build-up of the primary and secondary education system, setting the preconditions to the expansion of the higher education sector, and 1998 onwards as the take-off of the higher education sector (Gu 2012: 515).

The foundation of China's modern education system began with the 1985 "Decision on the Structural Reform of China's Education Policy".[3] It advocated decentralization, transferring administrative and financial autonomy from the central to the local governments as well as nine years of universal education (OECD 2010). The role of the central government was limited to setting educational guidelines and supervising the implementation of these directions. By shifting the financial responsibility to local governments, the central authority was able to promote expansion of education without running the risk of increased spending (Mok 2005: 232). Thus, local governments had control over tuition fees but also had to find ways to raise donations, as they were only modestly supported by the central government. Primarily fuelled by the fiscal considerations of the central government, governments at the local level secured funding for their schools through various means (Hawkins 2000).

This process of decentralization of education led to economically stronger regions having significantly higher teaching quality than poorer areas, and therefore, creating large regional disparities between rural and urban as well as coastal and inland areas (Gu 2012: 515). Although China re-emphasized the need to alleviate these disparities with the "Revised Law of Compulsory Education" in 2006 (Ministry of Education of the People's Republic of China 2006) and stressed the need of the harmonious society and harmonious expansion of education in China (Mok 2012: 230), regional inequalities will not only remain a fundamental problem of China's society and education system but are also an intrinsic characteristic of this system, in which local governments act as "the real entrepreneurs and change agents" (Hawkins 2000: 445) of the educational system. Equal access to and success in educational institutions is one of the most pressing social issues in China.

The effort to finance the school sector led to *privatization* of the educational system as local governments began to rely increasingly on private education providers in order to meet the demands of education. These private schools, the so-called *minban*[4] schools, offered poor regions the possibility to provide higher-quality education. These schools enabled China to realize its nine-year, nationwide compulsory education target. Between 1994 and 2006, the number of schools increased from 1280 to 10,366 at the secondary educational level (Chan and Wang 2009: 28) and from 37 to 228 (from 1999 to 2004) at the tertiary level (Mok 2009: 38). The central government has endorsed the development of private schools but with the limitation that they are not allowed to deviate from the school curriculum that the state sets (Hawkins 2000).

The expansion of education was induced by China's recognition of global pressures and the ongoing domestic demand for education, as exemplified in "Outline of China's National Plan for Medium and Long-term Education Reform and Development (2010–20)" (Ministry of Education of the People's Republic of China 2010: 5–6). Expansion, however, was not limited to the secondary education system. From 1999 onwards, it also occurred in the higher education sector (Liu 2012: 6). The two most important documents that enabled this shift were published in 1998, the "Action Plan for Vitalizing Education for the Twenty-first Century" (Ministry of Education of the People's Republic of China 1998a) and the "Higher Education Law of the People's Republic of China" (Ministry of Education of the People's Republic of China 1998b). Between 1999 and 2006, the number of Chinese higher educational institutions nearly doubled to 1867 (Hawkins et al. 2008: 223). There was a goal of having 35.5 million students enrolled in higher educational institutions by 2020, up from 29.8 million students in 2009. Similarly to the secondary education sector, the government shifted the financial responsibility to local governments, which increasingly became shouldered by students and their families. Between 1996 and 2008, the percentage of total funds for higher education rose from 13.7 per cent to 33.7 per cent, with a likewise decrease of government appropriation from 80.3 per cent to 47.6 per cent (Dong and Wan 2012: 2). Nevertheless, public funding has steadily increased. In recent years, the central government has taken a more dominant role in education spending.

## Actors' responses to the PISA Study

Within the dynamic field of educational policies, the PISA Study of 2009 played a controversial part in the ongoing reform process in China. Two groups of actors emerged that either expressed *voice* against or *loyalty* to

PISA. While *voice* took the form of criticism of PISA and its role in the reformatory process of the Chinese educational system, *loyalty* manifested itself in defence of the scientific quality of PISA as well as the education system and the cultural values that are represented by it in general. In the latter line of argumentation, PISA is perceived and used as a legitimation instrument for the ongoing reform process. Finally, the last category, *exit*, finds only a limited applicability in the Chinese case of secondary education, since more regions will participate in future PISA studies. Furthermore, because state schools are financially supported by the government and providers of private education are legally bound to accept state curricula, there may be some homogeneity in the type of education offered, but there are nonetheless different levels of quality in these educational institutions.

## Legitimizing the test results

The top scores received by Shanghai in the 2009 PISA test not only surprised the world but also China itself; scepticism regarding these results was aroused as well. For instance, Bingqi Xiong (2010), a well-known Chinese educator and the associate dean of the Chinese 21st Century Education Research Center, criticized that the form and content of PISA focused on testing basic knowledge and learning abilities. Thus, PISA focused on mechanical memorization rather than on developing students' active learning abilities and real-life skills (Jiang 2010). To respond to this criticism, Jing Lu, secretary of the Shanghai PISA team, stated that "the [PISA] questions bear the characteristics of openness and cultural diversity [which] has gone through four processes of review and modification" (Lu 2011). He continued by stating that PISA does not test what the students have learned, but what practical problems they can solve based on their knowledge and skills (Lu 2011).

Not only was the content of the PISA questioned, but also the reliability of the PISA results examined. Both domestic and international voices questioned the representativeness of the sample: Did Shanghai choose the best schools or the best students to test? The members of the Shanghai PISA team tried to explain the distinctiveness of the PISA project compared to China's present test system and justified the accountability of PISA. Two key members, Jing Lu and Xiaohu Zhu (2011), wrote a report specifically in response to these criticisms. They treated the suspicion of unscientific sampling as a deep-rooted Chinese stereotype and explained the sampling procedure at length: The sampling of schools had been conducted by the research corporation Westat. This was followed by the Shanghai PISA secretariat using the Keyquest software to randomly sample 35 students from every selected school. In this context, the evidence-based feature of PISA played in its favour. Local education authorities and the PISA team shaped the discourse based on this evidence-based feature.

## Reacting to Shanghai's PISA scores

Regarding the PISA results, two distinct positions emerged. On the one hand, local education authorities, Shanghai PISA team members as well as journalists affiliated with the government displayed *loyalty*, stressing the positive effect of reforms and underlining the innovative practices of the local education authority. On the other hand, independent educators and overseas researchers expressed *voice*, looking instead at the negative aspects and persistence of China's exam-oriented education system. Haiyan Hua, a Chinese professor at Harvard University, commented that "China emphasizes examination, scores of college entrance examination are very important, and students from this elite education can easily get good results from this PISA test" (Li 2010). Although the appeal for quality-oriented education started in the early 1990s, the public still remains sceptical of the effect of its practical implementation. Other educators and professors stated that the Chinese educational system is effective only at preparing students for standardized tests. Furthermore, independent educators and overseas researchers argued that Chinese students face pressures from various sources, including schools, parents and society, as an explanation for why they take the test more seriously than counterparts in other non-Asian countries (Xie 2010). Therefore, the high test scores of Chinese students are achieved at the cost of heavy workloads, low social skills and a hindrance to the development of creative thinking (Xie 2010).

In contrast, local authorities and members of the Shanghai PISA team displayed *loyalty*, stressing that the PISA results represented the outcome of Shanghai's successful education reforms. This reasoning was framed, reproduced and disseminated through various channels such as conferences, journals and newspapers, which are part of the government agency. The reasoning made its first appearance one week after the OECD announced the results on 7 December 2009. In an interview, Mingyang Xue, the director of the Shanghai Municipal Education Commission (SMEC), stated that PISA "demonstrates that Shanghai has gained certain achievements in quality-oriented education; the direction of Shanghai curriculum reform is correct" (Xue 2011). Indeed, the local education authority, the Shanghai PISA team and some local researchers

*Table 10.1*    The discrepancy of reasoning for PISA results (own account).

| Reasoning | Loyalty<br>Local Authority, PISA Team Members, Local Educators and Researchers | Voice<br>Independent Educators, Overseas Chinese Professors |
|---|---|---|
| **Successful Reform Policy** | Strong | No |
| **Social Cultural Norms** | Medium | Rare |
| **Developed City and Good Students** | Rare | Medium |
| **Exam-Oriented Education** | No | Strong |

and journalists affiliated with government agencies sought to explain and confirm that the results were due mainly to the education reforms that were carried out under the government's leadership. By attributing Shanghai's performance in the PISA Study to its successful implementation of state education policy, local political actors confirmed and legitimated their pre-existing policy stance and policy innovation as well as reaffirmed the role of government in regulating and planning future reforms.

### Summary of actors' reactions to PISA

Independent educators and overseas researchers showed more sympathy towards students who bear heavy workloads and face high pressures to achieve academic success, which arguably come at the cost of sacrificing social life and mental health. In this sense, China's current educational system is somewhat paradoxical: On the one hand, the whole nation places a strong emphasis on developing students' creativity and all-around development; on the other hand, students still suffer from tremendous examination pressure. Ultimately, for these actors, China's education reforms remained unsuccessful (Li 2010).

As previously discussed, local officials and members from the PISA team positively viewed the PISA results as a reflection of Shanghai's successful education reform; however, they also emphasized that these results should be interpreted with caution. First, it was argued that Shanghai's performance in the 2009 PISA Study is not representative for the overall performance of the entire Chinese educational system. Mingyan Xue pointed out that "Shanghai is just a city, [and] it doesn't represent the whole of China" (Fu and Shen 2010). Reminding the public of improved economic development and infrastructure as well as highlighting the wide gap between Shanghai and other regions, local officials tried to obviate the critics that used China's overall educational characteristics to attack Shanghai's education system.

Furthermore, the local education authority and the PISA team emphasized that Shanghai's performance did not indicate a poor-quality educational system in other countries. This caution mainly targeted the critiques and suspicions coming from international educators, commentators and overseas professors who found it surprising that Shanghai achieved better results than other countries. In order to stop these claims, the local education authority and PISA team members stressed the merits of other countries' education systems. Hence, they showed a modest attitude, recognized the value of other education systems, reaffirmed the stance of learning from international experience and promoted education reform.

Moreover, the Shanghai PISA team recognized that certain deficiencies needed to be improved upon in the future. Although the local education authority downplayed heavy workloads as the cost of high student scores, they still pointed out the need to reduce the workload.[5] They also addressed the gender balance in education performance. For instance, in the reading test, the average score for girls was 48 points higher than for boys. The researcher Mingyang Zhang noted that this result "reminds us to further study the cognitive and psychological differences between boys and girls" (Fu and Shen 2010). The third problem they identified was that "Shanghai's student performances at non-continuous texts reading are much lower than those on continuous texts reading" (Fu and Shen 2010).

The local authority, PISA team members as well as local educators and researchers highlighted the importance of continuing educational reforms and working on solving problems. For them, PISA 2009 has evaluated more than two decades of Shanghai's education reform efforts. The local education authority and PISA team framed their argument in such a way to make it difficult and unjustifiable for the public to use the PISA results to overhaul the educational reform attempts made by the government. Through interviews, talks and written reports, the local education authorities and PISA team developed and enhanced the legitimacy of PISA as an instrument to deepen education reform. In contrast, independent educators and overseas scholars demonstrated a more negative attitude towards the test results (see Table 10.2).

*Table 10.2*   The discrepancy of reflection on the test results (own account).

|  | **Loyalty**<br>Local Authority, PISA Team<br>Members, Local Educators<br>and Researchers | **Voice**<br>Independent Educators,<br>Overseas Chinese<br>Professors |
| --- | --- | --- |
| Major attitude | Positive | Negative |
| Warnings | PISA results representative;education in other countries is not bad;acknowledge problems | PISA results do not reflect Shanghai's education;it reflects the failure of China's education |
| Reflecting on theproblems | High costs for results;gender difference;low performance on reading non-continuous texts | Simplification of education, passive learning, no creativity; high costs for results;consider psychological health |
| Looking into the future | Continue reform process | Question reform process |

## Higher education in China

It should be kept in mind that the Bologna Process is a strictly European initiative, towards which other countries can orient their educational systems. However, the impact of the Bologna Process traversed European borders and was felt in China as well. Although the empirical evidence regarding the implementation of Bologna-style reforms suggests the same sets of actors as in the PISA Study, the delineation between these two camps is less straightforward than when compared to secondary education. Interestingly, *voice* is even expressed by university researchers appealing for government leadership to disseminate information about the Bologna Process and coordinate cooperation and exchanges with European partners. Our analysis focuses on how these two groups of actors interpreted and used the Bologna Process to relate to their current circumstances and reform agenda. Furthermore, in contrast to the PISA Study, the Bologna Process received remarkably little attention in China, judging by the number of relevant newspaper articles. Thus, we can label this lack of relevance of Bologna as an indirect type of *exit*. In the second step of the analysis, we will contrast the findings within a broader contextualization of *exit* and *loyalty* in the form of membership in international organizations dealing with education.

## Governmental reactions to Bologna

On many occasions, the Chinese government has emphasized its willingness to participate in international cooperation and exchanges in the field of higher education (Pinna 2009). The Bologna Process has provided an opportunity to advance such cooperation and exchanges with its European partners. Mr. Zhou, the deputy director of National Centre for Education Development Research in China, summarized the EU-China educational cooperation:

> [. . .] the Chinese government and education research institutes have been paying close attention to the development of the Bologna Process. These years, China has been actively participating in the Erasmus program, striving to facilitate joint curriculum development between China and European countries, and increasing mobility of undergraduates, graduates, and faculty. [. . .] It also provides more opportunities for exchanges of faculty and students, credit recognition, joint degrees, top talent training and other bidirectional educational trainings, and equal cooperation in science and research (in Gao 2010).

Education authorities emphasized that cooperation should be bilateral and equal. According to Pinna's interviews (2009) with Chinese professors and officials at the Chinese Ministry of Education, the cooperation between China and European partners has not been well balanced in the past. One challenge for China to integrate into the international educational system is to demonstrate its own higher education systems and receive recognition from its international partners for its quality. In October 2006, the communication "EU–China: Closer Partners, Growing Responsibilities" from the European Commission, suggested that the EU should actively respond to China's re-emergence and strengthen its partnership with China (European Commission 2006). Chinese education authorities are actively concluding bilateral agreements on the mutual recognition of degrees with over 30 countries, including Germany, United Kingdom and France; nevertheless, they are still trying to expand such bilateral agreements (Yang 2009).

Furthermore, attracting more foreign students to China was also a main point of emphasis. Chinese education departments noticed an imbalance of outgoing and incoming mobile students. Statistics show that from 2000 to 2011, 32.1 per cent of overseas Chinese students studied in the U.S. and 27.9 per cent in Europe,[6] while in a similar time span (1997 to 2009), only around 10 to 15.1 per cent of students from these regions studied in China (Yang 2011). In cooperation with its European partners, China has been increasing its effort to attract European students. For example, in 2005, China and Germany developed a new chapter of strategic dialogue in higher education and established a proposal for developing mutual learning programmes. The proposal pointed out that the Chinese government would develop more programmes to attract German students to China in order to conduct joint learning and research activities (Zhou 2006).

Finally, despite the relatively little attention that the Bologna Process received in China, examples where it was indeed acknowledged were mainly found when used to justify educational reforms. The Chinese education authorities, for instance, refer to the objectives of the Bologna Process and use its 2020 vision to resonate with the principles and priorities underlying Chinese higher education reform as well as to mobilize social resources to achieve its reform policy. This was well illustrated by Mr. Zhou, who advocated, among other aspects, the implementation of a lifelong learning strategy, increases in student mobility as well as multidimensional and transparent quality-assurance tools (in Gao 2010).

## Non-governmental reactions

Since the launch of China's higher education reform, Chinese educational researchers have *voiced* their concerns on the current management system in higher education. For example, Bao and Li (2010) point out that the traditional redistribution of educational resources by the government could not meet the increasing demand and competition for educational resources. In order to improve resource efficiency and promote resource sharing among universities, university alliances became a viable coping strategy. This idea appears to be implemented mainly at the regional level. For example, in 2006, leaders from universities in the Zhejiang province met at Xiasha High Education Park to cooperate. In January 2010, ten universities in the Hubei province also established an alliance. After evaluating the outcomes, Lei, Fang and Wei found that although alliances have been created, the transfer of credits is not proceeding very well. They argued that this is due to the fact that Chinese universities have been organized within a top-down administrative structure for a long time, impeding resource sharing and the development of common evaluation criteria among partner universities. The major obstacle, therefore, is derived from the conservative leaders at the universities who are reluctant to share their resources and break down institutional barriers (Lei et al. 2007).

Similarly, considering administrative barriers and conservative education philosophies, Bao and Li (2010) warned that there is still a long way to go towards any substantial inter-university cooperation. Therefore, they suggested referencing the experience and framework of the Bologna Process as a means to help Chinese universities step out of this dilemma. Chinese universities should take concrete actions, such as establishing a well-rounded credit transfer system, overcoming barriers of student and faculty mobility, providing quality assurance and establishing scientific assessment. They also advocated that, under the current Chinese higher education system, university autonomy should be ensured and a student-centred model should be promoted.

Paradoxically, while referring to the higher education reforms and university alliances, researchers advocate a reduction in government interventions in the administration of universities and an increase in university autonomy; however, on international cooperation, researchers appeal for leadership and coordination from the government. A research team noticed that in exchange programmes with the EU, China needs more effective coordination from an education authority (Centre for Higher Education Research Group 2009). In order to promote substantive cooperation, education departments need to establish permanent organizations to better communicate with European partners and provide relevant information and consultation for domestic educational organizations. They should also facilitate exchange and cooperation among governments, universities, research institutions, business sectors and social organizations.

## Internationalization and regionalization of Chinese higher education

The political elite plans further steps that are specified by the government and are to be implemented by the educational institutions. Higher education institutions are encouraged to foster further internationalization of their faculties, study programmes and students. Specifically, greater recruitment efforts are made for top international professors and scientists to permanently work at Chinese universities. These plans are paralleled by the intention to attract more foreign students to China. One way to realize internationalization is to offer more English study programmes. Another approach is to develop more cooperation based on mutual recognition of credits, ensuring that students can receive credit for their courses or even complete double degrees. The Chinese government stated that this cooperation has to be equal for institutions and students in both countries. China intends to be less of an education importer and more of an education exporter by attracting foreign students to its own renowned universities. The advantages are both financial, as tuition fees that are paid by foreign students, and reputational, insofar as increasing the awareness and recognition of Chinese universities worldwide (Zgaga 2005). Another goal is to encourage Chinese universities to open their own branch campuses in foreign countries. These university subsidiaries in other countries are connected to the Confucius Institute, which are official Chinese language schools. Via the Confucius Institute network, China can increase its international influence and use soft power to promote all facets of China (Yang 2010: 201).

There have been structures of regional cooperation in East Asia since the 1950s. For the first three decades these regional cooperation initiatives were exclusive, intra-regional and mostly concerned with economic and security issues. Since the 1980s, new patterns of cooperation could be noticed: Regional organizations became inter-regional, and these initiatives also started to cover social issues, for example, in higher education (Hawkins et al. 2012: 98). Among these organizations are the Brisbane Communique, the ASEAN University Network Programme (AUNP), the Asia Pacific Quality Network (APQN), the University Mobility in Asia and the Pacific (UMAP) and the Southeast Asian Ministers of Education Organization (SEAMEO) Regional Centre for Higher Education and Development (RIHED) (Zgaga 2005: 65). These organizations have varying memberships and cover a range of different issues, such as quality assurance, frameworks for the recognition of educational and professional credentials, common competency for teaching as well as generally enhancing "regional understanding, cooperation, and unity of purpose among the Member States" (SEAMEO 2013). Equally broad are the means through which these organizations hope to realize their goals, such as through conferences, education forums, workshops and seminars. These regionalization and internationalization efforts are conducted against the background of very different regional education systems, a lack of a common identity, numerous languages and disparity in the general quality of educational institutions (Nguyen 2009: 80).

It is this overall context in which the Chinese reactions to the Bologna Process need to be analysed. China and its partners strive to achieve their mission: First, to harmonize their higher education system with European universities by adopting Bologna-style reforms, and second, to engage in bilateral exchanges. Similarly, starting in the 1990s, the goal was shifted from increasing the quantity to enhancing the quality of the Chinese education system, and hence, becoming internationally competitive (Deem et al. 2008).[7] Second, China regionalized its own higher education system with neighbouring states, initiating a regional Bologna Process. Thus, on the basis of the evidence currently available, it seems fair to suggest that the Bologna Process had an effect on China's internationalization policy as a state and that little *exit* has been pursued.

## Conclusion

This chapter suggests that a study of China – with regard to its reactions to internationalization processes in education – paints a multifaceted picture that goes well beyond the usual Chinese political, societal and academic discussions. Despite the relative isolation of its political system, the limited participatory possibilities of its citizens, its only recent participation in the PISA Study and its non-membership in the Bologna Process, China's reaction towards internationalization processes is diverse. Although we can identify different actor coalitions as well as varying responses, a *new constellation of the state in education* is not apparent.

In the field of secondary education, the empirical evidence suggested the presence of two actor coalitions, one concentrating on government officials, PISA team members and journalists associated with the government, and the second consisting of independent *voices* and overseas educators. Essentially, we were able to identify *loyalty* and *voice* in the discourse, while *exit* – either as leaving the state education system or indifference towards PISA – could not be found. The data suggests that PISA is embedded within the reformatory process of the education system, influencing the discourse, and is being used to legitimize further reform efforts by local authorities. Moreover, critical *voices*, at least in appearance, contribute to a more open discourse in which the performance of Shanghai's students is evaluated based upon different opinions.

The political opportunity structure in China is not as open for social movements and protests as it is in Western democracies. From a rational choice perspective on ideas, resources and opportunities, it is not surprising that a coalition of government officials and PISA team members used the results to legitimize their reforms of the education system. Yet, *voice* has been raised from independent educational experts, especially from abroad. Even though the overall discourse is more open than it used to be in China, the cost of collectively organizing protest and asking for reforms is high and, more important, the expected chance of successful *voice* is very low if good PISA results can easily be turned into good arguments in favour of reform.

Regarding the field of higher education, the picture is far less clear. The delineations between *voice* and *loyalty* become fuzzy at times. The coalitions should, however, be considered in the light of the low number of related newspaper articles, hinting at the lack of relevance of the Bologna Process in the domestic discourse. Yet, contrary to these findings, China is massively engaged in the internationalization and regionalization of its higher educational institutions, efforts that are unquestionably linked to Bologna – even if an "East Asian Higher Education Area" would greatly differ from its European counterpart, the Bologna Process functions as a model. Thus, we are confronted with a conundrum: If arguably the most important, or at least the most dynamic, reform processes are initiated at the level of higher education, why is this not reflected in the domestic (or international, for that matter) discourse?

China is part of the internationalization of education, whether through PISA, Bologna or other initiatives. This has opened up the discursive space for critical and *loyal* comments, for taking internationalization seriously and finally shaping and influencing the policies of a rising power with a population of over 1.3 billion people. Notwithstanding China's excellent result on the 2009 PISA, the country is still catching up to its counterparts around the world. As stated by the Chinese Ministry of Education, "the destiny of our nation rests on education. People across the country are duty-bound to rejuvenate education. Education development should always be put in a prioritized position on Party and state agenda" (Ministry of Education of the People's Republic of China 2010: 6).

## Notes

1   CNKI is the largest online database covering nationwide newspapers, dissertations, academic journals, proceedings and so on. Overall we found six research papers.
2   This is only a short overview of the reformatory process of the Chinese educational system. For more details, see (Dello-Iacovo 2009; Mok 2012; OECD 2011).
3   This decision was formalized one year later, in 1986, with the Compulsory Education Law of the People's Republic of China (Ministry of Education of the People's Republic of China 1986).
4   For further discussion on the term *minban* and different types of these institutions, see Mok (2005; 1997).
5   The Outline of China's National Plan for Medium and Long-term Education Reform (2010–20) observes that "heavy schoolwork is harmful to the mental and physical well-being of youngsters and children" and that "governments at all levels shall regard reducing heavy school work burdens as a major task for education work" (Ministry of Education of the People's Republic of China 2010:15).

6 中国留学生超六成滞留海外 http://news.sciencenet.cn/htmlnews/2012/9/269556 .shtm 张冬冬 来源: 中国新闻网 发布时间, retrieved 17 September 2012.

7 Among the projects to achieve this goal was "Project 211", which was implemented in the ninth five-year plan, in 1995, to enhance the general quality of universities. The best 100 universities or faculties of the country are located and supported by the government (Liu 2007). "Project 985" selected 39 out of the 211 universities for additional funding. It was implemented in 1998.

## References

Bao, W. and Jingbo Li. 包万平,李金波 (2010) Promoting the 'Bologna Process' in Chinese Universities, 推进中国大学的"博洛尼亚进程", *Science Times*, 科学时报. Section B1, March 23.

Cai, Yongshun (2008) "Power Structure and Regime Resilience: contentious politics in China", *British Journal of Political Science*, 38(3), 411–32.

Centre for Studies in Higher Education Research Group, Central South University. 中南大学高等教育研究所课题组 (2009) Proposal for Establishing China's Coping Mechanism for the Bologna Process. 建立中国应对博洛尼亚进程机制的设想, *Modern University Education*, 现代大学教育, 6.

Chan, Raymond K.H. and Ying Wang (2009) "Controlled decentralization: minban education reform in China", *Journal of Comparative Social Welfare*, 25(1), 27–36.

Deem, Rosemary, Ka Ho Mok and Lisa Lucas (2008) "Transforming Higher Education in Whose Image? Exploring the Concept of the 'World-Class' University in Europe and Asia", *Higher Education Policy*, 21(1), 83–97.

Dello-Iacovo, Belinda (2009) "Curriculum Reform and 'Quality Education' in China: An overview", *International Journal of Education*, 29(3), 241–49.

Dong, Haiying and Xuehong Wang (2012) "Higher Education Tuition and Fees in China: Implications and impacts on affordability and educational equity", *Current Issues in Education*, 15(1), 1–10.

European Commission (2006) *EU-China: closer partners, growing responsibilities*, Brussels: European Commission.

Fu, Lujian and Zuyun Shen. 傅禄建, 沈祖芸 (2010) "PISA 2009: The Quality of Shanghai Compulsory Education in a Global Perspective. PISA 2009: 国际视野中的上海义务教育质量", *Shanghai Education*. 上海教育, 22–23. Section 12B, December.

Gao, Liang. 高靓. (2010) "What Does the Launch of Regionalization of European High Education Bring to the World? 欧洲高等教育区启动给世界带来什么? —访第二届博洛尼亚政策论坛中国代表团团长, 国家教育发展研究中心副主任周满生", *People's Daily, People's Daily Overseas Edition*. 人民日报海外版. Section 3, March 31.

Gu, Jiafeng (2012) "Harmonious Expansion of China's Higher Education: A New Growth Pattern", *Higher Education: The International Journal of Higher Education and Educational Planning*, 63(4), 513–28.

Hawkins, John N. (2000) "Centralization, decentralization, recentralization – Educational reform in China", *Journal of Educational Administration*, 38(5), 442–55.

Hawkins, John N., W. James Jacob and Li Wenli (2008) "Higher Education in China: Access, Equity and Equality" in Donald B. Holsinger and W. James

Jacob, eds., *Inequality in Education. Comparative and International Perspective*, Hong Kong: Springer, 215–39.

Hawkins, John N., Ka Ho Mok and Diane E. Neubauer eds. (2012) *Higher Education Regionalization in Asia Pacific Implications for Governance, Citizenship and University Transformation.* Basingstoke: Palgrave Macmillan.

He, Kai and Huiyun Feng (2008) "A Path to Democracy: In Search of China's Democratization Model", *Asian Perspective*, 32(3), 139–69.

Hirschman, Albert O. (1970) *Exit, Voice, and Loyalty. Responses to Decline in Firms, Organizations, and States*, Cambridge: Cambridge University Press.

Jiang, Hongbing 姜泓冰 (2010). People's Daily. 人民日报 "Using International Standards to Examine Chinese Education. 国际标准"体检"中国教育". Section 12, 20 December.

Kuah, Khun Eng and Gilles Guiheux (2009) *Social Movements in China and Hong Kong: The Expansion of Protest Space*, Amsterdam: Amsterdam University Press.

Lei, Wei, Yongping Fang and Weihua Hu. 雷炜, 方永平, 胡维华 (2007) "European Bologna Process and Its Implications. 欧洲博洛尼亚进程及其启示", *China Higher Education*,中国高等教育, 6.

Li, Dajiu. 李大玖 (2010) "How to View Shanghai Students' First Rank in PISA Test? Advices from Chinese American Educators for China's education. 如何看待上海学生 PISA 测评全球第一? — 美国华裔教育学家为中国教育建言. 参考消息", *Reference News.* Section 9, 16 December.

Liu, Jinghui (2007) "Das Bildungswesen in der Volksrepublik China: ein struktureller und statistischer Überblick", Fischer, Doris and Michael Lackner, eds., *Länderbericht China*, Bonn: Bundeszentrale für Politische Bildung, 513–22.

Liu, Jian (2012) "Examining Massification Policies and Their Consequences for Equality in Chinese Higher Education: A Cultural Perspective", Higher Education: The International Journal of Higher Education and Educational Planning, 64(5), 647–60.

Lu, Jing. 陆璟 (2011) "The Primary Thing Is the Balanced Development of Education. 第一的关键是教育均衡", *China Education Newspaper.* 中国教育报. Section 3, February 18.

Lu, Jing and Xiaohu Lu. 陆璟, 朱小虎 (2011) "How to View 2009 Shanghai PISA Result? The Review of the Reflection on Shanghai Middle School Students' First Participation in the International Test. 如何看待上海2009年PISA测评结果—中国上海中学生首次参加国际测评结果反响述评", *Shanghai Research on Education.* 上海教育科研, 17–19. January.

Martin, Michael F. (2010) *Understanding China's Political System*, CRS Report for Congress, Washington, D.C.

Ministry of Education of the People's Republic of China (1986) *Compulsory Education Law of the People's Republic of China*, Beijing: Ministry of Education of the People's Republic of China.

Ministry of Education of the People's Republic of China (1998a) *Action Plan for Vitalizing Education for the Twenty-first Century*, Beijing: Ministry of Education of the People's Republic of China.

Ministry of Education of the People's Republic of China (1998b) *Higher Education Law the People's Republic of China*, Beijing: Ministry of Education of the People's Republic of China.

Ministry of Education of the People's Republic of China (2006) *Revised Law of Compulsory Education*, Beijing: Ministry of Education of the People's Republic of China.

Ministry of Education of the People's Republic of China (2010) *Outline of China's National Plan for Medium and Long-term Education Reform and Development (2010–2020)*, Beijing: Ministry of Education of the People's Republic of China.

Mok, Ka Ho (1997) "Retreat of the State: Marketization of Education in the Pearl River Delta", *Comparative Education Review*, 41(3), 260–76.

Mok, Ka Ho (2005) "Riding over Socialism and Global Capitalism: Changing Education Governance and Social Policy Paradigms in Post-Mao China", *Comparative Education*, 42(2), 217–42.

Mok, Ka Ho (2009) "The Growing Importance of the Privateness in Education: Challenges for Higher Education Governance in China", *Compare: A Journal of Comparative and International Education*, 39(1), 35–49.

Mok, Ka Ho (2012) "Bringing the State Back In: Restoring the Role of the State in Chinese Higher Education", *European Journal of Education*, 47(2), 228–41.

Nguyen, Anh Thuy (2009) "The Role of Regional Organizations in East Asian Regional Cooperation and Integration in the Field of Higher Education", *Asian Regional Integration Review*, 1, 69–82.

OECD (2010) *Strong Performers and Successful Reformers in Education: Lessons from PISA for the United States*, Paris: OECD.

OECD, ed. (2011) *Education at a Glance, Country Note – China*, Paris: OECD.

Osa, Maryjane and Cristina Corduneanu-Huci (2003) "Running Uphill: Political Opportunity in Non-democracies", *Comparative Sociology*, 2(4), 605–29.

Pinna, Cristina (2009) "EU–China Relations in Higher Education", *Asia Europe Journal*, 7(3), 505–27.

SEAMEO (2013) *What is SEAMEO?*, http://www.seameo.org/index.php?option=com_content&view=article&id=90&Itemid=518, retrieved 29 August 2013.

Sellar, Sam and Bob Lingard (2013) "Looking East: Shanghai, PISA 2009 and the reconstitution of reference societies in the global education policy field", *Comparative Education* 49(4), 464–85.

Wang, Naixia and W. John Morgan (2012) "The Harmonious Society, Social Capital and Lifelong Learning in China: Emerging Policies and Practice", *International Journal of Continuing Education and Lifelong Learning*, 4(2), 1–15.

Xie, Xiang. 谢湘 (2010) "What Does Shanghai PISA Test Tell Us? The Balanced Development of Education Is Not Impossible. PISA 测试上海夺冠回答了什么—教育均衡并非可望不可. 中国青年报", *China Youth Daily*. Section 8, March 4.

Xiong, Bingqi. 熊丙奇 (2010) "Being World No.1 in Students' Knowledge Accomplishment Test Is Not Something to Be Proud Of. 学生知识素养世界第一未必值得骄傲", *Oriental Morning Post*. 东方早报, Section 22.

Xue, Mingyan. 薛明扬 (2011) "It Is the Government's Obligatory to Promote the Balanced Development of Compulsory Education. 促进义务教育均衡发展是不容推卸的政府责任", *China Education Newspaper*. 中国教育报. Front page, February 18.

Yang, Chao. (2011) "The Structural Change of Foreign Students in China and Its Influencing Factor. 来华留学生教育结构变化及其影响因素." *Modern Education Management*. 现代教育管理. 10, 111–115.

Yang, Linyu. 杨琳瑜 (2009) "Studies on Bologna Process in China: Review and Outlook. 国内关于博洛尼亚进程的研究：综述与展望", *Huibei Social Sciences*. 湖北社会科学, 9.

Yang, Rui (2010) "Soft Power and Higher Education: An Examination of China's Confucius Institutes", *Globalisation, Societies and Education*, 8(2), 235–45.

Yu, Lan and Hoi K. Suen (2005) "Historical and Contemporary Exam-Driven Education Fever in China", *KEDI Journal of Educational Policy*, 2(1), 17–33.

Zeng, Qian, John Adams and Andy Gibbs (2012) "Are China and the ASEAN Ready for a Bologna Process? – Factors affecting the establishment of the China-ASEAN higher education area", *Education Review*, 65(3), 1–21.

Zgaga, Pavel (2005) *Looking Out: The Bologna Process in a Global Setting on the 'External Dimension' of the Bologna Process*, Oslo: Norwegian Ministry of Education and Research.

Zhang, Yongjing (2011) "The Successor's Dilemma in China's Single Party Political System", *European Journal of Political Economy*, 27(4), 674–80.

Zhang, Chenjian and Alexander Akbik (2012) "PISA as a Legitimacy Tool during China's Education Reform: Case Study of Shanghai", *TranState Working Papers* 166, Bremen University.

Zhou, Mansheng 周满生 (2006) "Bologna Process: A Chinese Perspective. 博洛尼亚进程: 中国视角", *Forum on Contemporary Education.* 当代教育论坛, 8.

# Part III
# Conclusion

# 11
## Reforming Education Policy after PISA and Bologna – Two Logics of Governance and Reactions

*Michael Windzio, Philipp Knodel and Kerstin Martens*

### Introduction

Over the last decades, we have observed fundamental changes in education systems across Western countries. Although education has traditionally been a national policy concern or even regulated at the sub-national level, many of these recent changes were triggered by new actors in the international arenas of education governance (Martens et al. 2007). As one of the most important changes detected in Europe, the Bologna Process was initiated by the Sorbonne Declaration, which envisioned the harmonization of tertiary education in Europe. At the moment of signature, it was little more than a declaration of intent signed by four EU member states, but nonetheless served as a catalyst for a so-called 'big bang' of higher education policy reform (Toens 2007). Concurrent to this development was a further wholesale reform of education policy at the secondary level following the widely publicized results of the PISA Study, a collection of data surmising student achievement levels in OECD countries. While there was at least some consensus among national interest groups about the reforms in secondary and higher education, some groups responded negatively to the reforms; others welcomed the ongoing reform processes. To date, it is unclear what the actual real-life effects of these reforms are at present and will be in the near future. Thus, the consequences of the reforms are hard to evaluate. What are the outcomes of education reforms at the secondary and tertiary level? And which social groups react to these reforms for what reasons? What does it mean to the future structure of education systems and future reforms? These are the basic questions in our study.

We started this book by outlining our theoretical framework, designed as a multilevel approach that comprises political opportunity structures at the macro level as well as the choice of behavioural alternatives at the micro level. As we deal with organizations and interest groups, we investigate *collective actors* at the micro level. Theories since the 1970s on the limits of governance and control, systems theory (Luhmann 2008) and particularly results of implementation research (Bardach und Kagan 1982) challenged the assumption of a direct causal impact of policies on outcomes as summarized in the introduction to this volume. Even more problematic is the assumption that powerful political groups can put their specific political or ideological guiding principles into practice without any frictional loss in the political process (Mayntz 1997). In view of this situation, it is ambitious to analyse how the state has been transformed with regard to education policy as a result of internationalization – such as the OECD benchmarking by the PISA Study or the Bologna Declaration supported at the EU level. The core of this complexity is that explaining impacts and social processes implies statements on the difficult question of causality (Pearl 2000; Gangl 2010). From the researcher's point of view, this problem is not only an analytic one, but also one for practitioners who conceptualize their measures of political intervention. Is the current state of a social system really the result of a particular policy? Is a particular policy output in line with the original ideas of the political or ideological carrier groups, or is it just a result of bargaining and joint decision-making in differentiated modern political structures?

The issue of causal attribution of political measures or policies to observable outcomes is a general problem for policy-makers. Nevertheless, their situation is comparatively convenient because they decide within political institutions explicitly designed and adapted with the intention to facilitate policy-making. While current systems theory seems to be sceptical about control capacities in general, actor-centred approaches argue that the political actors' attempt at exerting control encounters resistance by highly organized and institutionalized power structures in subsystems, such as interest groups (Mayntz 1997: 200). Paradoxically, control at the state level is impeded because subsystems have high internal control capacities at their disposal.

Attributing changes in policy *outputs* and *outcomes* directly to the guiding principles of particular groups is even more problematic if international organizations only apply forms of 'soft governance' in education policy (Martens und Wolf 2006), such as benchmarking. From the social scientist's point of view, it is of interest to see whether soft governance has a similar impact on the desired *outcomes* compared with the traditional decision-making within political institutions. As we have seen in this volume, both perspectives are important. In Switzerland, for instance, education reforms were blocked for decades but received enough political support in light of the published PISA results for policy-makers to collaborate in conceptualizing and implementing reforms that had already been discussed but that could not be realized before PISA due to the reform-adverse political institutions. In this setting, benchmark-ing was a catalyst for such reforms, but it would not have had any effect without the consensus, deliberate action and organizational capacities of the policy-makers, as well as the institutional structure in which they deliberated and reached a consensus. Notwithstanding, ideas and guid-ing principles often become spoiled by compromises, making a direct causal attribution of outcomes to policies questionable in most cases. Accordingly, governance in the field of education is a problem per se, particularly if it happens at the supra-national level.

The theoretical framework of our study explains the problems of con-verting political ideas into education *outcomes* as well as *reactions* of relevant groups towards changing policies and outcomes. It combines arguments from different theoretical perspectives, and may thus be sus-picious of an eclectic approach. However, our explanandum is a complex social and multilevel process that requires an appropriate framework, one that captures rational actors as well as systemic processes. Moreover, *frictions* between reforms in education policy and their outcomes also result from task overload, especially in educational institutions (Windzio 2013). Ideologies that aim at deliberate changes of society try to influence educational institutions, as well as the content and forms of educating young members of the society. The idea of frictions between education reforms and their outcomes sensitizes us not only to the problems of reforming educational institutions but also to the large potential of reac-tions to changes in education policy (see chapter 1).

Our basic causal model states that the *new constellation of statehood* in secondary and higher education results in intended, but often also unin-tended, consequences. These consequences are the *outcomes*, desired or not, as well as the *reactions* of relevant actors. Regarding the actors' reactions, we argued that the explanation for who reacts in which way depends on *political opportunity structures* at the macro level and on *ideas* and *political resources* of each interest group on the micro level. Taken together, these variables result in specific *value expectations*. We employed value-expectation theory because it is a broad framework, open to the utility functions of specific groups as well as subjectively perceived opportunity structures. This enables us to analyse the subjectively perceived ability to realize the utility of a behavioural alternative. If we take all these components together – opportunity structures, ideas, resources and expectations – we are able to explain processes of collective actors' mobilization. In the view of Hirschman's (1970) typology, their reactions can be *loyalty, voice* or *exit*. Following Coleman's (1990) model of explanation in the social sciences, we argue that this macro-macro association can only be explained by analysing collective actors' positions and values at the micro level. Following this theoretical framework, the consequences of the transformation of education policy are analysed in different case studies as well as in two large-N comparative studies.

### The findings of the study

In a comparative research design based on data from the first four waves of the PISA Study, *Teltemann* shows that many OECD countries seem to have changed their education policy and show considerable changes in educational output factors at the secondary level. If there were a rather direct impact of 'best practices' in educational institutions, we would have expected, at least at the level of educational output factors (for example, standardization, stratification), a trend towards convergence and common goals. This is obviously not the case, albeit there is a growing importance of accountability practices. The empirical approach tries to detect causal effects between changes in educational output factors (for example, achievement and equality of opportunity) on educational outcome variables. If countries *change* their education policies, and thereby induce changes in the *output* of their education policy, this can indeed have an impact on outcomes. However, it is a rather specific change, such as ability grouping for some subjects, which shows the desired impact on educational inequalities. Admittedly, it is not easy to give a clearly justified theoretical explanation for these effects or for why other changes have no or even an undesired impact. The analysis also indicates that there is no clear policy concept in terms of best practices wherein countries converge.

By using a longitudinal data set of 39 to 41 countries, *Fulge* and *Vögtle* have shown that the share of students of a given country who move abroad in order to pursue their tertiary degree has only moderately increased in Bologna countries. This result is not in line with the basic intention of the Bologna Process to foster the international exchange of students. Moreover, they also showed that a high degree of institutional change in implementing the reforms of the Bologna Process do not change student mobility. However, exchange patterns are more balanced – compared to non-participating OECD countries – between countries participating in the Bologna Process. Increasing the mobility of students and facilitating the comparison of different degrees between multiple countries were ambitious goals of the Bologna Process. It did not only address specific organizations or even nation states but also a wider European higher education area. In line with our theoretical arguments, we observe again that governance also faces complex imponderables at the supra-national level. But if Bologna membership does only moderately increase student mobility, it does not necessarily mean that the reform is ineffective. There is a steady trend of increasing international student mobility in general, which can be a result of the Bologna Process as well. Rather than being a club with specific members, the Bologna Process can be also conceived as an idea of making tertiary education globally comparable, and the consequence of not following this idea could lead to the intellectual and cultural self-exclusion of a country in the long run. Indeed, there is evidence that countries that are not formally part of the Bologna Process also take the European reforms in higher education as a role model (Vögtle und Martens 2013). If there is a steady, nearly worldwide trend of student mobility, this trend – probably triggered by the original Bologna Process – cannot be measured by the dummy variable in a regression model.

One of the most interesting case studies at the level of secondary education is Germany. For decades, Germans perceived themselves as an economically powerful country with only scarce natural resources, but with a well-educated and highly qualified workforce. This was the precondition for the PISA shock, when the OECD published the results of the PISA 2000 wave. Reforms of the secondary education system were encompassing and based on a quick implementation process. Currently, the reforms and the fine-tuning adjustments are still ongoing. As one example, the German education system has accepted the increased demand for output-oriented policy-making as a result of the scientific evidence against the premise of institutional effectiveness. Rather than a convergence of the *Länder* to a uniform best practice in secondary education, there is a set of specific reforms that are overall widely accepted by relevant actors. However, some controversies regarding the general orientation in German secondary education remain. While some actors aligned to the output evaluation, others feared an overemphasis of market-driven education principles. A similar picture can be drawn in German higher education. As *Niemann* has also shown, there is a common support for the intentions of the so-called Bologna reforms, but there are still political struggles with regard to the implementation and organization of the two-cycle tertiary education system (that is bachelor's and master's studies). The political landscape of Germany consists of strong and well-organized political interest groups who either support a slight rollback of the policy reforms in education or an intensification of the process. In general, and as the theory of political opportunity structures assumes, support or resistance to the introduced reforms in education almost always took place in the usual political forums since the weak German state in education policy offered many access points for actors to participate in political decision-making.

In the case of England, as analysed by *Knodel*, the results of the PISA Study were not found to be of great, if any, importance as a period of far-reaching reforms had already taken place during the 1980s. Moreover, standardized evaluation procedures at the level of secondary education were already common, even though an internationally comparative assessment, such as the PISA Study, was new. England performed well in the first round but has dropped in the ranking since 2000. Even though the results have not been published, the decline in performance became obvious in the 2009 wave, eliciting both *exit* and *voice* reactions. Regarding higher education, reactions in the government changed from *exit* – or ignoring the Bologna Process after having co-initiated it – to *voice*.

For France, *Dobbins* finds that the structure of state governance changed at the tertiary level. In higher education, the organizational structure was indeed transformed due to numerous reforms resulting from internationalization. The fragmented nature of the French academic community and student unions made it possible for the state to reshuffle the organizational landscape. French secondary education policy-making is still highly corporatist to the extent that powerful teacher unions are integrated directly into ministerial policy-making. Thus, teacher unions apply a strategy that oscillates between cooperation and conflict with the ministerial bureaucracy. This strategy proved successful in hindering policies aimed at decentralization, which would have potentially undermined the collective clout and privileged position of the teaching profession. Blocking reforms of secondary education is therefore a strategy with good prospects in France.

*Popp* shows for the Spanish case that many actors supported the vision of Bologna but sharply criticized the way it was implemented. The government started late to adopt the national higher education system to the European model, and in some points, opted for isolated solutions (for example, study structure). Actors' reactions indicate that ongoing reforms offer new venues for participation in higher education, but transformation in this policy field has just begun. In secondary education, the results of the PISA Study have become an important measure for educational quality. By a variety of actors, PISA was used as a political instrument in order to legitimize the organizations' priorities. Spanish education policy is marked by a long tradition of rivalry between the private and public school sector. Thus, PISA was not able to alter the logic of this system.

The case study of *Bieber* is focused on the particular political opportunity structure in Switzerland. The strong federalism combined with direct democratic principles and consensus-oriented policy-making hampered education reforms for decades. As the author was able to show, most actors approved and supported the reforms of the education system because there was a broad consensus for its necessity. Rather, the complex political opportunity structure had prevented earlier reforms. It seems that both the PISA Study and the Bologna Process were again catalysts that triggered the action of political actors. In this sense, the international initiatives provided policy-makers with a legitimization of action that was intended by reform proponents anyway.

*Bieber et al.* state in the case of the U.S. that evidence-based education policy-making was rather common a long time ago and – similarly to England – the PISA Study is not considered to have had much impact. However, it shapes the belief of the political elite, which is, with some exceptions, *loyal* towards the study. Similarly, we also find *loyalty* as a dominant reaction to the Bologna Process. It is perceived as a *fait accompli* that cannot be ignored any longer and that requires political reactions in order to maintain future international attractiveness of U.S. study courses. Thus, *loyalty* is rational because the U.S. attracts masses of highly motivated international students at different levels (for example BA, MA, PhD) as well as academic researchers. The assimilation of higher education systems towards the American domestic structure facilitates the inclusion of international students.

In China, the central authority shapes local educational discourses, as *Akbik et al.* have highlighted, and is undoubtedly the most important actor in this field. Between 1978 and 1998, the system of primary and secondary education was established and strengthened. China participated in PISA for the first time in 2009, as represented by Shanghai. Members of the Chinese PISA team as well as local officials explained the unexpected success with these efforts invested in the 1980s and 1990s. However, this explanation was not based on a systematic pre-post evaluation design, but rather meant to legitimate the central authority. This *loyalty* is self-evident from our rational-choice perspective (see chapter 1): Stable authorities must seek legitimacy, as we learned from Max Weber's sociology (Weber 1978). In contrast to this *loyalty*, independent experts, particularly from abroad, raised their *voice* against China's exam-oriented education, the heavy workload and a limitation of creative thinking. The fact that *voice* has been raised from an independent side seems to be symptomatic for a restricted political opportunity structure, which is neither in favour of social movement formation nor of an open public discourse. Moreover, success in exams is highly valued in the broader society, as it is in line with the Confucian tradition and culture. Thus, opposition to this system is highly unlikely, as most, not just those segments in the Chinese society who benefited from this system with regard to their status attainment, remain *loyal* to it.

### Institutions, outcomes and actors' reactions

Pessimistic views on control capacities usually describe problems of government in democratic systems, when the process of governmental decision-making involves a broad set of more or less powerful actors. In our study, we have investigated only the effects of the Bologna Process and the PISA Study on outcomes and reactions of actors to reforms. Of course, neither the Bologna Declaration nor the OECD was endowed with capacities to control or govern national legislations. Nevertheless, in some education systems, their impact resulted in the most fundamental changes in education policy in decades.

Political scientists usually focus their analyses on the *output* of the political system and ascertain, for instance, that there are problems with the implementation of legal norms in multiplayer systems (Bardach 1980; Scharpf 1997). What is still lacking is an analysis of the effects of norms, or widely accepted declarations, on society, namely on social groups and collectives as well as on individual actors. That is, what are the *outcomes* of education policies? How do organizations deal with norms? Are they actually capable of meeting their clients' expectations? How some universities adopted the bachelor's and master's system gives insight into the frictions between output and outcomes. Universities are still occupied with handling and correcting self-created defects, not just in the structure of their bachelor's programmes, but also in their administration, for instance, with regard to issues concerning exams.

Regarding the *outcomes*, we find an important similarity between PISA and Bologna: In both cases, there is no direct link between the policy output and the desired outcome. In tertiary education, the formal introduction of the bachelor's and master's programmes in higher education did not result in a strong increase in international student mobility.

At the level of secondary education, changes in education policy do not seem to follow a common pattern, neither are they guided by any best practices. While specific changes in educational contexts at the national level moderate the effect of social background on the outcome, for instance, in terms of ability grouping for some subjects, effects of changes in other characteristics are only weak, at best, or even increase educational inequalities. Accordingly, regarding the *output* of changes in education policies, we can summarize that there is an impact of very specific changes, but overall, it is hard to identify any best practices of how to make secondary education efficient and equitable. Interestingly, we come to the same result if we regard either the impact of the PISA Study or the Bologna Process, despite the fact that the latter has been initiated and adopted by national governments that are endowed with institutionalized control capacities whereas the OECD does not.

Different and complex conclusions with regard to *reactions* are based on Hirschman's (1970) typology of *exit, voice* and *loyalty*. Tertiary actors often raise their *voice* against Bologna. For example, student protest against the implementation is also a result of open local political opportunity structures at their universities. In combination with a broad consensus about the utility to optimize the implementation of bachelor's and master's programmes, the expected probability of success is rather high. In contrast, the policy activism after the continual decline of the PISA results was rather a process of trial and error, indicating that political decision-making happens more in the form of *coping* (see below) than governmental control.

Regarding the huge complexity of social systems, the classical view on ruling a social system as developed in Max Weber's theory of bureaucracy is no longer applicable. Social systems theory highlights the self-regulation and autopoiesis, or self-maintaining and reproductive nature, of social systems, and particularly, the boundaries between systems and their environments (Luhmann 2008). These boundaries are a further reason why governance and social control become increasingly difficult. Governance theory was developed to address this challenge by developing new concepts about the phenomenon of different groups of social actors becoming part of a complex network of self-regulation, based on an existing legal framework. As Renate Mayntz has argued, self-regulation and decentralization of power is not just a new form of control, but also an abandonment of control (Mayntz 1997: 195). Yet, policy-makers still aim at controlling social systems by means of *coping* (Schimank 2011). Coping does not necessitate abandoning political control but rather adjusting actors' controlling behaviour to highly complex situations. While earlier theories of political control suggested piecemeal engineering, which means that policy-makers can only proceed in very small steps (Popper 2003), the coping concept is more radical. Here, political control is 'sub-incremental' (Schimank 2011: 459), which is not a passive way of being affected by the situation, but nevertheless far from being a successful and goal-oriented problem management, as we know it from the concept of 'active policy-making'.

Accordingly, the coping concept is a good substantiation of our theoretical arguments on frictions between guiding principles, policies and outcomes. Schimank (2011) provides six strategic recommendations for policy-makers in order to exemplify the coping concept. Firstly, do not aim too high and do not stick to your goals at all costs. Secondly, wait for opportunities. Thirdly, take time to sit the problem out. Fourthly, avoid decisions that have irreversible consequences. Fifthly, orient your policy-making to non-goals, which means, opt for those alternatives which are less harmful and do not cause too much damage. And sixthly, take your time and try to find out what has happened if the process goes in the right direction.

Against this background, we find obvious differences between actors' reactions to the Bologna Process and the PISA Study. The Bologna Process was a clear and well-defined concept that can be accepted, modified or rejected. The basic goal of the Bologna Process was to establish a common higher education area by increasing student mobility. At the end of the 20th century when the Bologna Declaration was signed, this goal was well accepted by all member states, as science and academic education had already an international issue for quite some time. Policy-making in the wake of the Bologna Process was not an example of coping, but rather a groundbreaking reform following a clear guiding principle, namely the two-cycle degree structure. Most student unions accepted the new model, even though they criticized details of its implementation. More specifically, their criticism was not an example of *voice* in a strict sense but rather *loyalty* as it was meant to optimize, not oppose, the reform. Aside from that, *voice* reactions occurred in the form of public statements and had a clear reference to the existing ideological lines. Those who favoured the Humboldt ideal of education as a guiding principle of self-actualization and personality development were in opposition to the Bologna Process, but these groups were outnumbered by the vast majority of *loyal* supporters.

In contrast, the PISA situation is quite different. PISA provided little more than a ranking of countries with regard to their educational performance and degree of inequality. It does not result in a clear reform programme, even though the top scorers in the PISA Study were regarded as role models. In countries ranking lower than expected, the publication of the results triggered a hot debate and hectic activity (Martens and Niemann 2013). In combination with institutional structures based on strong veto players, especially in federal systems, policy-making was more similar to the coping concept than it was in the Bologna Process. To not take action was no alternative; successful reforms were expected in the short and mid-term. For this reason, those reforms were conceptualized and implemented, as they basically caused no harm, were a good compromise and avoided political suicide (Schimank 2011: 461).

For instance, the stratified system of secondary education in Germany was highly controversial, but federal states could not completely abolish this structure. In the city-state of Bremen, the *Gymnasium* remained after the reform, but the lower strata, *Hauptschule* and *Realschule*, were merged into one school type called the *Oberschule*, where students can obtain a certificate of having passed the university entrance qualification in the 13th grade. The idea behind this reform was that the fusion of the lower strata would reduce educational inequalities, and at the same time, not to call existence of the Gymnasium into question. Yet, it is not clear whether this halfhearted reform will reduce educational inequalities. Indeed, the recent improvement in educational performance of German pupils in PISA 2012 could be one indicator of positive results from such reforms, but may also be a result of the fact that problem-solving, in the spirit of the PISA tests, has now been recognized as a competence and has therefore been introduced informally into the curricula. In other words, German pupils and especially teachers are highly sensitized to problem-solving skills as highlighted through PISA ('teaching to the test').

From this point of view, policy-making as a response to the PISA Study is much closer to *coping* compared with the response to the implementation of the Bologna guidelines. A clear pattern of actors' reactions to the reforms after the PISA Study is difficult to identify, because the political reforms were so heterogeneous, particularly in federal systems. If any coherently negative reaction was observable across countries, it was the criticism of the assumed economic view on education. There was no general reform plan like there was in the Bologna Process, but different attempts at politically coping with bad results in the PISA Study. Thus, the only alternative, given the complexity of governing social systems, was coping, which complicates the processes of identifying a clear concept against which actors can raise their *voice*.

## Outlook on further research

As in any study, our approach to the analysis of outcomes and reactions in the field of education policy also has limitations. We elaborated an actor-based theoretical model for the explanation of reactions. Our ambition was to explain why specific groups of actors either chose *exit*, *voice* or *loyalty*, regarding their resources and the political opportunity structures. However, a direct test of our model would have required data on political resources, utilities of each alternative as well subjectively expected probabilities of realizing the utility by choosing an alternative. As methods of data collection, we used document analysis and expert interviews, which did not include broad or detailed insight into our scientific constructs, such as utility, evaluation and expected probabilities. For this reason, our analyses can only be a first step in providing evidence for why actors show reactions of *exit*, *voice* or *loyalty*.

One of our expectations was to link actors' reactions to the outcomes affecting them. In other words, some actors might not respond to the Bologna Process or PISA-induced reforms in general. Rather, they raise their *voices* against particular problems or disadvantages. For instance, reactions of student organizations often referred to confusion induced by the implementation of the BA/MA structure. All significant actors involved in the reform, or who were affected by it, were interested in solving the problem and optimizing programme performance. As we have argued, the rationale behind the *voice* reaction in some cases was actually one of *loyalty* because the critique aimed to optimize the new system. Overall, however, we could not identify regular links between specific kinds of outcomes and specific reactions, which has also to do with the abovementioned problems of empirically analysing group-specific evaluations and utility-functions, as well as subjective expected probabilities of realizing utility $U$ by choosing alternative $i$. This study is the first that analyses reactions to reforms in education policy, a topic that is not yet well established. Rather, we ventured into uncharted terrain and therefore could not extensively draw on preliminary research in our field. Consequently, further studies could elaborate concrete hypotheses on the link between specific outcomes and reactions. Moreover, in further studies we should devote more resources to the development of new methods that enable us to collect better indicators on utility and subjective probabilities.

The theoretical model that we developed in this book could be easily used for studying education policy in other regions or countries. For different reasons and constraints we could only focus on some selected countries. Since this book is based on our earlier research, the main focus of our publication is on European countries. However, the cases of the U.S. and China have shown that it is highly informative to study education policy in regions beyond Europe. What can be learnt from the U.S. and China is that even though these countries were only partly involved in the international initiatives we analysed in our research, their higher education systems have been affected. Future research could thus, for example, take a closer look at internationalization of education policy in the Arab and African regions. Even though it might be challenging to access data in some countries, the general model of outcomes and actors' reactions could be applied and developed further. Hence, our study lays an important foundation for further analyses of changes in education policies and actors' reactions.

## References

Bardach, Eugene (1980) *The implementation game: What happens after a bill becomes a law,* Cambridge: MIT Press.

Bardach, Eugene and Robert A. Kagan (1982) *Going by the book. The problem of regulatory unreasonableness,* Philadelphia: Temple University Press.

Coleman, James Samuel (1990) *Foundations of social theory,* Cambridge: Harvard University Press.

Gangl, Markus (2010) "Causal Inference in Sociological Research", *Annual Review of Sociology,* 36(1), 21–47.

Hirschman, Albert O. (1970) *Exit, Voice, and Loyalty. Responses to Decline in Firms, Organizations, and States,* Cambridge: Cambridge University Press.

Luhmann, Niklas with the cooperation of André Kieserling (2008) *Die Politik der Gesellschaft,* Frankfurt: Suhrkamp.

Martens, Kerstin and Dennis Niemann (2013) "When Do Numbers Count? The Differential Impact of Ratings and Rankings on National Education Policy in Germany and the US", *German Politics,* 22(3), 314–32.

Martens, Kerstin and Klaus Dieter Wolf (2006) "Paradoxien der Neuen Staatsräson – Die Internationalisierung der Bildungspolitik in der EU und der OECD", *Zeitschrift für Internationale Beziehungen,* 13(2), 145–76.

Martens, Kerstin, Alessandra Rusconi and Kathrin Leuze eds. (2007) *New Arenas of Education Governance: The Impact of International Organizations and Markets on Educational Policy Making,* Basingstoke: Palgrave Macmillan.

Mayntz, Renate (1997) "Politische Steuerung und gesellschaftliche Steuerungsprobleme", in Renate Mayntz, ed., *Soziale Dynamik und politische Steuerung. Theoretische und methodologische Überlegungen,* Frankfurt: Campus, 186–208.

Pearl, Judea (2000) *Causality. Models, reasoning, and inference,* Cambridge: Cambridge University Press.

Popper, Karl (2003) *Die offene Gesellschaft und ihre Feinde,* Tübingen: Mohr Siebeck.

Scharpf, Fritz W. (1997) *Games Real Actors Play. Actor-centered Institutionalism in Policy Research,* New York: Westview Press.

Schimank, Uwe (2011) "Nur noch Coping: Eine Skizze postheroischer Politik", *Zeitschrift für Politikwissenschaft*, 21(3), 455–63.

Toens, Katrin (2007) "Die Sorbonne-Deklaration. Hintergründe und Bedeutung für den Bologna-Prozess", *Die Hochschule* 17(2), 37–53.

Vögtle, Eva Maria and Kerstin Martens (2013) "Bologna as a Fad or Fashion. The Bologna Process as a Template for Transnational Higher Education Cooperation Initiatives", in Sigrid Karin Amos, Josef Schmid, Josef Schrader and Ansgar Thiel, eds., *Europäischer Bildungsraum. Europäisierungsprozesse in Bildungspolitik und Bildungspraxis*, Baden-Baden: Nomos, 149–73.

Weber, Max (1978) *Economy and society. An outline of interpretive sociology*, New York: University of California Press.

Windzio, Michael (2013) "Integration and Inequality in Educational Institutions: An Institutional Perspective", in Michael Windzio, ed., *Integration and Inequality in Educational Institutions*, Dordrecht: Springer, 3–20.

# Index

Printed and bound by CPI Group (UK) Ltd, Croydon, CR0 4YY